Bus Stops on the Moon

Red Mole days 1974–1980

MARTIN EDMOND

OTAGO UNIVERSITY PRESS
Te Whare Tā o Te Wānanga o Ōtākou

Published by Otago University Press
Te Whare Tā o Te Wānanga o Ōtākou
533 Castle Street
Dunedin, New Zealand
university.press@otago.ac.nz
www.otago.ac.nz/press

First published 2020
Copyright © Martin Edmond
The moral rights of the author have been asserted.

ISBN 978-1-98-859251-0

Published with the assistance of Creative New Zealand

ARTS COUNCIL OF NEW ZEALAND *TOI AOTEAROA*

Editor: Anna Rogers
Design/layout: Fiona Moffat

Front cover photograph: Joe Bleakley
Author photograph: Joe Bleakley

Printed in Hong Kong through Asia Pacific Offset

MIX
Paper from
responsible sources
FSC® C136333

Fugue state: a psychiatric disorder characterised by reversible amnesia of personal identity. The state can last days, months or years. Usually involves unplanned travel or wandering and is sometimes accompanied by the establishment of a new identity.

Wikipedia (adapted)

We had to take that long hard road
To see where it would go
Yeah we took that holy ride ourselves to know

Warren Zevon

I want to go where there's no Beyond

Alan Brunton

BUS STOPS ON THE MOON

Contents

Prologue
Fugue States

THE SUMMER I TURNED 22 I WENT MAD. Or nearly went mad. Approached the borders of madness, perhaps, then retreated. Or crossed over and came out the other side. Yet madness has no borders; once you have gone there, there's no way back. Or so it seemed that summer. Even now, more than 40 years later, it's hard to say exactly what happened: not least because, as the borders of madness approach, memory becomes something other than we generally assume it to be. Less recall than trauma, if that makes sense. So does thought. So too does everything else. Consciousness alters and, with it, reality. All things become questionable, including the questions themselves.

It's a long time ago now but fragments remain in mind, images of estrangement, provocations and intuitions, and from these I may be able to make something comprehensible, perhaps even true, though truth might be too exalted an ambition. I'll settle for narrative coherence. Plausibility, in other words. Truth might thereby be served but only if, like beauty, it lies in the eye of the beholder. So I will try to say what my incipient madness was like. It seems important to do so because, once it passed, I was able at last to enter into the life I wanted to live. As if madness were a territory I had to traverse in order to get to the place I wished to be. A stage in learning how to live.

It may be like that for other people too, but I don't wish to implicate anyone else. Nevertheless, however much it might have felt that way, I was not alone. There were always others. Even at the precise moment when I realised I might be going mad, someone was there. Her name was Karen. Although we were lovers, I didn't know her very well. I'd heard that she and her brother were heirs to a high country sheep station but never asked if it was true. I don't remember her surname. Nor how we met. She was probably just as inexperienced, uncertain and afraid as I was. Most of us were back then. She was from Dunedin. Once, when I told her how I'd been infatuated with a woman from there, someone she knew, she cried – why, I don't know. Perhaps she cared for me more than I thought she did.

Karen was small and dark and good looking and didn't say much. The moment of truth came when we were in bed in my room at 56 Grafton Road one morning and I said – I remember the exact sentence – 'I've finally become a complete animal.' As soon as the words were out of my mouth, and I heard what they said, fear descended upon me. A cold, dark, numbing, airless dread. As if I'd pronounced a doom upon on myself. As if my erratic behaviour over the past year or so had been leading inexorably to this point, at which I would understand what I'd been doing, articulate it and then feel afraid. It was the coming to consciousness of the results of my willed dissolution. The culmination of my dérèglement de tous les sens.

I don't know what Karen said. If she said anything. I think my confession scared her. It was scary. I wonder now if that was the last time we slept together. I think she may have left that day and not come back. It was December 1973, and that room at Grafton Road was very beautiful: downstairs, at the back of the house, with glass sliding doors opening to a wooden deck that gave onto a wild garden full of weed trees. The Domain, over a hidden creek, began at the back of the section. It was all leafy green shadow and lemon yellow light, where grey warblers, riroriro, sang; but beauty is of no account when you are crossing the borders of madness.

I had two black and white kittens someone had given me. A male and a female. They had been taken too soon from their mother and still needed to suckle. I would wake up in the middle of the night and find one in each armpit, sucking industriously away at the hairs that grew there. This might have been after Karen left. I had nothing to do. No job, no work, no prospects, nothing. I'd dropped out of university to become a poet but that hadn't happened. There were poems, lots of them, but they were, like me, awkward and strange, and I believed in them as little as I believed in myself. Now they, too, had dried up.

Money? I don't know. I must have had some because the one thing I reliably did, every afternoon, was go up to the Kiwi and drink – often until I passed out. I woke up in some strange places. Once I found myself lying on an old mattress in the waste land behind the house next door, with no idea how I got there. Missed my way home probably. Another time I met an old girlfriend outside the pub and dragged her down to No. 56 with me. She came, but now I wonder why. That night I was singing, over and over again, the chorus of the Rolling Stones song 'Don't play with me 'cause you're playing with fire' while she looked on incredulously. How did the sweet boy she knew turn into this sottish oaf? Perhaps she felt sorry for me.

What did I even mean, a complete animal? That I had alienated myself from all finer feelings? All merely human responses? I think I thought that, if I could get back to operating on a purely instinctual level, I would find my true self. In the same way that many people then wanted to get back to nature, back to the land. I knew I was in trouble. After Karen, after meeting my ex, after the drunken nights at the Kiwi and the vague stumbles home, I had to do something. But what? And how about the actual animals, the kittens, who depended utterly upon me – the most undependable human being alive? I decided to go home for Christmas.

One of the kittens, the boy, Bill, came with me when I went to Wellington, although common sense says that must have happened later, after Christmas, when, using Laurence's van, I moved my things down. I gave Bill to a friend of one of my younger sisters in Brentwood in Upper Hutt, where I like to imagine he lived a long and happy life. Though I think he might actually have been run over. I don't know what happened to the girl kitten. Maybe Karen took her.

We hitch-hiked to Wellington. Just Dean and me. Dean was my best friend, my drinking partner, my confidante and my support. No matter how weird I got, he would always be there for me. Perhaps, being somewhat self-obsessed, he didn't really notice what was going on, but I think he did. We'd been in some extreme situations together over the past couple of years and took a proportion of insanity for granted. I don't know how mad I would have had to have gone before Dean abandoned me. Perhaps he wouldn't ever have done so. Anyway, he got me to Wellington. For which I am eternally grateful. The painter, Dean Buchanan.

The trip was a nightmare. By mutual consent, whenever we found a ride, Dean sat in the front and I sat in the back. In those days you were usually picked up by people on their own and the rule was, when hitching in pairs, that you alternated, because it was the job of the one in the front to do the talking, which could be onerous. And I was no longer capable of conversation. Even the most casual remark – 'How you going, mate?' – filled me with anxiety. More complex offerings seemed to disclose depthless ambiguities as I tried to work out what the person was saying, what they meant, how dangerous they really were. In this paranoid state people looked as well as sounded terrifying: bloated, bug-eyed, red-faced, snarling, sweating, their teeth shiny with saliva as they licked their chops.

I had lost the monitoring self, the one which says, no, that's delusional, that's not really happening. This is just another day, this is a normal person, a farmer perhaps, driving us through Taupō, along the shore of Five Mile Bay, past Waitahanui and on into the hills. That's the lake out there, a slight agitation upon the water, whitecaps, glints of golden light, pumice on the beach where I paddled as a child. The mountains blue against the distant sky. I was clutching a book the whole way. *Memories, Dreams, Reflections* by Carl Jung. It was a paperback and on the cover was Carl himself, avuncular, smiling, pipe in hand, the picture of sanity. Jung wrote: 'Who looks outside, dreams; who looks inside, awakes.' I was looking both ways at once and the only thing I could see was horror.

At that time my parents were living in a grand house in a leafy, expensive part of Upper Hutt called Heretaunga. An elegant white weatherboard dwelling down the end of a long drive lined with ornamental cherry trees. When I visited I didn't write or call or telegram ahead to say I was coming. I would turn up unexpectedly; it suited my sense of myself as a maverick, a free spirit. If Dean was still with me, that would have been all right – he was a friend of the family. But I remember walking up the gravel drive alone on a balmy summer evening, going in the back door, which was unlocked, and surprising them all doing whatever it was they were doing.

I have two memories of that visit over Christmas, 1973. Both are disturbing. One is of a family dinner, possibly on the night I arrived. It might have been a Sunday. Cold cuts, boiled eggs, a salad made with grated carrot, chopped lettuce and sliced tomato, potatoes tossed in butter and mint. Sweetcorn. I had taken to wearing around my left wrist a rusty metal chain I'd dug up in the garden at Puka Puka Road, Pūhoi, North Auckland, where Dean and I and some others had squatted in an old farmhouse for much of the past year. It was an undistinguished artefact, of unknown provenance, certainly not an item of personal adornment.

My youngest sister, who was 14, noticed and asked me what it was? I recoiled, I clutched my wrist and I snarled, 'It's mine!' There was a startled silence around the table as everyone contemplated my inappropriate response, the aggression, the lack of empathy, let alone manners, I had shown. I realised too, but I didn't apologise or explain, I just waited until normal discourse resumed.

The other episode must have taken place after Christmas, possibly on New Year's Day. My mother was hosting a party. For her new, her literary, friends, because she was on the way to establishing herself as a poet. She had already begun to work on her edition of the letters of A.R.D. Fairburn (1981); she must also have started publishing poems in magazines, ahead of her first book, *In Middle Air* (1975). And I, her son, the poète manqué, got hold of a bottle of brandy and drank from the neck until I passed out, on the sofa, in the middle of the afternoon, in the middle of the party. I remember my mother's fury. I had ruined her gathering and shamed her in front of her friends. She was beside herself with rage.

Ours was not a happy house. My father had lost his job as headmaster and had been hospitalised for alcoholism and depression. He'd had shock treatment but it hadn't worked; he wasn't cured. When he wasn't at work, a desk job in the Curriculum Unit in town, he spent his time, back turned, smoking and sipping from a continually recharged glass of sherry. He loathed my mother's literary friends yet insisted on being present whenever they came around: a baleful, accusatory presence in the corner of the room. My sister Rachel, two years younger than I, had survived a suicide attempt the previous August. She took sleeping pills and crawled under a boatshed in Herne Bay where the owners found her, unconscious but alive. After a period in hospital she came home to recuperate. Although nobody said so, I think we all knew the damage was irreparable.

In the context of these two unfolding tragedies my behaviour was of minor import, even though there were affinities with my father's and my sister's predicaments. The habit of drinking myself into oblivion was an imitation of my father's self-medication, and some of the symptoms of my mental state mimicked those from which my sister suffered, to a far more serious degree. In the throes of a schizophrenic attack she, too, became paranoid, had difficulty understanding what people were saying to her, believed the world to be full of threats and violent terrors. But there the parallels ended. I did not have, as she did, hallucinations. I did not hear voices saying I was worthless and telling me to die. I did not see demonic faces, slavering and grimacing, morphing from the walls. My 'madness', though real enough to me was, beside hers, inconsequential.

I have one more incident to relate. It is from later in the summer. I was lying in bed one night, in the room at the end of the hall, on a single divan just inside the door; with two other beds, both empty, under the window that gave onto the clothesline and the vegetable garden. This had been my room when I'd last lived here, four years before. I was lying there, drifting into sleep, when I saw loom over me Laurence, holding a knife with which, I knew, he was going to kill me. I saw him and I saw the knife, but he was not there. He was in Auckland, 650 kilometres away. The apparition was so real I tried to shield myself with my hands from the blow. Then Laurence disappeared, leaving me there, heart hammering, sweating, gazing into the dark.

Why him? Laurence Clark was a tall fellow who in those days wore a herring-bone overcoat, even in the heat of summer, and liked to cultivate an air of mystery. His lips smiled faintly beneath his walrus moustache; he rarely spoke. When he did, his remarks were cryptic, knowing, opaque. He was a cartoonist and his cartoons, too, were enigmatic, his characters almost wordless; if there was a speech bubble above their heads, it would most likely be empty. I remember he knew all of the words of the Bob Dylan song 'Lily, Rosemary and the Jack of Hearts'; he used to say he was the Jack of Hearts. Though that record came out the year after Laurence delivered my things to the Hutt.

His red Bedford van had a sliding door on the side, and during our rapscallion days at Puka Puka Road we used to career all over the peninsula in it, drinking and carousing and leaping out to chase game across the paddocks. If Cameron Thompson was with us, and had his .303 rifle, he would shoot the goats or the turkeys, which we would then take home to butcher, cook and eat. Laurence had a girlfriend, Philippa, who was tiny, a gamine with an elvish face and bright eyes. She spoke as little as he did and I always wondered if she left the note on my desk that read: 'Today is the day for fucking.'

It might have been guilt over Philippa, or Laurence's game-playing – if that's what it was – which caused me to focus my fears upon his person. Even so I knew, as soon as he disappeared, that the presence I had seen was an hallucination. Knowing that did not lessen its power, however; nor the fear it provoked. If my mind could do that, what else could it do? What might happen next? I would still like to know if this visitation came before or after Laurence, out of the goodness of his heart, trucked my worldly goods down the island; but the chronology is lost.

I didn't have much: books, records, a stereo, a few clothes, the tartan blanket that has been on my bed since childhood. No furniture and no kitchen things. Andrew McCartney, another lost soul from those far-off days, travelled with us, on one of his flights between one rural job and another. We drove down through Te Kūiti and Taumarunui and Raetihi, parked on the banks of the Whanganui and spent the night above the river. Somehow, probably in consultation with my parents, I had decided to move to Wellington. It was to be a new start. I was going to go back to university to finish my degree.

What about the madness? There are a couple more things to say about it. One is that, over the course of 1973 my friends and I had became enamoured of the poetry of Sylvia Plath and Ted Hughes. Hughes' *Crow* (1970), along with Plath's posthumous collection *Ariel* (1965), were sacred texts to us. We read and reread them; we imitated them. I took from Hughes a conception of the natural world defined by violence and tried to mirror that in my writing. No wonder I thought I was turning into an animal: I was trying to become a Ted Hughes poem.

Meanwhile Plath romanticised death as a fate she would inevitably embrace, as in time she did. My sister was a Sylvia Plath fan: her own suicide attempts, the third of which succeeded, imitated Plath's appalling example. The only extenuating circumstance I can offer for this calamitous enthusiasm is that we reckoned our obsession with violence and death to be, paradoxically, life-affirming. Our worship of the mortal and the transitory would make our days more intense, more momentous, more real. Needless to say, or perhaps not, I no longer think that way.

The other insight gained from the events of that summer is genuinely life-affirming. Those distortions of perception and apprehension characteristic of mental illness, once experienced, do not go away. Like the sensory alterations consequent upon the use of drugs, which don't go away either, they become a part of your psyche, your memory, and so enrich both your interior landscapes and your view of the external world. Having felt the terror of my own animality, and the fear of what it might do to me, or I with it, I cannot dismiss the testimony of those who have undergone similar things; even when, as in my sister's case, those experiences are far more powerful, and far more deadly, than mine ever were.

Not only do the insights of madness persist: I believe my schizotypal episode increased my potential for empathy. So that, gradually, over the course of the summer, in the undemanding routines of the parental home, even one as afflicted as ours was, those insights sank into my mind, taking their place as things that might not have been desirable but were certainly possible. To which attention must be paid. They added to my knowledge of what could happen in a life. As a result, when I moved out of home again and resumed an independent existence, I found myself ripe for the chances that came crowding thick upon me.

How peculiar, it seems, looking back: so much of my despair in that last year in Auckland had been focused upon my inability to write and the seeming lack of any prospect of publishing the meagre bits and pieces I did manage to complete. In Wellington, without my even trying, publishing opportunities presented themselves; to satisfy them, I had to learn how to write. How serendipitous. One February day I went in to Victoria University and, from the noticeboard outside the Student Union building, copied down the telephone number of a household seeking a flatmate. I don't know why, from the dozens available, I chose that one. It was the only number I rang and it was the address where I lived for all of the four years I spent in Wellington.

A member of that household was music writer and political journalist Gordon Campbell. He put me in touch with Roger Steele, editor of *Salient*, the student newspaper; Roger said he'd publish anything I might like to offer to him. I decided to try art and theatre reviewing. I had few qualifications: I'd stayed in the Living Theatre house for a while in Auckland; I'd spent a fair amount of time watching Dean paint. I went to all the shows and began a course of self-education in art history, reading through the 750s on the shelves of the Wellington Public Library. Otherwise, I had my eyes and ears, and my curiosity, and that turned out to be enough. It was 1974 and, in Luang Prabang, in an opium den behind the Shell service station, Red Mole had already begun.

I
96 Kelburn Parade

THE HOUSE AT NO. 96 was a big old wooden two-storey weatherboard pile built up against a cliff on a crumbling bluff above a blind corner on Kelburn Parade, with views to Hawkins Hill to the south and, to the east, a rectangular lawn lined with pine and pōhutukawa and other natives. It belonged to Russell Bond, the theatre critic for the *Dominion*, who had the house divided horizontally and rented out as two separate dwellings. Russell lived up the coast somewhere, Waikanae perhaps, and we never saw him. It was disconcerting to find, some time later, after I went to live upstairs, that he had cached family photographs and sundry other documents in the back of a wardrobe: what were we supposed to do with them? We just left them there.

When I first moved in, however, it was to the downstairs flat. You walked up a steep path to an enclosed porch and then went through the front door into a wide hallway that must once have housed a staircase and now constituted the sole communal area, with a battered sofa along one wall and a couple of nondescript armchairs upon the other. Unless we were interviewing potential flatmates, none of us ever sat there. We entertained guests in our rooms.

Or in the kitchen, three steps up, which looked out onto a cliff of dripping terrane. The bathroom was off the kitchen: this seems unhygienic now but was in those days unremarkable. There was a hole in the kitchen floor out of which Bill the Big Brown Bush Rat, so-called, climbed nightly looking for food scraps in the compost bucket. Was he a kiore? We hoped so but we never knew. When the exterminators came for Gordon's white rats, Bill was collateral damage. I remember his corpse lying along the yellow linoleum floor. He was much bigger than I thought he would be.

The two front bedrooms, to the left and right of the entrance, belonged to Gordon and Mary, respectively. Mine was at the back, also on the right, with sash windows through which you could see the vegetable garden I dug at the end of the lawn, and the underside of the external staircase that led to the upstairs flat. Ivy grew over the veranda above, which creaked and sighed and shook to the tread of the heavy feet of the young men who lived there.

I was surprised to find among them two boys I had played rugby with at school in Greytown and even more surprised when I realised that, though scrupulously polite, Gary and Roger didn't want to know me any more. They were law or commerce students and I, with my long hair and hippie clothes, was some kind of freak: in those days, without shame, I used to wear a pair of skin-tight scarlet crushed velvet bell-bottom trousers my sister had sewed for me.

Mary was a librarian, and pathologically shy: when she spoke to you, she gazed at your chest, as if the buttons of your shirt were of consuming interest. I can't remember her second name. And Gordon was – Gordon. As a music-obsessed teenager growing up in Whanganui he had heard, probably on the radio, the Summer of Love going off in San Francisco. Our winter of 1967. Possessed of insatiable curiosity, energy and a desire to see for himself, he got together the money for an air ticket and flew to California, where he remained for some months.

Unquestionably the experience changed his life. When he told me about it there was a hush in his voice. Pride, bordering upon incredulity. He had been there! Just seven years before. Gordon was eccentric and I sometimes wondered if he was an acid casualty. Or had he smoked too much dope? He was a reggae buff, after all, with a magnificent collection of sides of Jamaican music. At this time, however, he didn't smoke ganga, never drank alcohol, was abstemious rather than indulgent. He was also, as he still is, to an almost alarming degree, politically astute.

Gordon was vegetarian as well, though without any of the sophistication you find among that tribe these days. He lived mostly on baked beans and toast, which he always burned: the kitchen smelled of burnt toast and I woke most mornings to the abrasive sound of a knife scraping off the carbonised crumbs. Another of his causes was animal rights: the first person I knew of that persuasion. It may have been connected to his vegetarianism. He and a group of desirous young women rescued white rats from the university psychology department, saving

Martin Edmond, upstairs at 96 Kelburn Parade.

them from the cruelties of experiments in operant conditioning. Some of these rats lived in Gordon's room; and thereby hangs a tale.

They were caged, and he had scrupulously divided male from female; nevertheless, one of the males chewed his way out and got among the females. Copulation ensued, followed by reproduction. Gordon's dilemma was exquisite. The whole point of saving them was that their lives were precious; how then could he murder their young? Nor did he seem able, probably for logistical reasons, to prevent further sexual encounters; thus an exponential growth in numbers. Gordon had a single divan bed in the centre of his room; members of the burgeoning rat population took up residence in its base. I never understood how he could sleep above their rustlings, their squeakings and their scuttlings; he was tolerant far beyond what most of us can manage.

I recall the number 67; he must have made a count. That many rats were running around the mazes in Gordon's room! There was the smell, too. It filled me with anxiety. I suspect Mary felt the same, but Gordon was imperturbable. Something had to happen but we did not know what. Then the rats took matters, as it were, into their own paws. They escaped. As if from a sinking ship. Over a period of not many days they gnawed their way out of the house and disappeared. Neighbours reported an influx of white rodents to the city council. A pest control officer came to our door and asked if we had a problem, too. I said, truthfully as I thought, there are no rats here. Though Gordon may have kept one or two. Perhaps even the progenitor of that fecund line.

He had other peculiarities. His hat, for instance. A unexceptional soft khaki felt hat with a narrow brim and a faded floral band which he always wore perched upon his head of straggly dark hair. Perhaps it came from San Francisco. His myopia. Once or twice in the early days of my residence at No. 96 I passed him in the street, going to or from the university just down the road, and was flummoxed by his lack of a greeting, or of any acknowledgement whatsoever. Later I found out he was short-sighted but refused, for some reason, to wear glasses. Despite his girls, I'm pretty sure he was celibate in those days; there was a feeling of solitary grandeur about Gordon. That might have come upon him in San Francisco too. Even when you saw him walking down Kelburn Parade with his entourage of girls and dogs, he seemed to be alone.

His dogs were three. Eva, a wise old black Labrador cross, patient and kind; Teddy, an emotional black and tan with some farm dog in him, and maybe some German shepherd, and only three legs. The back left one had been amputated and it was hilarious to watch how he would still cock the phantom limb when pissing against a lamppost or a tree trunk. When Teddy got his remaining back leg caught between the bars of a stormwater drain grille one day his piteous yelping could be heard as far away as Salamanca Road. Later Teddy and Eva were joined by a terrier called Gavin, who had been so badly treated by a previous owner that his spirit was broken and his only mode of engagement a craven appeasement which masked a snarl. 'Teddy! Eva! Gavin!' Gordon would yell whenever they bailed up some nervous visitor or hapless passer-by.

What I liked about Gordon was his generosity. He wasn't a student. He never took any university course that I know of, but remained alert to currents of contemporary thought and was as educated in the arcana of post-Wittgensteinian philosophy as the Ethiopian politics of Haile Selassie. You could talk to Gordon about anything; he was as well informed and open-minded as anyone I have met. A good writer too: mostly of record reviews in those days, which he published in *Salient* to whose editor, Roger Steele, he led me.

~

Impossible to exaggerate the importance of that meeting: it led, in a dream-like fashion, to everything that was to follow. When I think of the *Salient* office now I see a long, narrow room, windowless, with back issues piled upon every flat surface. Colours grey and yellow. Half a dozen people in there working. A sense of unremitting activity that would, whatever else it did, inevitably add to those piles. Roger himself, a spider spinning in the heart of a vast web, is sitting at a desk at the end of the room, looking inwards. Well, perhaps not vast. And maybe there was a sheeted or a blinded window behind him.

He was older than me, from Rotorua, the son of an army officer, with a beard, an attitude (he liked to disparage those who would rhyme 'June' with 'moon') and a commitment to one of the popular forms of socialism: neither a Stalinist nor a Trotskyite; was he a Maoist? It is unlikely that, like the New Zealand Communist Party, he followed the Albanian line. He was attempting to change the world but he wasn't doctrinaire. Radicals of all persuasions contributed to *Salient* in those days. Conrad Bollinger. Alister Taylor. Trevor Richards. Chris Kraus, who wrote an article about the People's Theatre in Communist China.

Roger gave me complete freedom. Every couple of weeks I would sally forth into town to look at what was on in the galleries: Antipodes, in the Hope Gibbons Building on the corner of Taranaki and Dixon streets; Elva Bett's and Peter McLeavey's, opposite each other on the first floor of a dingy building in Cuba Street; the Rothmans Cultural Centre in Marion Street; the Academy of Fine Arts upstairs at the Dominion Museum building in Buckle Street where, across the hall, the National Art Gallery had its premises. It was during these trips to town that I first saw works by Rita Angus, Philip Clairmont, Robèrt Franken, Tony Fomison, Jeffrey Harris, Milan Mrkusich, Joanna Paul, Ian Scott, Robin White and Wong Sing Tai.

Any show I thought I could say something about I reviewed and handed the typescript to Roger. There was never any discussion, evaluation, opinion, proofs or excisions: he printed what I wrote in the form in which I wrote it. Nor did he ever try to direct my attention in any particular way, except when he offered me complimentary tickets to a theatre show at Downstage or Unity or some other theatre in town.

Roger was also, unusually for a Pākehā at that time, fluent in te reo. This was important for me because when I re-enrolled at university I was told that, even though I was completing a BA which would, in time, be awarded by the University of Auckland, I still needed to satisfy the requirements of Victoria University of Wellington, which included a compulsory unit in a foreign language. I didn't want to revive my schoolboy French or embark on learning any other European tongue, so I asked if I could study Māori. There was consternation in the faculty but it turned out no regulation prohibited it.

Otherwise I completed my degree in philosophy and anthropology, not English: an excellent decision, as it turned out. The philosophy mostly passed me by; the anthropology was revelatory. The department at Auckland, headed by the Australian Ralph Piddington, who'd studied under Bronisław Malinowski, was functionalist. The components of a society were to be described according to what they did; each aspect contributed to a whole of pre-existent, unquestionable integrity, like a clock or an internal combustion engine. Piddington was austere, courteous, precise – and in decline. In tutorials he shook so badly inside his green tweed suit I thought he must have had a fever; but it was Parkinson's disease.

The department at Victoria was structuralist: elements of human culture were to be understood in reciprocal relationship to each other and to an over-arching system of belief, which might not ever become explicit outside the interactions between the actual things people do, think, perceive and feel. In other words, in ritual and in myth. *The Comparative Study of Myth* focused on the work of Swiss linguist and semiotician Ferdinand de Sassure; and French anthropologist, Claude Levi-Strauss. It was also for me, among much else, an inoculation against the coming excesses, and the frequently impenetrable jargon, of post-structuralist theory.

Art writing became my métier, one I still practise today. Yet I reviewed as many theatre shows as exhibitions. A John Banas production at Downstage, called *W.A.S.T.E.* (*Wait And See The End*): an eerily prophetic piece about pollution; *Adventures in the Skin Trade*, based on Dylan Thomas texts, staged by the Victoria University Drama Society; a capping revue; children's theatre; the New Zealand premiere, at Unity, of James Joyce's *Exiles*; a Molière, *The Misanthrope*, designed by Grant Tilly. I walked out of a version of Beckett's *Waiting for Godot* because the actors, unable to memorise the lines, were reading them instead. I saw Francis Batten's Jacques Le Coq-incubated Theatre Action and read Peter Brook's *The Empty Space*.

Then there was Amamus, founded by Paul Maunder in 1971. Of its 1974 production *Gallipoli* I wrote, 'It is, quite simply, the most powerful piece of theatre I have seen here this year. I would recommend that everyone who can see it (especially anyone who is bored, unhappy, dissatisfied with things as they are) should see it.' A clarion call, then. The review mentioned Ken Rea's Living Theatre, then in abeyance, and Theatre Action, which was reconstituting itself. 'Amamus can claim to be the only experimental theatre group at present performing in NZ.'

I didn't then know the term 'poor theatre', in which the actor's body is the primary resource; didn't know that its Polish originator, Jerzy Grotowski, had visited Wellington the year before, giving workshops and attending a performance of a previous Amamus production. By 1974 Grotowski had moved on from the concept of poor theatre into his paratheatrical phase: 'to attempt to transcend the separation between performer and spectator through communal rites and interactive exchanges'. When Amamus took *Gallipoli* to Poland the following year, the aficionados in Warsaw, hilariously, pronounced it inauthentic, the result of a provincial misunderstanding, though intriguing for that reason. Grotowski had by then gone into exile; his legacy in his home country was still in dispute.

The tone of my Amamus review, like that of my review of *W.A.S.T.E.*, was one of youthful idealism, of someone looking for, and thinking he may have found, the revelation that will allow change. This wasn't anomalous in the pages of Roger's *Salient*, but it wasn't typical either. Some of my other contributions, some of Gordon's, some by Roger himself, had a different tone: knowing, combative, smart-arsed – as if we were a kind of elect, superior in our knowledge of how things ought to be, with an undercurrent of jejune disappointment in even our most strident proclamations.

But you never know who's reading you, nor how you're being read. One evening around the middle of the year I went to an event at Downstage Theatre. A room full of people standing around talking, drinking beers or wines, snacking on canapés. Among them, Sally Rodwell and Alan Brunton. Sally I knew from Auckland. I'd last seen her in Queen Street the year before. She'd been about to embark on travels overseas. England, I thought. She looked different: a slimmed-down version of herself. Next to her, this braw, red-haired fellow, wearing a cloth cap, with a belligerent look on his face. Alan. I knew who he was, knew his work, but had not met him before.

He pointed to a woman on the other side of the room: Who was she? Sandy Duncan was stylish, beautiful. A friend had had a fling with her recently; there was a fashion in those days for older women to seduce good-looking younger men. Sandy lived alone in a small cottage perched on the side of the hill on Talavera Terrace. You could see it from the cable car. That's where my friend went for their trysts. I told Alan who she was and then repeated a piece of gossip: 'Some people call her a professional mistress.' He looked sideways at me. 'I've already got one of those,' he said.

Startled, I looked around to see if Sally had heard; maybe not. If she had, there would have been some riposte. They were like that. Anyway the shock didn't last. Alan went on to say he had read my work in *Salient*, that I wrote well – and that he was starting up a magazine to which I might like to contribute. This was the publication called *Spleen*. The invitation was an entrée into a milieu I had hitherto regarded from afar, with my nose pressed, as it were, against the sweet-shop window. That pane of glass, illusory as it was, in a moment dissolved, and I stepped through into another world.

~

Alan was born in Christchurch and grew up in Hamilton in the care of his paternal grandmother. The family were radical Christians, an extreme Protestant sect. Your faith, he said, had to be total: 'the man of vision comes from the provinces/where the flesh believes the soul.' He was named after his uncle, his father's brother, a printer by trade, who'd worked on a soldiers' newspaper edited by Geoffrey Cox and published during the Battle for Crete in 1941. This other Alan Brunton was wounded in the fighting, evacuated to North Africa, and died when the SS *Chakdina*, commandeered by the Royal Navy as a hospital ship, was torpedoed by an enemy aircraft off Tobruk in December of that year.

Alan only saw his father, his two full brothers and his various half-siblings, intermittently. They were good, solid, working-class people; his father, George, was a cook in the army and a cheesemaker in civilian life. I don't think he ever knew his mother Maisie. It was as if he was both self-born and a reincarnation: a vivid, isolate and intimidating figure, ungovernable, idiosyncratic, with a turn of phrase that could cut to the bone. I was already in thrall to him.

I'd seen him read, with Russell Haley and David Mitchell, during orientation at Auckland University in 1970. It was my first poetry reading and unlike any I have been to since: chaotic, delirious, irreverent and theatrical, it called forth from the audience of hundreds of undergraduates the kind of foot-stamping, fist-raising response you'd expect from a crowd at a rock concert: 'shouting erotics!' It

Alan Brunton with his grandmother (Nana Steele).

might sound like an exaggeration but that reading really did change the way I saw
the world and its possibilities.

Later that year, with my new girlfriend, I went to a party at the house in
Hargreaves Street, Freemans Bay where Ted Sheehan, editor of *Craccum*, the
University of Auckland student magazine, lived. Brunton was there and I watched
him covertly throughout. Parties in those days generally consisted of wall to wall
people who drank and smoked and raved while music belted out from another,
darkened room where there would be dancing. Alan was performing in the kitchen
with a petite raven-haired woman at his side. She had a mullet, panda eyes, pale
skin. A hairdresser from Hamilton, someone said. Someone else told me that
Alan had 'stolen' her off a lecturer in the History Department. The lecturer was at
the party too and Alan's shenanigans were aimed at him: skiting in a provocative
manner while the woman clung to his arm. I was simultaneously appalled and
impressed by this demonstration of flagrant egotism and sexual power.

Alan went overseas soon afterwards, via Australia (Sydney, Melbourne,
Darwin) to India, Nepal, Afghanistan, then London and many other places in
Europe, North Africa, Ireland, Britain. He remained a presence in Auckland,
however, because the work he sent back kept appearing in magazines, notably the

three issues of *Freed* which came out between 1970 and 1972, and *A Charlatan's Mosaic*, the 1972 Literary Society yearbook edited by Stephen Chan. Then there was *The Young New Zealand Poets*, edited by Arthur Baysting and published by Collins in 1973. I bought each one as it appeared and read, as an avid, unknown, unknowing acolyte, the poems they contained. They were wild and strange, intensely musical, too esoteric for me to work out what they meant, but I loved them anyway.

Sally Rodwell was a theatre-obsessed doctor's daughter from Rotorua. I'd met her in 1972 when I moved into 28 Sentinel Road, Herne Bay, where most of Ken Rea's Living Theatre Troupe, including my sister Frances, lived. Ken, Brian Divers, John Darville. My cousin Murray Edmond, the poet, was often there. Russell Haley, sometimes, too. Linda Taylor, the dancer, languished with a broken foot in her yellow room under the stairs. We had a brief, heart-breaking love affair. In those days Living Theatre did agit-prop in the streets, indoor productions that were partly scripted, partly improvised, and, in summer, toured the beaches in a big white bus called Stanley.

Sally lived, with her boyfriend Paul Carew, in the room next door to mine upstairs. I was in awe of her – her grace, her allure and her kindness. In the afternoons I used to sit in the corner of my trapezoid-shaped room typing on the portable Smith Corona I'd bought for $30 on Karangahape Road. When Sally was passing she would always put her head around the door and smile and ask what I was doing. Her curiosity, amusement and possible approval gave me hope. Sally was buxom in those days, wore diaphanous scarves and long interesting dresses, had white skin, warm brown eyes, a thrilling voice. Dean used to call her 'Shirley Rockwell, the famous film star'.

When I'd last seen her in Queen Street, she was actually on her way to meet Alan in Bali; they spent the year travelling in South East Asia, going from Java to Sumatra to Thailand to Laos, with an afternoon in Burma. The Vietnam War was still raging so they couldn't go there. They went instead to Sarawak, Brunei, Kalimantan and Sulawesi; home via Timor and Darwin. It was during these travels that the idea of Red Mole was mooted: the legendary occasion in the opium den behind the Shell service station in Luang Prabang. When I met them that night at Downstage they were not long returned. It's salutary to remember how young we were: I was 22, Sally 24, Alan a hoary old 27.

~

Sally Rodwell (passport photos).

I had already met Jan Preston. I came home one day and there she was in the hallway at No. 96, sitting opposite Gordon, talking non-stop, as she was wont to do. She was vivid and striking: short red hair, a black and white knitted pullover with the sleeves pulled up, grey slacks rolled just below the knees, sneakers. Mary was moving out; Jan had come about the room. She'd completed a music degree in Auckland the previous year and was now enrolled at teachers' training college in Karori. And she wasn't well. She was recovering from the hepatitis B infection she'd contracted from her previous boyfriend, a Māori guy called Arthur Mita.

Mita wasn't his surname, it was an alternative Christian name. His Māori name perhaps. He was a tall, slender, handsome man who was always laughing, showing a wide mouth lacking a few teeth. I used to play chess with him. I'd go round to his big old three-storey house, a squat, at 14 McDonald Crescent, between Willis Street and The Terrace, and we'd convene to an upstairs sitting room and play a game or two. Arthur was a superb tactician and invariably won; I felt good if I came even close to troubling him. He played as much above the board as on it: the mind games were incessant and, despite his unfailing good humour, deadly serious too. Especially after I got together with Jan. 'What you doing with her, man?' he would say.

Arthur was co-owner, with a couple of others, of Macavity's, a hip restaurant off Plimmer Steps in the city. It was housed within an enterprise called Plimmers Emporium, created between 1968 and 1972 by architect Ian Athfield out of the old Rutland Hotel. Redmer Yska recalls: 'Amazing circular Euro-style wooden staircase, hard on the waiters. Massive architectural refit of old dead building, across two floors, maybe three. Carmen had an antique shop upstairs. Alister Taylor opened a ground floor counterculture bookshop called Printed Matter. Malcolm McSporran was founding manager. But no-one ventured up those steep steps from Lambton Quay and place soon died.'

Rachel Stace was the manager, or was she the maître d'? Peter Fantl was the cook. The food was magnificent, especially the salads, full of exotica, including nuts, like pecans, we'd barely heard of before. Servings were huge. Usually, around 10.30, they'd close the door and the partying would begin in earnest and go on until after midnight. The restaurant guests, mostly friends anyway, would stay on to drink and smoke and carouse. There was always music playing. Steely Dan. The Rolling Stones. Roxy Music. Redmer remembers seeing *Deep Throat*, the porn movie starring Linda Lovelace, projected on the wall at Macavity's.

Peter Fantl, like Arthur Mita, was a tall, handsome, slender man with curly black hair and a wide white smile, though his didn't lack any teeth. He was generous to a fault. Charming, too. He was the son of the architect Robert Fantl, who'd escaped to England from Prague, aged 15, by train as part of the Kindertransport, on the eve of World War II. Bob had come to New Zealand in time to enlist in the air force and fight in the Pacific. He married a German woman called Claire Wolff and they built an elegant house in Wilton. Bob was a colleague of modernist architect Ernst Plischke, and a pioneer environmentalist. Pete sometimes lived at home but usually had a place in town. In Fairlie Terrace, for instance, just around the corner from 96 Kelburn Parade, a house his parents owned. Later he bought at 1 Haines Terrace. His only sibling, a sister, Judi, died by her own hand in 1971. He told me about this after my own sister Rachel committed suicide in 1975.

Pete was a dealer. As I recall, in Wellington in the mid-1970s, you could buy just about anything – with the exception of drugs like Ecstasy, which hadn't yet come on the market. And maybe not opium, which had been obtainable in Auckland earlier in the decade but was then rare. Heroin, certainly. Buddha sticks were starting to arrive, very strong marijuana heads that came threaded around small skewers of bamboo. Speed, of course. Pills of all descriptions, generally divided into two categories, uppers and downers. Acid. Traffic lights were ubiquitous, small cylindrical tablets in red, orange and green. Cocaine was available if you had the money. Everything else was cheap as. Halcyon days. Though I was never a serious drug user. I just took a bit of whatever was on offer.

~

Jan was the talented daughter of working-class parents, born in Greymouth on the West Coast of the South Island. Her family, like many Coasters, migrated north to sunny Hawke's Bay, where her father, Ed, a bluff, kindly fellow, was a milkman in Napier. He had escaped from a POW camp in Italy during the war and walked to Switzerland. While Ed was missing, Jan's mother Tui had fallen in love with someone else. But there was already a child, Edward, and so when Ed turned up again she returned to the marriage. Tui had the aspiration, the drive and the displaced ambition that may compel children towards outstanding achievements of the academic and/or the artistic kind.

Jan was the youngest of three. Her brother, Ted, was a primary school teacher; her sister Gaylene, still at that stage in England (she returned in the summer of 1976–7), an art therapist who became a well-known and accomplished filmmaker.

Jan Preston.

27

And Jan was a classical pianist. She had her B. Mus., her LRSM, her ATCL. She was a compelling solo performer, playing the works of Scarlatti, Schubert, Scriabin, de Falla, Stravinsky, among others; worked as a répétiteur for opera singers; and composed music for film, dance and theatre shows.

We were already an item before I knew much about this; even so, my love for her was composed partly of admiration for her considerable gifts. This was not simple. When we met I was already seeing another woman, Bernadette, a bit older than me, a computer programmer, who liked to dress me up in satins and velvets and with whom I used to party, drink, take drugs and fuck. It was a liaison composed of, and for, unthinking pleasure. Who knows where it might have led? Jan, however, impressed me with her high art credentials, which I felt I lacked and which I wanted to possess. In a way, it was the same yearning to associate with the prodigiously talented that drew me towards Alan, though I wouldn't have been capable of that insight then.

As for Jan, I'm not sure what she saw in me. I was young and good-looking, I suppose. I wore interesting clothes. I wrote art and theatre reviews, studied English literature and wanted to become a poet. I was, by nature, unassuming, well-mannered and kind. Beyond that, it is hard to tell. My insecurities, of which there were many, I kept very close to my chest. I didn't want anyone to see them. And maybe that made me seem more confident than I was. We were the same age, or nearly: she was six months older than me. We were good together for a while; and then we weren't. Unfortunately, by then, we were married.

One thing quickly became apparent. She was highly strung and inclined towards outbursts of anger, especially when she was due to give a solo piano recital. It was my role to absorb, like a lightning rod, these bursts of emotion; and, more generally, to provide support for her professional career. I was happy to do that, at least at the outset, but matters became more complex later on. When we each, in our different capacities, began to work for Red Mole, that support was extended to the ongoing enterprise. Our commitment to each other became part of our commitment to the group but I sometimes found myself in an invidious position: when they were in conflict, where did my loyalties lie, with Jan or with the Moles?

In Auckland Jan had been recruited into the avant-garde performances which composer Jack Body, principally, staged during the late 1960s and early 1970s. In 1972 Jack's multimedia production *Sexus* debuted at the Māori Community

Centre Hall in Fanshawe Street in Freemans Bay. Six dancers performed, to taped music, in front of two screens upon which two films were shown. 'Body invited choreographer Jennifer Shennan to work with him to produce *Sexus*, an erotic and gritty stage-performance. The dancers were paired to represent a spectrum of bodily encounters – male/male, male/female, female/female. Their movements were enacted in conjunction with the projected image of an ambiguously gendered man, who repeatedly performed a series of gestures and actions that confused the coded behaviour of conventional masculinity.'

The second film showed, simultaneously, in excruciating detail, the butchering of a sheep in an abattoir: the bio-luminescent guts spilling in slow motion from the body cavity into the offal trough. Dancers moved before the two large screens. In the half-light they seemed remote, abstracted, tranced. One of them was Deborah Hunt. The boy in the movie, young, androgynous, was filmed with his long, straight, glossy hair cascading over his face and shoulders and his hands caressing his naked torso. His name was Jerry and he was, briefly, a campus hero. Jennifer Shennan, the choreographer, was Jan's good friend and the two women resembled each other so strongly they were sometimes taken for sisters. After *Sexus* there was a performance of Karlheinz Stockhausen's *Kurzwellen*, for six players with short-wave radio receivers; Jan was one of these players.

I saw the show with a frisson of excitement but without understanding much of what was going on. I don't remember Jan being in it. I hadn't met her in Auckland, had never even heard of her, though another of her boyfriends, the mercurial Wilton Roger, was an acquaintance of sorts. It turned out Jan had a ghostly encounter with me too. In 1972 I had been a member of the Scratch Orchestra. Under the direction of Philip Dadson, we performed Cornelius Cardew's *The Great Learning*, a setting for percussion and voice of a Confucian text translated by Ezra Pound. Cardew had worked with both Stockhausen and John Cage; Philip had studied with him in London in 1969, then founded his own Scratch Orchestra on his return to Auckland. You didn't have to be able to play an instrument: 'a large number of enthusiasts pooling their resources (not primarily material resources) and assembling for action (music-making, performance, edification),' Cardew wrote.

We convened over the week of 21–26 August, during the New Zealand University Arts Festival, and performed the seven paragraphs of the work at three venues: St Paul's Anglican Church in Symonds Street, St Matthew-in-the-City and the Union Rugby shed in Wynyard Street. As part of the lead-up to *The Great Learning*, or perhaps during the week of performances, I cut a stencil and one night, with a couple of friends, took a spray can and inscribed the words 'The Streets Are Laughing' across the veritable streets of Auckland. Jan had seen this inscrutable message on the path leading up from Wellesley Street into Albert Park and wondered who its author might have been. It was a line from a poem I wrote.

Either Sally or Alan, or both, knew of Jan's work as a musician and a performer in Auckland. The same night Alan asked me to contribute to *Spleen*, he and Sally asked Jan to do the music for the upcoming, and inaugural, Red Mole show, *Whimsy and the Seven Spectacles*, in November of that year. This was the beginning of her association with them as their musician of choice and de facto composer in residence, or on the road, which would continue for the rest of the decade. She quickly became intrinsic to Red Mole, an outstanding contributor to the live shows. I still think the music she wrote and performed – most of it, alas, unrecorded – included works of genius.

~

Towards the end of 1974 Roger and Gary and the other boys moved out and Jan and I moved in to the spacious three-bedroom flat upstairs at No. 96. It was in every way an improvement on the dank, dark, doggy, cramped quarters down below. The sitting room, which we painted dove grey, was light and airy, with a red carpet and spectacular views over the hills and valleys to the south and the east; there was a bathroom with a bath; a kitchen table we could all sit at; a back door leading out to a small garden with a lasiandra tree, secluded and sunny enough that I was able to grow marijuana plants in pots there. I had, for the first time in my life, a study: a small rectangular room built over the landing where the staircase had once emerged. I put my desk under a window with panels of red and blue stained glass, facing Hawkins Hill; and sat, with my back to the household, tapping away at my Smith Corona.

I was only ever part time at Victoria; without a bursary or a scholarship I had to work in order to support myself. One job, which I loved, was taking newspapers off the end of the conveyor belt out the back of ramshackle old Press House at 82 Willis Street as the late afternoon edition of the *Evening Post* chuntered down from the printing presses. These were stacked into bundles, secured with a blue plastic band and sent off to be delivered to paper boys and dairies and newsagencies all over the metropolitan area. It was the smell of the ink, the rattle and roar of the presses, the sense of being in the very guts of the business of communication, which I loved. That, and the fact that the job was over almost before it began – about 45 minutes later, cash in hand, I could go to Barrett's Hotel for a beer.

There I might meet Redmer Yska. Or Neil Rowe, down from Masterton to visit his girlfriend. Or other more shadowy denizens of Wellington night life. There was an Englishman who haunted me. He went by the unflattering sobriquet of Fluffy, perhaps because of the blond fuzz that covered his cheeks. He carried with him at all times a copy of Salvador Dali's prophetic novel, *Hidden Faces* (1943), which he considered a sacred text and would urge upon you, though not to the extent of actually offering to lend his own battered and dog-eared paperback. It goes without saying that he was an artist himself, though I don't recall ever seeing any of his work.

Another job, which I loved as much as the one at the *Evening Post*, was situated, as it were, at the other end of the blockchain. It was for a firm called Information Research Consultants, who had a small office up above Cable Car Lane off Lambton Quay. Reg and Chua were the principals. Reg was an earnest, hard-working, red-headed man in a suit; Chua, svelte, subtle, also besuited, was Singapore Chinese. Their business was a clipping service: they harvested material from the press for a number of clients. It was my job, and that of my co-workers, to scan through the newspapers and then to cut out, paste up and annotate any articles that mentioned, for example, the Wool Board.

There were four of us: Denise Keay, a writer, somewhat reclusive, who later published a fine historical novel called *The Stove Rake* (2002); her good friend Jackie Wotherspoon, married to a potter called Paul, and with a very new baby, Lottie, whom she used to bring to work in a bassinet; and Neil Rowe, who was soon to become, or had already become, as an art reviewer, a (friendly) rival of mine. Neil, who ran an art gallery in Masterton, was courting Jenny Neligan, a young woman who worked at the university library. In time she would become a successful gallery owner herself.

My abiding memory of those mornings in Cable Car Lane is of unrestrained mirth. We laughed ourselves silly as we scanned the daily press: because newspapers are inadvertently hilarious anyway, because the work itself was ridiculously easy – you just had to spot headlines – and because Reg and Chua were broadly tolerant and uniformly cheerful as they bustled in and out on their way to secure more clients or to cultivate those they already had. It was fascinating in another way: a window into the world of business. Reg and Chua, for instance, idolised a guy called Henry Newrick, former encyclopaedia salesman and founder of the *National Business Review*, publisher, tourism promoter, art collector, treasure hunter, direct marketeer. He was, to them, everything a successful entrepreneur should be. I saw him sometimes, a suave fellow in a grey suit.

When, in the lead-up to the 1975 general election, property developer Bob Jones 'authored' a book called *The First Twelve Months: A study of the achievements of the third Labour government in 1973*, I went to the launch. Henry was its publisher. The book itself, a handsome, expensively bound hardback, contained 300 thick white pages of nothing whatsoever. It was blank, empty; that was the point. An elaborate joke. The launch was well attended and many people bought one of the copies stacked up on a table in the middle of the room, presumably as a form of political donation.

This was a time when sponsored graffiti on a wall in Willis Street said, 'Mat Rata reads comics.' Then, below: 'No, he doesn't, he just looks at the pictures.' (Matiu Rata was Minister of Māori Affairs and later helped to found the Waitangi Tribunal.) Bill Rowling, who inherited the prime ministership when Norman Kirk died on 31 August 1974, was regularly lampooned, in a cartoon that appeared daily on page two of the *Dominion*, as shivers looking for a spine to run down. Or even less polite assessments. It startled me that Reg and Chua, whom I liked, were aligned with this ruthless right-wing business faction, but I never said anything.

My other source of income, intermittent but more satisfying than either newspaper job, was writing itself. There was a short-lived (17-issue) ambitious, independent publication, a left-wing review called *The Week*, edited by Keith Ovenden, a tabloid on good-quality newsprint, and I contributed to that. Alister Taylor published a monthly magazine, *Affairs*, with a coloured cover and rather more inferior newsprint inside, which went out to secondary schools, and I wrote for that as well. The work I did for *Salient*, like the work I would soon be doing for *Spleen*, was, of course, unpaid. To be given money for writing seemed miraculous to me then; it still does.

The work and income issue was soon resolved, however. I heard that Wellington City Transport employed casual and part-time bus drivers, went down to the depot in Wakefield Street and signed up for training. It was fascinating watching the experienced Samoan and Tongan drivers manoeuvring the Big Reds, diesel or trolley, within inches of each other in the yard where the buses were marshalled. I never attained their level of expertise but did enjoy negotiating, with some competence, the narrow city streets, the twisting upland roads, the hills and valleys, in both kinds of bus. Dealing with the public had its own stresses and I learned, quite quickly, the saving grace of maintaining an even temper in the face of any provocation whatsoever.

It was shift work. Mornings started around 6am and went to 2pm; afternoons ran from about 2 until 10 or 11 at night. You alternated, week and week about. They would despatch a cab for you if your start or finish time fell outside the rostered shifts of your fellow workers. Or you could, like most of the older drivers, work a broken shift, which meant driving through both rush hours, having a few hours off in the middle of the day and then an early finish. I always worked straight shifts. The money was good and I could save up enough in the holidays to get through the next term of study. I stayed on the buses until I was offered a job at the university at the beginning of 1977.

~

When, at the end of 1974, I completed my BA, I did enrol for an MA: in English language and literature. I decided against taking the option of writing a thesis and set myself to complete six papers instead. Before I could begin, however, I had to do a course in Old English and to inaugurate the study of my 'foreign language', Māori. I never became fluent in te reo but some vestigial understanding remains, so that I don't feel entirely ignorant when I hear it spoken and can get the gist of written Māori if the text is not too complex or too ancient. And I have my dictionaries still.

There were the formal lessons and then there was the Māori Club, where I began to learn to whaikōrero alongside people like poet and performer Brian Potiki, then called King; Mark Derby, the radical historian; actor Wiki Oman and film director Lee Tamahori; and our language teachers, Ruka Broughton and Amster (New Amsterdam) Reedy. Koro Dewes, head of department, was a more remote, even forbidding figure. It was said his lack of academic qualifications troubled him, but I think it more likely that it troubled some of his university colleagues. His traditional knowledge was secure; his attitude, a mingling of pride and protectiveness.

In his other life he was a farmer up on the East Coast and one memorable Sunday night, during a marae restoration project at Tikitiki north of Ruatoria, out the back of the whare kai, he did open up. He was in his work clothes: checked shirt, grey woollen trousers held up by braces, gumboots. 'You Pākehā,' he said, enunciating the word with relish, like an especially potent insult. 'You Pākehā are like moths to the flame. When it flares up you all come around. When it dies down, you disappear.' Candlelight flickered across his face, danced in reflection in the whisky glass in his hand, like a warrant of the truth of what he was saying.

It was under the auspices of the Māori Club that I re-entered the world of stage drama for the first time since I'd appeared in Shakespeare's *Richard III* at Huntly College 10 years before. At the Ngāti Pōneke hall in Thorndon in September 1975, Brian Potiki directed Harry Dansey's two-act play, *Te Raukura: The Feathers of the Albatross*. The first act concerns the doings of Te Ua Haumēne, the prophet of Pai Mārire, 'the good and peaceful religion', which degenerated into the bloody cult Pākehā called Hauhau. The second is about Parihaka resistance leader Te Whiti o Rongomai. Written in 1971–72 and premiered at St Mary's Cathedral in Parnell during the Auckland Festival, who commissioned it, in 1972, it was the first professionally produced play by a Māori author.

Koro Dewes played Te Ua. Roger Steele was John Bryce, the so-called butcher of Parihaka, the police minister who led the armed raid on the town, an alarming performance which still lingers in the mind; perhaps he was channelling his father's military background. Rua Bristowe was among the cast of 38, as was Mark Derby. I played a couple of small roles: an angel; and a constabulary officer. Our uniforms were authentic period costumes borrowed from the Ballet and Opera Trust.

The thing I recall best about my contribution, however, is curious, a mere detail: I made a papier-mâché mask with a painted tattooed face, which represented (at least in my mind) the decapitated head of the posthumously moko-ed Captain Thomas Lloyd, sent around the country as a call to arms among the Hauhau. Lloyd led a crop-burning patrol that was ambushed south of New Plymouth in Taranaki in 1864. I wore the mask as the Angel Gabriel when he appeared to Te Ua.

I made it by sculpting a wet clay mould into the shape of the face, smearing it with petroleum jelly (Vaseline) and then applying layer after layer of torn-up bits of paper soaked in Selleys wallpaper glue. Each layer of paper was dried in front of a heater before the next was applied. After a dozen or so layers had been applied, the mask would be left to set, then taken off the mould, given eye holes, whatever fixtures it needed so it could be worn, and painted.

This was the mask-making method used in all of the Red Mole productions I was subsequently involved with. But *Te Raukura* was staged before I started working with Red Mole. I must have seen masks and puppets being made on the evenings we used to spend around at Sally and Alan's place in Tinakori Road. We would smoke dope, or heroin if there was any around, and listen to music. There was never a great deal of conversation; what there was would be focused upon forthcoming shows.

I was much more interested in these extra-curricular activities, so why did I keep on studying? I didn't really have a vocation as a scholar or as an academic. And, in fact, the first chance I got, I abandoned my putative university career. I probably persisted because, like so many others, I didn't know how else to occupy myself. Study postponed the question of what, in the old phrase, I would do when I grew up. It was, perhaps, a way of not growing up. And then, after that meeting with Sally and Alan at Downstage in 1974, and increasingly during our interactions over the next few years, my ambitions came to be defined by, and then wholly merged with, those of Red Mole.

II

Reversible Amnesia

WHAT WAS RED MOLE? When all external descriptions are exhausted, the enterprise still encodes a mystery – one best explored, perhaps, by looking again at that originary moment in Laos: the chance meeting of a group of New Zealanders in an opium den behind the Shell service station. Michele Leggott examined in some detail the circumstances of that meeting: 'Downriver at Luang Prabang,' she wrote, 'a dangerous cocktail of regional and personal turmoil explodes.' She concludes that some violent sundering occurred and was then, just as quickly, repaired. Red Mole was the result of the ensuing pact.

Sally and Alan were just a few months into their Eastern journey when that explosion happened. There are traces of it in the written record but, characteristically, nothing that can be called a documentary account. Certain motifs recur: the opium den; the Eros Cinema, where skin-flicks are shown; a meal of pancakes with condensed cream poured across them; a walk up to a temple upon a hill; a walk back down to the Mekong River; a departure for the south. These elements are combined and recombined in various ways in the poems and theatre pieces Alan made about the sojourn in Luang Prabang, and in them it is clear that two paths opened before the travellers, both of which are explored in the writing, but only one of which 'in reality' took place.

There is a version in which Alan, or rather his alter ego, Alias Monk Turnblazer, leaves Sister Mercy behind and goes alone down the river; in another, they go down river together; in a third, the crisis is existential and involves more than just the lovers: 'I want to go where there's no Beyond.' In other words, in Luang Prabang, Sally and Alan came to a point of personal crisis after which they might easily have split up and gone in different directions, but instead reunited in fealty to a shared enterprise that would consume their energies for the rest of their lives. Red Mole, then, was, first and foremost, a lovers' pact. This is why the initial imperative in the 1974 manifesto was 'to keep [the] romance alive'. This is what you joined, perhaps unknowingly, when you joined the group: a lifelong conspiracy that was also a love affair.

What about the other New Zealanders, met there by chance? At Pete Fantl's wake in the Alleluya Café in St Kevins Arcade on Karangahape Road in Auckland in February 2001, Sally delivered the eulogy, then read an unpublished poem of Alan's called 'Leaving Luang Prabang'. It begins:

> *Luang Prabang sits under strange skies*
> *at the edge of the universe.*
> *They walk down the moonlit road*
> *to the river.*
> *They smoke cigarettes then someone says, Go!*
> *White Angel*
> *White Flower*
> *Go!*
> *Holy*
> *Holy …*

Contemporaneously, in the programme notes for the show *Alias Monk*, which Alan was rehearsing in Wellington (it was why he didn't attend the wake), he recorded, 'one of the people encountered by coincidence on that trip, in a small riverside hotel in Luang Prabang, was Peter Fantl from Wellington'.

Pete's companions were his then girlfriend, Marcia Tuohy, his boyhood friend Steve Melchior, and Steve's wife Annie. They, like Sally and Alan, are best described, as they are in one of the Red Mole histories, as merchants and travellers. They were all, ultimately, on their way back to Wellington to sell their wares. And those wares included the shows that Red Mole would make. Many of these early shows, and especially after he got together with Deborah Hunt, featured Pete Fantl in a variety of roles, both on and off stage. 'PR, stuntman and baritone', is one descriptor; 'a one-armed circus shouter' is another; 'actor and advance man', a third. More importantly, perhaps, he was a direct route into the heart of the sophisticated alternative scene in Wellington, and especially its hedonistic, anarchic and oppositional drug culture.

Martin Edmond and Sally Rodwell, c. 1975.

Other crucial people in Wellington in 1974 were Jim and Jenny Stevenson. Jim, a lawyer, had joined the Department of Trade and Industry in 1970. He was an unusual kind of civil servant, a covert Mole perhaps. He had been Alan's co-conspirator in setting up the Cultural Liberation Front (CLF) in Auckland in 1969. They published an incendiary manifesto, 'Who as a Slug...': 'We must return all disciplines to a coherent order and resurrect the silent ghost of the Imagination.' The CLF was designed 'to infiltrate organisations through their weakest link, their cultural clubs and societies'. Jim and Alan had gone together by ship to Australia in 1970, but while Alan travelled on to Calcutta and beyond, Jim returned to New Zealand, probably to marry Jenny. In 1971 he negotiated the lease on the old Astor Recording Studios, which Sally turned into the Grafton Arts Centre.

Jenny was a dancer and in Wellington ran a studio that nurtured the talents of the young of the bourgeoisie, as well as those who might contribute to avant-garde productions in the capital. Members of her Can Can company, under the exquisite moniker Courtney Lace, appeared in early Red Mole shows, as did Jenny herself. And, somewhat improbably, Jim, too. Their presence in Wellington gave Red Mole entry into other circles: political, legal and, increasingly, corporate.

That corporate sphere was, however, mixed. It included, for example, the wildly successful Merchant Adventurers of Narnia, with their emporium full of exotica, mainly from the East, in upper Willis Street.

In those early Wellington years Sally and Alan lived in a basement flat on Tinakori Road in Thorndon. In keeping with every other place I knew them afterwards to rent, it seemed clandestine, Tardis-like. Nondescript from the outside, curtained against the light, it expanded within to make worlds – in both senses of that phrase. It was both a world, and a place where worlds were made. The first of those worlds, at least for public consumption, was *Whimsy and the Seven Spectacles*, performed for one night only, on 30 November 1974, in the Student Union Building at Victoria University.

The gig, part of a fund-raiser for the Newtown Adventure Playground, under the auspices of the Newtown Community Centre, inaugurated a long relationship between Red Mole and that community, as well as with community groups generally. The event made $692, covering expenses, with a couple of hundred dollars left over to go towards the playground. Other acts on the bill included poets Sam Hunt and Dave Mitchell who, during the performance of *Whimsy*, threw a beer bottle at Sally. Mitchell, despite the dramatic nature of his own readings – he sometimes appeared dressed as Harlequin – had an ingrained prejudice towards what he called 'the painted whore of theatre', especially when it seduced poets away from what he thought were their proper concerns.

The cast included Sally and Alan, Jim and Jenny Stevenson, dancers Ann Hunt and Erola Whitcombe, Jim Spalding, a Canadian who lectured in the Drama Department, and Jan on piano. I understood very little of what went on. Afterwards, perhaps in response to a similar perplexity, Alan told Jan there were always 77 levels of meaning to everything that he wrote, but it was up to audiences to work out what they were. This became, for years afterwards, a running joke between us. Jenny Stevenson was also mystified: 'I was dancing en pointe and Jim was eating a bowl of cereal – that's all I remember!' In the archives, however, is a phantasmagorical scenario which makes it clear that the primary inspiration for the piece was the arrest and trial of Dr W.B. (Bill) Sutch.

The Sutch Affair, so called, broke in late September 1974. Sutch (1907–1975), distinguished economist, historian, public servant, intellectual and sometime chairman of the Queen Elizabeth II Arts Council, was arrested in Aro Street, Wellington, and accused of passing information to Dmitri Razgovorov, first secretary at the Russian embassy in Karori. The SIS (Security Intelligence Service) bugged Sutch's office and, on multiple occasions, illegally broke in and examined his diary. They observed previous meetings between Sutch and Razgovorov, one under a lamppost just down the road from SIS HQ in Abel Smith Street. On the night of 26 September, along with police from Special Branch, they intervened and detained Sutch.

His arrest came less than a month after the death, from heart failure, of Norman Kirk – a death that at the time appeared suspicious to some. One popular rumour was that Kirk, on a scheduled visit to the Royal New Zealand Air Force base at Ohakea, had been taken in a jet fighter higher than medical advice considered safe for a man as overweight as he was. It was alleged that after landing he went, in distress, straight to hospital and never came out again. Another story was that he had been poisoned by the CIA. Sutch's arrest, coming so soon after Kirk died, can be understood as an early act in anticipation of the Muldoon putsch that succeeded the following year.

The SIS apparently thought that Sutch, caught red-handed, would confess, but to what? In the event he did not and, at the subsequent trial, was acquitted for lack of evidence. The Sutch family suggested that Razgovorov was in fact trying to defect and this was the reason for the meetings; if so, SIS incompetence spectacularly detonated that possibility. There were farcical elements: a sudden shower of rain caught the intrepid SIS agents unprepared (they had no umbrellas) and in the confusion they failed to detain Razgovorov, who fled down Aro Street and escaped in a car with diplomatic plates. He was questioned later on; his ultimate fate is unknown.

Nor was it clear that Sutch had actually given him the alleged 'package': a photo of the KGB man (taken by Peter Bush, then under contract to the SIS), umbrella furled, hat on, running through the rain, does not appear to show him carrying anything at all. The farce continued when the case went to trial. An SIS man was asked what time the sun set on several different evenings in the year during which Sutch had been under surveillance: in April, in August and in September. Apparently unaware of the seasonal variation in daylight hours, he said the sun went down at 6.30pm on each occasion. Sutch's acquittal was not, however, the end of the matter; there are still suggestions that he was guilty as charged.

~

41

Whimsy and the Seven Spectacles was staged using a wardrobe with a concealed entrance at the back and a levitating bed, under which, presumably, Reds might be found. The narrator was a figure reminiscent of Joel Grey, who played the MC in the 1972 film *Cabaret*. Out of darkness, two secret service men, X & X, enter. They wear trench coats and homburg hats, à la Humphrey Bogart, and have pig snouts for noses. They examine the joint carefully, professionally, then flee when they hear someone coming: a troupe of dancers.

Subsequently two other agents, Y & Y, enter, evidently in pursuit of X & X. They are comic, absurd, more Marx Brothers than Bogart-inspired; they wear bird masks. One opens the wardrobe door to reveal Jim Stevenson standing there in blue striped pyjamas eating cornflakes, but when he attempts to show the other agent, Jim, the skeleton in the closet, has disappeared. This agent also looks under the levitating bed and, when it descends, becomes trapped there.

The agents are disturbed once more by the troupe of dancers. The stage directions say, 'a different dance. Full sound. Full lights. A joyous dance. Cossack, maybe.' And then: 'Enter immediately the news media. One is a page of newsprint. One has a television camera for a head. The last, a microphone.' These masked figures are intricately sketched in the scenario; they have enormous feet. Then comes the re-entry of agents X & X, pursued by Y & Y, and, subsequently, repetition of the above, faster and faster – reminiscent of the old *Mad Magazine* strip 'Spy vs Spy'. At some point the Sutch figure is beguiled by the dancing of a Russian ballerina, played by Jenny Stevenson. It was a kind of fantasia, only very loosely related to the actual events upon which it was based.

The finale was Igor Stravinsky's *Circus Polka for a Young Elephant*, composed in 1942 for a ballet George Balanchine choreographed for the Ringling Brothers and Barnum & Bailey Circus. It was first performed by 50 elephants and 50 ballerinas; the elephants wore pink tutus. The title is another joke: Stravinsky said he would compose the piece for Balanchine only if the elephants were young ones. Jan played a version scored for solo piano: a lumbering, belting, grossly exaggerated piece of whimsy with which to conclude the parade of absurdities that was the *Seven Spectacles*. Someone is reported to have remarked, following this first incarnation of Red Mole, 'You'll never last.'

~

Whimsy and the Seven Spectacles: scenario, Alan Brunton, 1974.

The next Red Mole show took place just a few months later, on 8 and 9 March 1975, at the Jack Body-organised second Sonic Circus in and around the Wellington Town Hall. (The first Sonic Circus had been held the previous year, on 9 March, at the same venue where *Whimsy* was performed.) Sonic 2 utilised every available space: the main auditorium, the concert chamber upstairs, the green room, various corridors, the kitchen, the foyer, the stairs, the fire escape stairwell, the area under the stage, the public library (now City Art Gallery), the lawn and the gardens, including both the sunken garden and the rotary garden.

Performances included that of the antique gamelan orchestra ethnomusicologist Allan Thomas imported from Indonesia the previous year. In 1973 Allan was doing fieldwork in Cirebon, West Java, where the former royal court culture bequeathed a distinctive heritage of music and dance. An opportunity arose to buy the gamelan and Allan, aided and abetted by Jack Body, did so and had it shipped to New Zealand: 'About 25 years ago we set out on bicycles into the countryside with the price for the instruments and wayang puppets (the equivalent cost of a certain number of bags of rice).'

Thirty-three new New Zealand compositions were premiered at Sonic 2, including the Red Mole show, *Siddhartha*. It is the most mysterious of the early performances, partly because so little documentation of it survives. There is an A4 poster, landscape format, in pale aqua, with stencil lettering which gives only the title of the piece, misspelt, above the image and the name of the group below. The image, from a photograph, shows three female figures beside a river bank. One crouches down, picking up a container before her on the ground. The other two, robed, stand with fluted jars, no doubt containing water, on their heads. Beyond, a ship with a lateen sail floats at anchor before a line of palm trees on a distant shore. On a nearer shore, to the left, a line of camels steps down through more palm trees to drink from the river. There is a glimpse of a far horizon.

No scenario has been found in the archive. With a single exception, there do not appear to be any photographs of the two performances either. There was just one review, by Cathy Wylie, in the *Listener*: '[T]he Red Mole theatre used Chinese inspired movement in dialogue with a score, heavily accented with percussion, to play out the Siddhartha Legend. Behind you one of the poets slowly descended homewards through Asia, presenting the snapshot of his soul every sensitive traveller is bound to record for home consumption. Meanwhile Siddhartha was deflected from meditation on the Illusions of Life by a lissom houri who painfully relived Face to Face with Death in Varanasi.' The review was accompanied by an image showing ghostly figures before a screen, with a ladder-cum-palm tree and a ship-like shape stage left. The image in the photo, which I have seen only as a photocopy, bears an eerie resemblance to the picture, as described, on the poster.

If, as Murray Edmond remarked, *Whimsy and the Seven Spectacles* introduced many of the essential elements of future Red Mole shows – dance, music, mask, poetry, satire, a mix of low farce and high art – then *Siddhartha* added a no less essential thematic concern: the journey to enlightenment, the quest for revelation, the attempt towards the attainment of satori. It was also, in some sense, a rehearsal of Alan's personal story, as he told Chris Bourke in a 2000 interview: 'That's the reason I went to Australia; in the back of my mind I was heading for India and living out somewhere there. *Siddhartha*, the [Hermann] Hesse book, was a huge influence on me. The idea of walking beside the river with your bowl, dressed in a robe and nothing else was happening in the world, it was your world. This became a very interesting idea to me.'

When asked if he did in fact go walking by the river, Alan replied:

I went from Calcutta, which was amazing. First day I walked out and there's a body on the footpath right outside the Salvation Army. Where do you stay when you're poor, you stay with the Salvation Army, it said so on the little bit of paper someone had given you in Darwin: 'Stay at the Salvation Army dadada in Calcutta'. A dead person lying on the street, just starting to ooze the bodily waste, and people there standing looking, and that was the first thing I saw in the East. It was like the Buddha enlightens you, on the Buddha's turf the Buddha sends a sign: 'Beware of Maya, it's all illusion'.

Of course there is a paradox here: the journey to enlightenment is also the voyage towards death; if death is not in fact the enlightenment. All of the many journeys to paradise that featured in subsequent Red Mole shows, especially those in the later 1970s and early 1980s, explore this paradox. Cathy Wylie identified a further dimension of it when she wrote, somewhat inscrutably, that Siddhartha was 'deflected from meditation by a lissom houri'. Generally speaking, in theatrical terms, Alan played the pilgrim seeking enlightenment, and Sally the lissom houri who either distracted him from, or helped him to achieve, the quest.

The Sonic 2–Red Mole connection was notable for another reason. Rose Wedde (now Beauchamp), like Jan a classically trained pianist who moved into the exploration of other forms of music- and art-making, was there. Sally suggested that they might join forces to make a puppet theatre. Rose went home and began to read up on puppet-making. She and her husband Ian Wedde, who had been living in Dunedin, had just come north for a variety of reasons, some personal, some political. As Wedde remarked in 2018, 'they basically amounted to time to get the fuck out of there'. He also wanted to do whale research in the North Island. Rose's brother Allan Thomas, the gamelan man and Jennifer Shennan's partner, was living in Roseneath, where the Weddes also set up house. Rose and Sally's collaboration began the other half of Red Mole Enterprises in its first decade: White Rabbit Puppet Theatre.

Deborah Hunt was also at Sonic 2, performing with Theatre Action. She had encountered the Living Theatre troupe at Rawene in Northland, where she grew up, when she was just 16. 'They were wild university students performing commedia,' she said. 'I wanted to belong to a group of people like that.' She trained as a dancer and worked with Theatre Action from 1972; she was, as mentioned, one of the performers in *Sexus*. Over the winter of 1975 she went to Sydney, where she learned fire-eating from Tony Radcliffe of Whirling Brothers Circus. Radcliffe, aka the Elephant Man, was a New Zealander from Taumarunui; Whirlings, until it closed in 2006, was New Zealand's only home-grown touring circus.

~

Sally and Alan moved out of their underground flat sometime before June 1975. When they got married, at the winter solstice, the wedding party was held at their new place in Upton Terrace, off Tinakori Road. It was upstairs and you reached it via an external staircase and a catwalk to the back door. I didn't go to the ceremony, only to the party afterwards. It was riotous; there were lots of drugs; I recall only fragmentary images.

Alan in confrontation with Sally's father, for instance, a moment when blows might easily have been exchanged. Sally's father was a gynaecologist, a big, confident, assertive man, accustomed to getting his own way by means of natural authority and a degree of intimidation. Alan couldn't help but take him on. Someone, perhaps Sally, perhaps her stepmother, stepped between them. I can't now remember if Sally's mother, Audrey, was there. None of Alan's family were.

Another image also features Alan. It must have been later on, in the front room; he was flying high, in an intoxication of egotistical power. We were standing in an impromptu circle and he went around the ring, identifying each person's role in the unfolding enterprise. 'Jan, she does the music. Jim looks after legals.' And so forth. He came to me and paused, seemingly lost for words. 'Martin,' he said. 'Martin is the … critic.' I was deeply offended; I was sure that wasn't my role, but what was? If only I knew. Now I can perhaps say historian, but even as I write it, I'm listening out for a ghostly voice – Alan's sardonic riposte.

~

About 10 days after the wedding my sister Rachel died. She was 21. I have written elsewhere about her death and the effect it had on our family, but have never attempted to describe, insofar as I understand them, the circumstances. Now, nearly half a century later, perhaps it is time. She had been living at home, at 401 Fergusson Drive, Heretaunga, for most of that year. She had a job, working in a hospital, and was affiliated with a group of charismatic Christians based upon the Kapiti Coast and presided over by a Scotswoman called Margaret. Both job and affiliation provided support in her ongoing affliction, a mental illness diagnosed as schizophrenia, for which she took medication. However, an indeterminate time before her death, she discontinued the drugs, because of their flattening effect upon her perceptions, her thoughts and her mood. This is not uncommon among schizophrenics.

The last time I saw her, she came into town to visit me and we went to the movies. To the Lido, in Willis Street, to see *Julius Caesar* (1953) with Marlon Brando, John Gielgud, Deborah Kerr and James Mason. It is an excellent film and we both enjoyed it. Rachel was always good to go out with. She was intelligent and perceptive, never dogmatic; a wise, calm, quiet presence. She had come up to Kelburn Parade for a bite to eat before we went out. Afterwards I walked her down to the railway station where she caught the train back to Heretaunga.

Whether she'd ceased medicating by then, I don't know, but there is one final trace of her in which she was certainly drug-free. It's a black and white photograph taken by our youngest sister, Katherine; there was some camera shake and the image is slightly, heart-breakingly, blurred. Rachel has just washed her hair and is happy, smiling, perhaps even laughing in that helpless, side-splitting way she sometimes did. It is the last photograph of her real self because, a few days later, she recognised the warning signs and realised another psychotic attack was on the way. Her suicide was not an effect of that attack but a response to its inception.

In other words, she chose to die rather than endure what she knew was coming.

There are still mysteries, unresolvable now, about the events on the day she took the poison that killed her. One is that, at some point during the Thursday afternoon, she had a conversation with our mother, during which she put the case for her impending suicide. 'I have a good life,' she said, 'but I don't want it. Unlike Father, who doesn't have a good life, yet still wants it.' Or words to that effect. The mystery is that, following this conversation, during which she was apparently half-persuaded by Rachel's clarity of thought and strength of purpose in wanting to die, Lauris let her go. Or perhaps Rachel slipped away when Lauris's back was turned: she was adept at silent departures. She walked up Fergusson Drive to a gardening centre in the next suburb, Brentwood, and there bought a bottle of the herbicide called paraquat. It was used, among other things, to spray marijuana plantations in South and Central America.

It wasn't until my father came home from work later in the afternoon that anyone went looking for her. Years later he told me, in harrowing detail, the stages of his search, and how he found her at last in the grass down by the river in nearby Trentham Park. She had drunk the paraquat and lain down to die, but was still conscious. In those days the highway on the western side of the Hutt River had not yet been built. There was a wild bank of willows and natives on the far bank. And it was winter, so the river would have been high, rushing south, its sibilants drowning out whatever last thoughts she might have been having. I see my father now, picking her up in his arms, a pietà in reverse. She was taken by ambulance to hospital in Lower Hutt.

Here is another strange thing. I was due to fly north the next day, Friday, to join Jan for a weekend in Auckland; she was on a schools tour as the pianist for the New Opera Quintet. My parents rang to say that Rachel was in hospital but that it was thought she would survive. There was no need for me to cancel my trip. I could see her when I got back. So I went up as planned and, on the Saturday morning, at a house in Parnell called Sarnia Lodge, where the pianist Denys Trussell lived, received the phone call from my father saying that Rachel had died. The paraquat caused massive organ damage; the ultimate cause of death was liver failure. I flew back to Wellington. I remember weeping uncontrollably on the car journey from the airport to Upper Hutt.

There is one more thing to relate. In the hospital, as her life ebbed away, Rachel told our father that her imminent death was an accident and that she regretted it. To our mother she said the opposite: it was deliberate, willed and what she wanted to happen. This was an act of generosity, saying to each of them what they needed to hear in order to continue without her. But which was the truth? I suspect she wasn't delusional, that she made a rational decision based upon her conviction that she could no longer manage her illness, but I might be wrong. It's certain that the medication available for people with her condition is better targeted these days: you don't necessarily have to lose the things that make life worth living in order to dampen down the manifestations of those things that render existence insupportable.

Those mid-winter weeks of 1975 remain a blur, cut through with images of disturbing clarity. At the service, in a funeral parlour in Lower Hutt, an anodyne place, I know I recited lines from Shakespeare's *Cymbeline*:

> *Fear no more the heat o' the sun,*
> *Nor the furious winter's rages;*
> *Thou thy worldly task hast done,*
> *Home art gone, and ta'en thy wages:*
> *Golden lads and girls all must,*
> *As chimney-sweepers, come to dust.*

But I don't remember saying them. Rather, what I recall is Rachel's friend and mentor Margaret, the cult leader saying to me as I went up to speak and again when I came back down the aisle: 'She's no' in the box. She's no' in the box.' And thinking, you silly woman, that's precisely where she is. Now, though, I wonder.

Most people, faced with news of a death in the family, are kindly disposed but don't know what to say. Sally and Alan were exemplary in their empathy and their care. Others were brutal in their unconcern; or worse, toxic in their peculiar relish, even glee, at witnessing, from a safe distance, high drama. But distance seems in fact to be the key: the event, however devastating at the time, gradually takes on an emblematic character, something enacted upon an ancient frieze or in a play from the era before realism conquered our theatres. Rachel came to resemble a tragic heroine playing out a fate she had not chosen and yet was determined to embrace. She was, you might say, Greek in her forbearance and in her acceptance of an intolerable predicament.

Such distancing is probably a survival mechanism. What is more surprising, and ultimately more comforting, is the way fragments of her speech, her intonation, characteristic expressions, moments of laughter or tears, remain alive in my memory as testaments to her brief time on earth. Still, today, decades later, a certain set of the head in the figure of a dark-haired young woman, on a bus perhaps, or walking in the street, will have me turning to look, half-expecting to see her again. I don't think I'll ever lose that expectation. And then there are the regular appearances she makes, preternaturally alive, in my dreams.

~

I wrote my last review for *Salient* in the 20 June 1975 issue. It was a piece called 'Sunrays and Pain', which surveyed two international exhibitions, one at the Academy of Fine Arts and the other at the National Gallery. The first was a show of Picasso etchings from *The Vollard Suite* (1930–37). Three copies of the book, from a print run of 300, had been bought by local entrepreneur Barrington Cramp and dismantled – some said vandalised – so that individual images might be framed and sold. They were disturbing, often erotic prints, showing artists, models, bulls, minotaurs, nudes, in various liaisons or contretemps. The suite begins in joy and ends in darkness: a blinded minotaur, led by a little girl, wandering in the night.

At the National Gallery across the way was *The Graphic Art of German Expressionism*, toured through Australasia by the Institute for Foreign Cultural Relations. Wood- or linocuts, mostly portraits, the images burned themselves into my brain. I encountered for the first time original works by Max Beckmann, Otto Dix, George Grosz, Erik Hackel, Ernst Ludwig Kirchner, Emil Nolde, Karl Schmidt-Rotluff and many more. 'A gallery of faces looking out of the darkness of their setting or situation,' I wrote, 'with their dark staring eyes; the strength of those faces adamant before the forces that threaten them and which are nevertheless part of them'.

I stopped contributing to *Salient* because I was about to begin writing for *Spleen*, which debuted later that year, more or less coincident with the first Red Mole cabaret, *Cabaret Paris Spleen*, at the Performers Theatre upstairs at 106 Courtenay Place. The Performers had a curious genesis. Trevor Wells, technical director at Downstage, just up the road, leased the premises as an alternative theatre space. Alternative, that is, to the moribund middle-class theatre-restaurant Downstage had become. Director and writer John Banas and actor and designer Grant Tilly agreed to come in with him. Trevor signed a year's lease on the premises, whereupon Banas and Tilly ghosted. Wells, $10,000 out of pocket,

Cabaret Paris Spleen: Jenny Stevenson and Sally Rodwell,
The Performers Theatre, 1975.

was left holding the lease and without any shows to stage. Red Mole, sensing an opportunity, stepped in.

I have a set of colour slides of *Cabaret Paris Spleen* taken by Richard Turner, who was preparing to make his film, *Three Poets*, with Alan Brunton, Russell Haley and Ian Wedde at the time. Richard had just come back from a sojourn in Britain. He arrived in Wellington with long blond hair, wearing platform heels, flared trousers and glam rock shirts. He had been hanging out with William Burroughs and Brion Gysin, and a malodorous Allen Ginsberg, in the gay version of swinging London. He'd worked at the Royal Opera House in Covent Garden and on a music video for prog rock band Genesis. Russell Haley had been Richard's mentor at Auckland University and that was the connection which got him into making *Three Poets*.

The film has alternative titles: *In Search of the Garlic Seed* and *Souvenirs of Egypt, 1944*. It was meant to be a single work in three parts, but these somehow ended up having lives of their own. They became *Garlic Seed* (Brunton), *Weekend* (Haley) and *Angel* (Wedde). Funding from the Education Department had something to do with this: they were sent out to schools as separate items. Richard's cabaret slides, then, concentrate on the performances of those three poets, all of whom appeared in *Cabaret Paris Spleen*. But they also give some glimpses of the décor and the ambience on those long ago September nights.

The stage was along a side wall of the narrow rectangular room so that the audience sat, spread wide, very close to the performers. There was no set to speak of, no curtains, threads of carpet laid here and there over bare boards. A few posters: one from *Gone with the Wind*; another, hung deliberately crooked, announcing an exhibition of the works of Oskar Kokoschka; a third, an English newspaper billboard, proclaiming, white on black, 'I won't drop my Standards for anybody.' Somebody must have brought that back from London. There was an old sofa. A pile of books. A lamp. It could have been a share house sitting room.

Ian Wedde, in a white shirt and a black waistcoat, wearing a badge saying 'Mark Twain Lives', had a glass of water poured over his head by Sally Rodwell. He was reading *Angel*, his satirical attack upon a certain kind of person who was also a version of himself. Commissioner Haley performed with a bunch of arum lilies tucked into the waistband of his checked trousers, so that their white trumpets and golden tongues swayed gently above his head, sprinkling his cloth cap with orange pollen dust. Alan, in a trilby and a scarf, was impersonating an Apache but looked more like a wide boy exiled from the Marylebone Road.

Greta Campbell and Deborah Hunt, the Slitsky Sisters, danced together, one in a voluminous gown, the other wearing men's clothes and ballet pumps; it was a precursor of the routines Deb and Sal would perform in later years. When Francis Batten's clown, Swede, made his entrance, a grand jeté, he broke a hole in the stage through which his leading leg plunged; it became, perforce, part of the act. Jan played piano: Satie, Offenbach and the tango 'Hernando's Hideaway' from *The Pajama Game*. Rose Wedde contributed percussion and piano accordion. This replication of 'a night in old Montmartre' was a cross between a poetry reading, a literary salon and a variety show. The poster, by Jean Clarkson, was a collage: six can can dancers on the keys of an upright piano.

A feature of the slides is the number of images of dances performed by female couples, in various pairings, wearing slinky ball gowns and feather boas, bearing fans: Sally and Deborah; Greta Campbell and Frances Edmond; Jenny Stevenson and an unknown companion. Perhaps this was the inception of Courtney Lace,

Jenny's can can troupe. Steve Matthews, a drama school student like Greta and Frances, appeared in a leopard skin as a strongman, the Amazing Zardoz. The theme of Paris in the nineteenth century was visited only lightly: more mood than theme. Even so, the hero of Baudelaire's 'Spleen' – 'like the king of a rain country, rich / but sterile, young but with an old wolf's itch … whose food/is syrup-green Lethean ooze, not blood' – didn't really manifest. Everyone was too young and too sexy, too good-looking and too carnal, too much in flagrante delicto, for a pose of world-weariness really to convince.

~

The foundation myth of White Rabbit Puppet Theatre is as seductive, in its way, as that of Red Mole's beginnings in Luang Prabang. Sally answered a newspaper advertisement seeking children's entertainers to perform in the school holidays at James Smiths, the grand old emporium on the corner of Manners and Cuba streets in Wellington. White Rabbit were hired. The first shows took place between 25 and 29 August 1975 in the toy department on the second floor and featured a script by Ian Wedde called *The Crocodile and the Butterfly* aka *The Crocodile Who Went to Pieces*.

The croc, a denizen of the Mississippi and 'a nasty character', fell hopelessly in love with a butterfly called Flutterby; poignant absurdities ensued. The performers were Alan, Sally and Greta Campbell; Rose Wedde did the music. Alan carpentered the booth and the cast manufactured the puppets, glove and

White Rabbit Puppet Theatre: *The Crocodile Who Went to Pieces*, c. 1975.

stick, themselves. Greta played a life-size, mute, masked character called Ernie who stood outside the booth and, for and with the children, mimed watching the play unfold.

Most kids who went to school in New Zealand in the 1950s and 1960s had seen puppet shows, Alan among them: 'I can remember a puppet show. I don't know which troupe it was, the Burtons probably. I was seven or eight. The puppets talked, I was taken away; I wanted to do that.' Jim and Edna Burton were a Scots couple who emigrated from Glasgow to New Zealand in 1955. They used wooden puppets, marionettes, animated by sticks; Jim carved them and Edna made the costumes. Their material, from Hungarian, Russian, Turkish, Chinese and Japanese folk tales, was refreshed each year for the upcoming tour. After their shows, they would hold workshops, teaching school kids to make puppets out of junk.

Alan, born in 1946, might not have seen the Burtons. Perhaps it was the Goodwin Marionette Theatre, which also toured schools in the 1950s, and featured in their repertoire a version of Shakespeare's *The Tempest*. The Goodwins used both glove and wooden puppets and, like the Burtons, travelled by bus. Or it could have been the Puppet Theatre, formed in 1957 by Raymond Boyce and Geraldine Kean which, among much else, performed Aristophanes' *The Birds* and Ben Jonson's poem, *Hero and Leander*. Or someone else entirely. I remember a Punch and Judy show that came to Ohakune Primary School some time before 1962. Hundreds of us sat on the floor in the hall watching tiny figures animated within their vivid red and yellow booth, entranced, as if looking into the mouth of an eternity.

White Rabbit continued putting on puppet shows at the Performers Theatre for the rest of 1975. In December they returned to James Smiths, and, again, in the May holidays the following year, by which time Deborah Hunt had replaced Greta Campbell, who had followed her Divine Light guru overseas. In November 1975 they were temporarily approved by the Board of Education for performances in schools. That approval was made official in July 1976, though not without this assessment by Sunny Amey of the Curriculum Unit: 'Both parts of the programme are too long, there are too many characters, some scarcely developed e.g. the Scotsman who appears briefly with a donkey and reappears at the end. The content is rather adult.' It is likely that children did not agree with this opinion: when was variety ever a problem for kids? Or Scotsmen on donkeys?

White Rabbit Puppet Theatre: *The Adventures of George Washington Pratt,*
c. 1975.

In the repertoire by then were *The Billy Biter Show*, about a dragon with an insatiable appetite for gingerbread; *The Adventures of George Washington Pratt*, from a scenario written by Rose Wedde after her discovery in the Turnbull Library of the story of an American of that name abroad on the Central Otago goldfields; *Once Upon a Taniwha*, adapted from Māori folk tales; and *The Girl Who Lost Her Head*. Later shows included *Igor's Strange Tale* (a stepmother/stepdaughter story), *The Useless Policeman* (self-explanatory) and *After Midnight at the Kentucky Burger Bar* (starring the burger). Meanwhile, *The Crocodile and the Butterfly* remained a staple. Like the Burtons, White Rabbit held puppet-making workshops with children after the shows were over.

Puppetry has a central place in the Red Mole oeuvre, even though White Rabbit only lasted until June 1980. An Indonesian shadow puppet play Sally and Alan saw behind a bus station in Jakarta is as important in the genealogy as the events in Luang Prabang; in terms of technê, maybe even more so. In the early years puppet shows provided a more reliable flow of income than theatre and it was directly, palpably, influential in the way that adult theatre was not. You could see the effect on the children, the way the puppets liberated their imaginations.

White Rabbit Puppet Theatre: Ernie
(Greta Campbell), c. 1975.

The archive contains many letters of gratitude, not just from schools but from old people's homes, community centres, hospitals and the like.

Greta Campbell's appearance as Ernie at James Smiths was prescient too. Puppets, and especially shadow puppets, would become intrinsic to Red Mole's mask and gallanty shows; so too, inevitably, the combination of puppets and live actors. The apotheosis of this tendency was *Dead Fingers Walk* in New York in 1979: a mix of puppetry and live action which provoked a rave review from that doyen of theatre critics, Erika Munk. After that separate puppet shows vanished from the repertoire, but puppets didn't disappear; they became an integral part of the enterprise.

~

The magazine *Spleen* ('a useful organ') is often said to have been launched at *Cabaret Paris Spleen*, but this cannot have been so. The gossip column therein, 'Parish Spleen', is illustrated with photographs from the two nights at the Performers Theatre: the Slitsky Sisters, Swede, Commissioner Haley, the Amazing Zardoz. 'Parish Spleen', a regular feature over the eight issues of the magazine, would reliably ruffle feathers, but it also functioned as a source of news, detailing, for instance, with frequently acerbic commentary, grant money given out by the Queen Elizabeth II Arts Council.

Another regular feature was 'The Splinterview', a transcribed interview with someone from the art world or similar, conducted in a leisurely fashion and at some length. *Spleen 1* chose Robertus (sic) Franken, a displaced sixth-generation artist from den Hague, for its subject. The cover showed a Tibetan mask and robe, with Robèrt inside it, next to an elaborately framed Renaissance print: *Portrait of a Lady* by Rogier van der Weyden (1460). The centrefold was an A2 reproduction of *The Many Faces of My Genie*, one of his meticulous, grotesque, black and white, pointillist pen drawings of 1972–75 in which animal forms and human body parts, in free association, seem in the process of the invention of hitherto unknown creatures.

When you unfolded *Spleen 1* there was a poem by Mountain Jim Jantipur called 'Twelve Strings to the City', about an encounter with a blind blues singer. 'We found him at a pig/ pig'n'whistle stand in Atlanta./My wife said,/There is a negro man/with a guitar.' Jantipur is in Uttar Pradesh; most people assumed that the

Spleen 3: cover, Jean Clarkson, 1976.

pseudonym was Alan's. An anonymous sequence of six poems, 'New Jerusalem Sonnets', a parody of the late style of James K. Baxter, was so tonally perfect you felt Hemi must have come back from the grave to take himself off. They were addressed to Baxter scholar and biographer John Weir: 'The fires of wrath, John! Sometimes I think/My poems speak from the bronze arse-pipe/Of the bull that the Romans roasted slaves in.'

Bill Manhire republished the sequence in his book *Doubtful Sounds* (Victoria University Press, 2000) with a credit for his collaborator, Brent Southgate, whose performance as the oracular ghost of Baxter at *Cabaret Paris Spleen* was the sequence's inciting incident. The poems also appear in *Big Smoke: New Zealand Poems, 1960–75* (Auckland University Press, 2000). Brent Southgate remembered: 'I'd come up with the bit about JKB's poems speaking from the 'bronze arse-pipe' of the Roman torture machine, and so on – felt things were going well – and Bill suddenly topped it with the lines, "Man, how can you take the *via crucis*/And still be humble?" After twenty-odd years that still cracks me up.'

Tony Fomison contributed an essay/review, 'The Cart Horses of Paris', about the recent exhibition of eight Van Gogh paintings at the Auckland City Art Gallery. It was a caustic piece, illustrated with a full-page reproduction of a Fomison pencil drawing of Van Gogh, with glowing eyes, at the easel. A small, dubious face, a self-portrait, looking upwards at the artist, appears in the bottom right-hand corner. And then there was a despatch from filmmaker Geoff Stevens who had taken his debut feature, *Test Pictures*, to a festival in Iran.

The other regular feature in *Spleen*, 'Princes Wharf', usually appeared towards the back and contained reviews of various art events. In the inaugural issue reviewers were identified by their initials. NS, at a CANZ (Composers Association of New Zealand) conference in Hamilton, took a tilt at the barbarities and absurdities of the classical music tradition resuscitated, but on life support, in the South Pacific; ST previewed Amamus' coming trip to Poland; IW cast a cold eye over some recent coffee-table books featuring New Zealand landscapes ('Ah, Marti Friedlander and James McNeish, *Spleen* salutes you'); and ME went to see Sound Movement Theatre's *Anatomy of a Dance* and *Song Cycle*. NS was the composer Noel Sanders; I don't know who ST was; IW was Ian Wedde; ME was me. It was a confused review but I remember feeling delirious with happiness when it came out, as much because of the company I was keeping as for any other reason.

Spleen was meant to antagonise; an alternative title was *Stool*, as in stool pigeon but also as in turd. Although all of the issues now look tatterdemalion, because newsprint yellows with the years, then disintegrates, it was a stylish publication. Alan Brunton and Ian Wedde were co-editors of the first four issues, and both had a strong visual sense. Layouts were inventive and often incorporated visual puns. The standard of graphic illustration was high too, with contributions from Gil Fraser and Jean Clarkson, among others. The potential of black and white offset printing was fully used. And the editors were complementary in their networking.

Probably it was Ian who solicited the 'New Jerusalem Sonnets' and the Fomison essay. Alan would have interviewed Robèrt Franken and, although contributions came from all over, written most of 'Parish Spleen'. He also laid out the magazine, working nights until it was ready to go up by bus to be printed by the *Levin Chronicle*. His felt-tip was all over the final mark-up, making additions and alterations, signing articles, writing captions. That gives an endearingly home-made cast to the magazine. Issues cost 50 cents each. On the back cover of the first issue was a full-page advertisement for Frank Sargeson's novel *Sunset Village* bought and paid for by A.H. & A.W. Reed.

~

In August 1972, during the University Arts Festival in Auckland, Theatre Action organised a street parade to protest against the Vietnam War. Masked, robed figures moved silently down Queen Street, lamenting the death and destruction visited upon a country whose only crime was its desire for self-determination. Everything stopped. Cars, people, shopping. A similar event was staged in Wellington in 1975 in protest against the imminent election of a National government under Robert 'Piggy' Muldoon. One of our placards read: 'If you are white Anglo-Saxon and rich/vote National for NZ the way you want it.' We wore cardboard rosettes with the words 'I Want' upon them. We moved to the beat of a drum. The theme was greed.

Francis Batten, who was living at publisher Alister Taylor's ranch in Martinborough in the Wairarapa, made regular trips into Wellington to take mask-making workshops at the newly rebranded (1974) New Zealand Drama

Theatre Action: masked street parade, Wellington, 1975.

School. One day a student, John Davies, a young man off a farm near the small Waikato town of Piopio, noticed two women making masks downstairs at the school's premises at 172 Taranaki Street. They were Sally Rodwell and Deborah Hunt and the masks were to be worn in the coming street parade. Deb and Sal invited John to join them and make a mask himself; he did – and in 2018 still had 'the funny little mask' he made.

This was his initiation into Red Mole, the start of a relationship which would last a decade. John, who seems youthful even at sixty-something, had the energy and the optimism to take on any task and make something splendid of it. He could sing and dance and play guitar, and set words to music. His scholarly side emerged later, in his study of Japanese Noh theatre and his investigations of the synergies between Greek tragedy and contemporary Māori performance. He also looks like Robert Redford.

As everybody knows, Muldoon swept to power in a landslide at the end of November and stayed there for nine years. There was a party on election night at Upton Terrace, though party is perhaps not the right word for such a sombre occasion. Late in the evening, when people were starting to drift away, Noel Sanders lay stretched out full length and supine on the catwalk leading to Sally and Alan's door, singing the national anthem. The words had never sounded so desolate: 'From dissension, envy, hate,/And corruption guard our State,/Make our country good and great,/God defend New Zealand.'

Something else happened around this time that had a profound effect upon us all: Peter Fantl lost his arm. He was an injecting drug user; one of the puncture marks made by a hypodermic needle in his left arm became infected. Pete was already in a relationship with Deb Hunt; she took him to see a doctor, who did not seem unduly alarmed and sent him home with antibiotics and painkillers. By the wee small hours of the next morning, however, gangrene had set in and was accelerating at an alarming rate. They rushed to the emergency department at Wellington Public Hospital, where the arm was amputated below the elbow. A drastic action, though not as drastic as death from organ failure had the wet gangrene spread through the blood to other parts of the body.

I never heard Pete complain about the loss of his arm. He was right-handed, and seemed hardly impeded by the loss of his left. He relearned how to drive, for instance. His green Peugeot 404 had a column shift and he would secure the steering wheel in the crook of the elbow of the amputated arm, then reach across

Vargo's Circus: Ensemble (sitting: Helen Panckhurst, Rose Wedde, Carlos Wedde, John Davies; standing: Sally Rodwell, Deborah Hunt, Greta Campbell, Ian Wedde), The Dell, 1976.

with the other to change gears. I once drove up to Auckland with him in that car and felt not the slightest anxiety at his driving competence. It was the same with everything else he did, from bartending to cooking to catering to acting. I remember him at our wedding, for instance, a washing basket full of flowers under the remnant of his lost arm, scattering pink and white camellias with his good hand before the bridal path.

~

Pete recovered soon enough to join the Red Mole 1975–76 summer tour of North Island beach places. He acted as advance man on the East Coast before returning early to Wellington. Jan didn't go. Rose Wedde made the music along with various other members of the ensemble, which included John Davies, in the first flush of a romance with Greta Campbell. Another new recruit was actor, now Sydney-based film producer, Helen Panckhurst. Her husband, Kevin Davidson, provided technical support. In other words, he did the sound.

The Weddes travelled en famille; their son Carlos was still a toddler. The other members of the travelling show were Sally and Alan. Part one was from a script by Ian called *The Lion and the Gypsy*, a dramatisation of the famous *Sleeping Gypsy* painting by 'Le Douanier' Rousseau. Or, as Wedde described it, 'involving Henri Rousseau's relationship with a sleeping lion while on holiday at a North African beach'. Part two was a collective production that culminated in Deborah blowing fire; it was the first of many shows with this incendiary climax.

Red Mole travelled under the name of Vargo's Circus which, a man from Leonardo's Circus told Wedde in Ruatōria, was copyright and shouldn't be used without permission. They stayed in motor camps and travelled in a hired truck that was always breaking down. They were following in the tyre tracks of Living Theatre and Blerta earlier in the decade and, more distantly, of the Goodwins and the Burtons. It was one of the wettest summers in years. They were rained out in New Plymouth, headed north to Raglan and Kāwhia, then went across the island to Rotorua and the East Coast: Ōhope, Te Kaha, Te Puia, Tolaga Bay, Gisborne, Māhia. In that last place, after the show, the fish and chip man, who'd stayed open to serve them dinner, lifted up the lid of a freezer and there inside was the body of a baby sperm whale, two or three days old and with the birth marks still upon its skin: an image that reappeared in Ian Wedde's 1986 novel *Symme's Hole*.

After three weeks on the road Vargo's Circus returned to Wellington where there were more shows: in The Dell in the Botanic Garden, on the library lawn in the city and at Kilbirnie Park. Ans Westra took a series of photographs of audience members for the show on the library lawn. Di Cadwallader documented The Dell performances and her images, along with 'snapshots by Artie Bates' (Arthur Baysting), were used to illustrate Ian Wedde's diary of the tour published in *Spleen 2* under the title 'Smokestack Lightning: Rolling Thunder with Vargo's Circus!' 'Rolling Thunder' was the codename for the US military's bombing assault against North Vietnam; Wedde's diary included a call to arms to the counter-culture as represented in the rural hippie communities on the East Coast, and admonitions against certain individuals for not sticking with the plan.

I saw Vargo's Circus in The Dell. They performed on the grass before a triptych of landscapes painted on free-standing screens. A tent functioned as the dressing room. There was a rudimentary drum kit, with accessories. John played guitar; Rose, piano accordion. Sal and Deb danced wearing masks. Deb was a lion, Sal a gazelle: a mask of refined delicacy that she would continue to use and which I still

Vargo's Circus: Deborah Hunt (lion) and Sally Rodwell (gazelle), The Dell, 1976.

associate with her. There were lots of acrobatics, strenuous though not particularly skilful. Alan appeared wearing a diving mask and flippers, with Helen next to him in a striped jacket and a boater. The truck was parked at the back of the set, with Vargo's Circus, that purloined name, painted upon the side.

Promotional material was hyperbolic. 'Vargo's Travelling Circus presents The Land of 1000 Joys … from the far reaches of Empire, a world premiere: *A Lion with a Song in his Heart* … scenes of unimaginable oriental splendour.' The other acts were listed: 'The Fat Lady's Acrobats & Jugglers; Clapper Cassio the Mountebank & the Mighty Atom Miracle Cure; Can Can Dancers (Marigold and Mignonette from Manners Street); Clowns & Magic; the Sensational Ambulatory African Love Worm; sizzling delight from the nation's Number One Female Fire-eater.' This from a flyer for the last show of the tour, in the packed out Mokotahi Hall at Māhia Beach.

~

Spleen 2 came out, I think, in March 1976; the early issues are undated. It had on the cover a Gene (sic) Clarkson drawing of a woman resembling one of Sally's stage personas and, when you opened it up, another pseudonymous poem, 'How to Smoke "Lucky Strikes"' by Charming Cole Tundra. However, in contrast to the never republished poem in the earlier issue, this turned out to be a central work in Alan's oeuvre. Rewritten and retitled 'Slow Passes', it became the title poem of his 1991 selection from Auckland University Press. The subject matter was exemplary: taxi drivers crossing the Thai–Burmese border in order to have a smoke. 'I had decided to have nothing more to do/with John Locke's world,' it began. 'I wanted to find out where heroin/could be obtained.'

Other stalwarts of Red Mole in succeeding years debuted in *Spleen 2*. Arthur Baysting contributed a 'School Project Resource File on The Plutonium Economy'; the accompanying illustration was a five-frame comic strip drawn by Barry Linton. Arthur, with his wife Jean Clarkson, had come down to Wellington to work on screenplays with Dave Gibson of the Gibson Group; he would later receive a writing credit, with Ian Mune, on Roger Donaldson's 1977 movie *Sleeping Dogs*. This adaptation of the C.K. Stead novel *Smith's Dream* starred Sam Neill who, a couple of years before, had made his screen debut in Paul Maunder's 1975 experimental feature, *Landfall*.

Vargo's Circus: Deborah Hunt, Ian Wedde, The Dell, 1976.

On the page opposite Arthur's resource file were four photographs by Di Robson of a dance performance called *Kinekis*. The central figure in three of the images, although he was not named, was Ian Prior, opulently moustachioed, with naked torso. Ian would go on to perform in Red Mole cabarets the following year, 1977, join the group in 1978 and remain a somewhat elusive member for five more years. He was from Nelson; with a degree in physical education, he had attended Francis Batten's clown workshops. In a group full of talkers and writers, Ian remained for the most part silent, on and off stage. He preferred dance and mime to acting; his body was eloquent beyond what his tongue would say. His clown was called the Essential Kropotkin.

The impromptu clan was gathering: 'Parish Spleen' announced Deborah Hunt 'has departed Theatre Action on amicable terms to pursue a career in fire eating'. It did not say she was joining Red Mole, but she was. This decision was the outcome of a long, subterranean struggle, during which various members of the arts community in Wellington attempted to exert pressure on the outcome. Deborah was a prize: a highly skilled dancer, actor, mask and prop-maker, with that indefinable quality which made her a star. Many thought she should remain with Theatre Action, where her skills would flourish alongside the professionals, some of whom were French and had trained with Jacques le Coq in Paris, who made up the Francis Batten-led troupe.

In this view Red Mole was a group of amateurs, more or less untrained, who might have charisma but lacked the necessary gravitas to make significant theatre. As if they were just playing dress-ups perhaps. It seems incredible that so many people thought they had a stake in what was a clearly a private matter for Deb. To me, the real difference between Theatre Action and Red Mole was philosophical, not theatrical. Francis Batten was an austere man who later became a psychotherapist; his 'autonomous theatre' was black and white, you might say, rather than multi-coloured, as Red Mole was. Or grey, like Amamus. There was something puritanical about both of them, whereas the Moles were hedonistic, carnivalesque. Perhaps Deborah's decision to learn fire-eating was her way of making the transition from one to the other.

~

There were three more issues of *Spleen* in 1976, making a total of five for the year. I loved working on them and gradually took on various production responsibilities. I found every part of the process absorbing: from clearing the mailbox to see what submissions had come in to posting out subscription copies once an issue had been printed. I had the key to PO Box 214, down at the GPO in the city, and, later, the account book in which the sales and subscriptions were recorded; I have it still. In between there was the editing, the typesetting, the making of bromides and the laying out to make the camera-ready copy that offset printing required.

I was happy with my contribution to *Spleen 2*: an essay on turn-of-the-twentieth-century Scottish émigré artist James Nairn, whose work was on show at the National Gallery. Proud because it was an essay on the painter rather than a review of the exhibition; pleased because I had researched his life and times and found out things I imagined no one else knew; happy, most of all, because I thought the essay might make an actual contribution to New Zealand art history. Perhaps it did.

For *Spleen 3* I took a trip to the second South Pacific Festival of Arts in Rotorua and wrote up my diary in a ramshackle piece, which was rigorously edited by Alan – while I watched, aghast and impressed. *Spleen 4* featured his profile of the painter Philip Clairmont, with photographs by Bryan Staff, who was then doing a one-year photography course at the polytech. Brunton allegedly said to Staff, on

Five *Spleens*, 1976.

their way out to Waikanae, where Clairmont lived at the time, that he'd better take some decent shots because Phil would die soon. As indeed he did.

The profile explores Clairmont's expressionist roots and traces the European tradition's development in New Zealand, with particular reference to artist Flora Scales' influence on Toss Woollaston. Scales had studied in Munich in the early 1930s with the godfather of the American abstract expressionists, Hans Hofmann, and had shown her notes on these lessons to Toss. Clairmont, as a boy, lived for a time in the Woollaston house in Greymouth; his mother was the family's housekeeper. A small show of Scales' work, selected and introduced by Colin McCahon, toured the country in 1975.

Spleen 4 also included an inquiry by Flick Bromide into the rotting stocks of nitrate film in the New Zealand Film Unit archives: 'Soon it's going to jelly, let off gas and decompose into its "gaseous compounds". It's going to turn into a smell.' Flick Bromide was Richard Turner who, 'thanks to some long-forgotten misdemeanour, had been incarcerated in an edit suite to trawl through vast amounts of old footage rotting away in ex-army bunkers'. He was a perforce anonymous source of controversial information which did, in fact, contribute to Jonathan Dennis's founding, in 1981, of the New Zealand Film Archive.

Pseudonyms were common in *Spleen*. Ray Bowie, Ace Rock Writer, wrote a piece for the third issue about Split Enz's imminent journey to England to rerecord, with Roxy Music keyboard player Phil Manzanera producing, their debut album *Mental Notes*. Not all the songs off that album were used but some did appear on the follow-up, *Second Thoughts*. The next year, when Split Enz toured on the back of that record, Red Mole was their support act. In issue four, a new writer appeared and continued to contribute until the magazine's run ended: Hob Nails, whose dystopian and hilarious rural diary was called 'Country Notes'. Ray Bowie was Arthur Baysting; Hob Nails, Gerard Smithyman.

My favourite part of the production of *Spleen* was the laying out. It was always done at night around at Sally and Alan's house, wherever that happened to be at the time. We would sit, mostly not talking, listening to music, smoking cigarettes, using scissors and glue, Letraset and felt-tips, with just the odd remark to break the companionable silence. People were always dropping in. There would be joints going around. Cups of tea. A sense of vast encroaching darkness, in which our little magazine functioned as a small beacon of light. We were capable of a sense of mission as messianic as that; along with a proper appreciation of the absurdity, perhaps even the futility, of the ambition.

It's the music that stays in my mind. Link Wray's *Beans and Fatback*, for instance. I remember particularly the instrumental 'Water Boy'. Ry Cooder's 1970s trilogy, *Boomer's Story*, *Paradise and Lunch* and *Chicken Skin Music*. Albums by the Grateful Dead (*From the Mars Hotel*), J.J. Cale (*Naturally*), Warren Zevon (*Warren Zevon*). Zevon's songs resound: 'Carmelita', a junkie lament; the achingly prescient 'Mohammed's Radio'. Little Feat's *Sailin' Shoes* and the follow-up, *Dixie Chicken*. Willie Nelson's 1975 concept album *Red Headed Stranger*. Most of this was American, country inflected but also alternative music. Patti Smith's *Horses* and *Radio Ethiopia* fit here too, along with anything by Bob Dylan and Bob Marley.

Lists such as these are endless; there's always another name to add. The Neville Brothers. Dr John the Night Tripper. Professor Longhair. But we listened to English music too, and from the contemporary English avant garde came the album that for me best defines the next Red Mole show: *Cabaret Pekin 1949*. It took place over two nights, 6–7 August 1976, at Unity Theatre up the end of Courtenay Place, next to the fire station. Here Arthur Baysting made his stage debut with Red Mole, as did Bryan Staff. Both of them are better known today for their contributions to music: Arthur as a song-writing lyricist and Bryan as a record producer (Ripper Records) and a DJ. The album was Brian Eno's *Taking Tiger Mountain (By Strategy)* (1974).

~

Taking Tiger Mountain (By Strategy) was one of just eight model plays allowed to be performed in China during the Cultural Revolution. It was based on a novel that was in turn based upon a real incident, in 1946, during the Civil War. A soldier disguised himself in order to infiltrate a gang of bandits who were, in time, destroyed by communist forces. Eno found a booklet about it in San Francisco. Revised collectively by the Taking Tiger Mountain by Strategy group of the Peking Opera Troupe of Shanghai, it was published in English by the Foreign Language Press in Peking in 1971 and included 16 colour pictures of a 1970 production of the opera, a partial script, words and music of songs, and notes upon percussion instruments played by the orchestra.

The title intrigued Eno: 'the dichotomy between the archaic and the progressive. Half Taking Tiger Mountain – that Middle Ages physical feel of storming a military position – and half (By Strategy) – that very, very 20th-century mental concept of a tactical interaction of systems'. He and artist and teacher Peter Schmidt devised a set of instruction cards, called Oblique Strategies, which Eno used to determine the next (otherwise unconsidered) action in the recording studio. They were later expanded to form a set of over 100 worthwhile dilemmas, which Eno has continued to use in the making of his recordings. The lyrics, 'composed in a spirit of idiot glee', are surreal despatches from William Burroughs' cut-up London.

Phil Manzanera was there, 'just doing anything we felt like doing at the time. There was a lot of experimenting and a lot of hours spent with Brian Eno, me, and Rhett [engineer Rhett Davies] in the control room doing all the things that eventually evolved into those cards, the Oblique Strategies, and it was just a lot of fun.' Scored for keyboards, guitar, bass, drums and percussion, *Taking Tiger Mountain (By Strategy)* is a series of jaunty tunes with extravagant sound effects and sombre lyrics. Some tracks sound pre- or proto-punk; others prefigure the Eno-produced albums David Bowie made in Berlin later that decade. At least one track from it was played at *Cabaret Pekin 1949* on those August nights in 1976.

At the time we were also enamoured of Stomu Yamashta's Red Buddha Theatre. Yamashta, the Kyoto-born composer, keyboardist and percussionist, working mostly in England, in the 1960s and 1970s pioneered a fusion of traditional

Japanese percussive music with Western progressive rock. He was later, with Steve Winwood and others, a member of the supergroup Go. We listened to the eponymous *Red Buddha* (1971) and *Man from the East* (1973), the soundtrack for a show of the same name. Stand-outs from the latter included the 10-minute long 'What a Way to Live in Modern Times', recorded live in Paris, and the lengthy closing track, 'Memory of Hiroshima'.

We had a sense that the East was not just a source of folk tales, like *Siddhartha*, but held potential for social and political transformation. *Cabaret Pekin 1949* evoked a Walter Benjamin-like moment of crisis, when forces from the past rise up in the present to determine the future. Like Baudelaire's Paris, Pekin (Beijing) was a city on the cusp of change: the ostensible setting was the foreign enclaves just before the entry of Mao Tse Tung. The cabaret appears in the Red Mole chronology as a collective production but with a credit to Alan for *Holyoake's Children*, alluding to Robert Patrick's 1973 play, *Kennedy's Children*, and the subsequent hit Broadway production of the same name.

Keith Jacka Holyoake, aka Kiwi Keith, was New Zealand's prime minister from 1960 to 1972; his children are we who grew up in the 1960s. Music for *Pekin 1949* was provided by the progressive rock group Schtüng: the first, but not the last time Red Mole would collaborate with a rock band. As for oblique strategies, it's hard to think of a better description for Red Mole's modus operandi.

Another advance made at *Pekin 1949* was that the poets, Arthur Baysting and Alan Brunton, appeared without the usual piece of A4 paper in hand. They were no longer reading, they were reciting from memory, they were improvising and ad libbing, they were ranting. Alan overheard, in Darwin in 1970, someone saying the words 'cripple cockroach'. They remained in his mind and *Pekin 1949* was the first time he voiced the character they named. He would continue to do so, on a variety of stages, for the next quarter-century.

> *It's Cripple Cockroach*
> *taking his last walk tonight*
> *past the cinemas on the fantasy circuit*
> *a dollar bill in his hat band*
> *for the Sister of Mercy*
> *and Milk*
> *who will abandon him*
> *within reach of the red limit*
> *tonight.*

70

It's the contra of the journey to paradise: a galactic derelict, like someone out of a Tom Waits song, stumbling towards his demise. Sister Mercy, played by Sally, is a paradox: she who both salves and yet stands at death's door. You can't say if it is a blessing or a curse she brings. Both, perhaps; or neither.

The interaction of Cripple Cockroach and Sister Mercy was followed by a version of the last track off the Eno album. It's about five minutes long on the record but in *Cabaret Pekin 1949* was longer: not Eno, but Schtüng playing Eno. The album track has a weird, high whistling wind sound through it, making you feel you are indeed part of a cadre of soldiers abroad in a blizzard on a snow mountain. The lyrics are stark, simple, and they repeat:

> We climbed and we climbed
> Oh how we climbed
> My how we climbed
> Over stars to the top
> Of Tiger Mountain
> Forcing lines through the snow
> We climbed and we climbed
> Oh how we climbed…

~

Ace Follies opened in the concert chamber of the Wellington Town Hall just three weeks later, on 25 August 1976, for a six-night run; then it toured the South Island. The most ambitious Red Mole show yet, and the most cohesive. The basis of the plot was the first overseas trip Muldoon made as prime minister, to Britain, Northern Ireland, Europe, Korea, Japan and China, where he had an audience with a failing Mao.

In April 1976 he set out for London, making a single stopover on the way at Disneyland, where, Barry Gustafson writes, his advisers were astonished by the glee with which he responded to the exhibits. He'd been told it was no longer de rigueur, indeed rather old-fashioned, for a New Zealand PM to see the Queen before visiting anyone else, but he replied that he was old-fashioned and would so do.

He met her, Labour PM James Callaghan, Leader of the Opposition Margaret Thatcher, Sonny Ramphal, Secretary-General of the British Commonwealth and various others before, under heavy security, visiting Northern Ireland. In Paris,

Ace Follies: Alan Brunton,
John Davies, Dunedin, 1976.

Gustafson wrote, 'the state banquet ... started disastrously and became worse as the evening progressed'. Muldoon lost his trousers (to an inefficient laundress) and, wearing a borrowed pair, overheard French women discussing his attributes in their own language: 'they had obviously been briefed about some of the less favourable aspects of his personality'. Muldoon caused bewilderment later in the evening when, during the speech the ambassador had written for him, he broke into execrable Française, having picked up rudiments of the language in the Pacific during the war.

After Europe he went to Korea, Japan and China, where he had an audience with Mao Tse Tung. Mao was old and frail; his contribution to the discussion was limited to a few 'short grunted comments' which his advisers struggled to interpret as statements of purpose. More substantive discussions were held with Hua Guofeng, who had replaced the recently deceased Chou En Lai as premier; and who would, after Mao's death later that year, remove the Gang of Four from power. New Zealand and China signed a Most Favoured Nation Trade Agreement but Muldoon was furious when, at Chinese insistence, the agreement was inked, not at executive level, but by unelected officials.

~

These events provided the spine for the Red Mole show. Ace, the Muldoon figure, played con brio by John Davies, followed more or less the same itinerary. The *Greymouth Evening Star* reported:

> *He wins his way to the top of the NZ's political arena by cheating and lying. He meets with a man who calls himself Uncle Sam, who offers Ace a world tour if he signs a contract. Ace goes off on his tour selling NZ products, butter, cheese and*

meat ... he finds out he is not quite the great man he thinks he is. He is laughed at in England, ripped off in France and signs away his country's products in Japan for electrical goods that break down five minutes after he buys them.

He then goes to Korea, where he meets the Red Peril and finally ends up somewhere, which is really nowhere, and tells his troubles to a wise-looking bearded man who sounds like God. He then finds himself in a place with no-one but a voice that turns out to be Uncle Sam, who tells him to put on the cloak of power and return to New Zealand. He does so and is greeted by his friends, who are stunned by his change. He left the country a jovial and friendly man and returns a tyrant. The ministers leave the stage on their knees ... they reappear as an angry crowd and overthrow their tyrannical leader.

That last scene was of course wishful thinking. Or an exhortation towards an uprising.

Ace Follies began with the actors – 'strange-looking people carrying stranger-looking dolls' – coming in from the back of the auditorium. The stage set was minimal; the lack of scenery was made up for by an abundance of excellent props. The most outrageous of these were the papier-mâché breasts Deb Hunt wore

Ace Follies: John Davies, Helen Panckhurst, Alan Brunton, Deborah Hunt, Dunedin, 1976.

73

outside her clothes in the French nightclub scene. One of these she ripped off and used as a receptacle into which she poured Ace a drink of champagne. In the Japanese sequence Helen Panckhurst assumed the mask of geisha. Alan, as Uncle Sam, in a tall Stars and Stripes hat, striped trousers, smoked a big cigar. Ace had the sausages, the cheese, the lamb chops, hung from the lining inside his overcoat, like a street-seller's dirty postcards.

In the *Evening Post* Michael Nicolaidi wrote: 'If you wondered what Our Leader might have been up to on his peregrinations ... earlier this year, drop into the Concert Chamber before next Tuesday.' It was a recognition that Red Mole had persuasively re-presented Muldoon's boorish and alcoholic buffoonery abroad. Nicolaidi continued: 'One senses that Red Mole's eye is more steely and more challenging. They have tougher edges – appropriate to the times – and no tears for New Zealand the way you hoped it was.'

Jan composed and played the music for the Wellington performances of *Ace Follies* but she didn't go on tour. The Vargo's Circus ensemble, with the addition of Tim Hunt, Deb's younger brother, and minus Greta Campbell, supplied the accompaniment. It was led by Rose; this was the Weddes' last outing with Red Mole. Graeme Nesbitt, as technical director, designed and set up the sound and lights at the town hall but was never actually able to see a performance of the show. He was a prisoner in Wi Tako and, although allowed out on day release, had to be back at the jail in Silverstream by the nine o'clock curfew each night. He negotiated this predicament with grace and good humour.

Graeme had been, in 1972, the first director of the New Zealand Students' Arts Council, an influential organisation in the 1970s. He managed rock bands Mammal and Dragon, guiding the latter to antipodean fame. He was in Wi Tako for drug offences. One story, perhaps apocryphal, is that police had staked out a motel in Glenmore Street, Wellington, where a meeting of significant players in what became the Mr Asia Syndicate had gathered to discuss strategy and divide up the territory. The cops became distracted when they saw Nesbitt, with a briefcase, crossing a nearby park and arrested him instead. The briefcase turned out to contain 400 Buddha sticks and he got two years, while the Mr Asia heavies continued to transact business as usual.

In the South Island *Ace Follies* played Blenheim, Nelson, Motueka, Murchison, Westport, Greymouth, Kumara, Hokitika, Ross, Fox Glacier, Wānaka, Queenstown, Cromwell, Clyde, Roxburgh, Alexandra and Dunedin. There were an additional 58 performances at 42 venues by White Rabbit Puppet Theatre, and a late show at Dunedin's Fortune Theatre called *Shoot-up at Shotover River aka Cabaret Gone West*, which included a scene that became notorious in the annals.

Lee Hatherly remembered Sally and Deb coming on,

> one in lime yellow and one in lilac coloured tailored shirts, with pants in matching colour. They were untypically groomed. They began to sing 'The Streets of Laredo' … there was a hiccup. They began throwing lines back and forth, then throwing things and insults with the lines, leading to throwing, slinging mud – actual mud on their beautiful costumes. In the end there was mud all over each other and all over the stage. The music was wild. The mud was flying into the front row of the audience.

Spleen reported:

> We remain grimly determined while the Fortune hierarchy goes nutsville, the stage covered in mud gets them hysterical, the shit hits the fan. The hierarchy stoops so low they pull the plug on us. For fifteen minutes we sit in the blackout. They try everything to destroy us and we go on remorselessly. They even keep the box office! They cannot credit the absolute vulgarity of the cabaret, the low humour, the democratic touches, the slaughter of dramatic sacred cows.

Further performances of *Ace Follies* in Dunedin played to packed houses and, as a consequence, the tour as a whole broke even, although the actors were not paid. More significant was the impetuous arrival of 'the absolute vulgarity of the cabaret'.

~

The Incredible Ace Follies South Island tour was written up and published in *Spleen 6*, along with a scenario which, like all Red Mole scenarios, had only a tangential relationship with the work as performed. What the *Greymouth Evening Star* interpreted as a meeting with God was called in the scenario 'The Guru Scene' and featured a group of gangsters, gamblers in dark glasses smoking cigars, who transformed into Red Guards for the duration of the encounter with Ace, then returned to their former guise once he had gone. The ambience was Tibetan rather than Chinese: 'Temple bells, trumpets of the puja, saffron robed monks. Ace enters on all fours, licking the floor.'

Ace Follies: Sally Rodwell, Deborah Hunt, John Davies, Dunedin, 1976.

For *Spleen 6* I wrote an essay on Colin McCahon's recent show at the Peter McLeavey Gallery: 'About as Visually Splendid as Road Signs'. I was delighted when Peter told me Colin had read and liked it. 'And Martin Edmond,' McCahon wrote. 'I like him. He is kind. It is good to have kindness sometimes.' But the issue was controversial for two other pieces. One was a review of Vincent O'Sullivan's 1976 poetry collection, *From the Indian Funeral*; the other, a transcription of an interview Richard Turner had done with a couple of Black Power gang members.

The O'Sullivan review, unsigned, was provocative. It excerpted 25 similes from O'Sullivan's book, numbered and quoted in the order in which they appeared and printed as a list down the page. The only comment came at the very end of the review: 'Ah, fuck it …' The point was that O'Sullivan had imbibed so much of the work of Pablo Neruda and César Vallejo before making his trip to South America that he had become addicted to using 'like' and 'as' to make up his lines. It did not help that, in a more measured (though at the same time cruelly funny) review, opposite, of the second edition of O'Sullivan's *Anthology of Twentieth Century New Zealand Poetry*, Alan had taken to calling him 'Vinnie'.

It looked like a concerted attack and it probably was. Some correspondence ensued between Brian Turner, of John McIndoe Ltd, who published *From the*

Indian Funeral, and Ian Wedde, printed in a subsequent issue of *Spleen*. The tone was elaborately polite but most sentences were barbed and no one really conceded any ground, though Turner at one point allowed he might have been a bit over-sensitive. His boss, the grandson of the eponymous John McIndoe, was quoted as saying he found this sort of thing deplorable but recommended making no response; it was O'Sullivan who insisted upon one. To what end? It is difficult to say. Perhaps it was just a generational call and response.

The other matter was more serious. Richard Turner interviewed two young Black Power members in preparation for a film he was going to make about the gang. I transcribed the tape and we published it in good faith. There was nothing overtly controversial in the piece, which gave a detailed account of and insight into the upbringing, the ethos, the pride and the shame, the grievances and the triumphs, of two members of that subculture. It was called 'Yeah, We're Bringing In the Real Shit' and was the first thing you saw when you opened the magazine. There were photographs, one of which showed a tattoo that reconfigured some chubby male's navel as a vulva.

We were astonished, some weeks later, to find, on the editorial page of the *Dominion*, under Warwick Roger's by-line, a feature called 'Anatomy of a Murderer'. After our interview was recorded, one of Richard's subjects, Waki (Denis Luke, aged 16), had been charged (with Rufus Marsh, aged 18) with the murder of Taffy Williamson in Hopper Street in Te Aro. It was alleged that Williamson, who was drunk, had called the two men 'black cunts' and that they had kicked him to death. Charged but not convicted, Waki was awaiting trial. Roger plundered the *Spleen* interview for quotes with which to write 'his' profile. There was no attribution; readers would have assumed he gathered the material himself. They would also have assumed 'his' subject was speaking as a convicted murderer. The series was to run over five days, Monday to Friday. There were billboards. It was portrayed as a scoop.

That Roger had used the interview without permission and without attribution was the lesser offence. The major issue was that he had taken a matter that was sub judice and written it up as a fait accompli. Waki was entitled to the presumption of innocence, but Roger took no notice of that. So far as he was concerned, the boy was already a murderer. We rang the *Dominion* and demanded they cease publication. They refused. We demanded they acknowledge *Spleen* as the source for those articles already published: this was done, reluctantly, on the Wednesday.

On the Tuesday Alan and I had gone in to talk to someone in a position of power at the paper; it seems extraordinary now that he agreed to see us. We were in the *Evening Post* building in Willis Street, at lunchtime, in an office in a glassed-off corner of the press room. He was a bluff, hearty man in a woollen suit. Or he would have been hearty if he had not been so defensive. The *Dominion* and the *Evening Post* were already owned by Rupert Murdoch; but I didn't know that then.

Alan's invective was coruscating. When the suit tried to justify himself, he called him a casuist. The suit did not know what he meant. Neither did I; but it sounded good (or bad) enough to be true: a person who uses clever but unsound reasoning, especially in relation to moral questions. It was because of that meeting that the paper agreed to acknowledge *Spleen* as Roger's source. But there was no apology. And the series continued for the full five days. We could have sued, but how to pay the lawyers? We took it to the Press Council instead and won our case. The *Dominion* was obliged to report the council's findings and to acknowledge culpability. They did it below the fold on page six.

Waki was convicted of murder and went to jail. In 2019, after more than 40 years in jail, he was released on parole. He had been imprisoned again, in 1996, for an unrelated crime of which he may not have been guilty. How far the prior conviction influenced the judge who sentenced him for the second offence is hard to say. It was certainly a factor in the long denial of parole. Warwick Roger went on to have a brilliant career as a journalist and food writer. I never met him; he made himself scarce when we went looking for him in Wellington. Despite his success, I still think his transgression, and his refusal to own up to what he had done, shows that he knew he was acting in a devious and self-serving manner.

~

There was one more Red Mole show that year. It was called *Towards Bethlehem* and was a retelling, in vaudevillian style, of the nativity story. The three wise men were Persian astrologers and magicians who delivered their visions in mime and acrobatics. There were masked dancers 'whose swirling motions communicated the idea of the poor suffering under harsh Roman law praying for a powerful new king or Messiah to lead them to freedom'. The episode of the trip to Bethlehem, after the half-mad Herod ordered a new census so he could increase taxation, was told with a shadow puppet play.

Towards Bethlehem opened with the dance of the Nazira, 'while all about .../

Black Power members, Waki (Denis Luke) centre, with cigarette, Wellington, 1976.

reel shadows of the indignant desert birds'. Joseph, a builder of houses, has to be convinced to marry his pregnant niece Mary, but who is the father of her child? A Roman soldier? An angel? The divine genealogy was recited. The Annunciation was performed by Sally and Deborah in bird masks. Mary's ordeal, drinking bitter water in the temple to prove or disprove her adultery, turned into an auto-da-fé worthy of the Spanish Inquisition. The crowd in Herod's palace was represented by puppets: a masterwork by Deb, a platform of papier-mâché bodies and heads transported by an actor concealed under a black cloak, wearing the crowd like a city on her back.

The wise men – a priest, a scholar and a merchant bearing the frankincense, the myrrh and the gold – were appointed by Herod as his envoys, but they returned to the East without bringing him the news he wanted to hear. The shepherds watching their flocks by night were played as low farce. Like the journey to Bethlehem, the flight into Egypt was a shadow puppet play. When Herod cried out 'Kill all sons!' the puppet city fell in confusion to the floor. Then the finale: 'Joe and Mary go past to begin the future. All characters suddenly form a crucifiction (sic) scene. Tableau is held then – fin.'

Towards Bethlehem was my debut as an actor with Red Mole. We performed the show that December in Christ the King church in Cannons Creek and St Columba's in Miramar, the Petone hall, Unity Theatre, the Newtown Community Centre, the Ngātitoa Lodge in Porirua and the Island Bay Surf Club (to an audience of seven). I remember standing at the lectern in St Andrew's Presbyterian Church on The Terrace reading from *Genesis* 5: 'And Adam lived one hundred and thirty years, and begot a son in his own likeness, after his image, and called him Seth.' It was the first time I had read aloud in public.

There were other moments: Alan as a shepherd doing a hand jive, with chant, with a second shepherd, the one-armed bandit Pete Fantl. It was complex, elegant and tender too. Jenny Stevenson, a woman of luminous beauty of soul and body, appeared as an angel. The circumcision in the temple, with John as Simeon and Sally as Anna, waiting through the ages for a glimpse of the Messiah, occurred on a bare stage. We achieved, among the low farce and the vaudevillian acrobatics, moments of mystery and revelation. When that happened, whether in a church, a surf club or a community hall, everybody witnessed the secular miracle theatre can be. There is no other feeling like it. I was hooked.

III

Oblique Strategies

WE ARE SITTING IN THE WELLINGTON TOWN HALL one night in January 1977. The room is packed, buzzing. The lights go down; silence, more slowly, descends. Shards of green and orange glint from the cymbals of the drum kit, red pilot lights glow on amplifiers. Pools of yellow and of white. Then we hear a subterranean rumble, voices groaning as if from deep wells, transforming into an exaltation of *a capella* angels: a Gregorian chant. The stage lights intensify but there is no sign of anyone there yet. The chant, too, builds. And then we sense a rustle, a commotion, doors opening behind us. As one, we turn to look. There, from the rear of the auditorium, come four three-metre tall masked and robed figures. They are monks, evidently, and they are processing towards the lighted stage.

This was how *The Adventures of Sir Real Janus* began. The papier-mâché monks' heads were almost a metre in diameter, painted in pinks and yellows and reds, with tonsured hair; and carried by actors concealed beneath black robes and holding them upright with sticks. They processed, in solemn order, two in each aisle, up to the stage, ascended – then heads and robes were cast aside to reveal four lithe, lycra-suited players from a commedia show; or, since the ambience was medieval, a mystery play. The music changed too, from solemn chant to carnival roundel. It was market day in Chaucer's England; it was April: 'Thanne longen folk to goon on pilgrimages.'

Sir Real Janus was a comic figure, a Quixotic knight who, 'with his sword, his lunch and his orangeade', sought the Holy Land. There were adventures at various European destinations along the way, most memorably, perhaps, in Greece where, in atavistic memory of satyr plays, one of the actors strapped on an enormous cock and made love to one of the others. It needed to be big because the auditorium was: the audience was there for a rock concert. Any introductory theatre piece had to approximate the level of intensity that bands achieve primarily though the amplification of sound. Red Mole did it with large props and even larger action. That gargantuan fuck.

The band was Split Enz, newly returned from their sojourn in England, promoting *Second Thoughts*. They had already toured Australia, to acclaim, and would soon leave from Auckland for California and a 23-day, 40-show American tour called *Courting the Act*. The poster resembled a shield bearing chivalric devices and their own costumes and hairstyles suggested a set of seven characters cut from some mutant, medieval tarot deck. They wore tights and slippers and face paint, pantaloons and jerkins and gowns, and no one, not even themselves, seemed to know exactly what to make of it all. They were, everyone said, zany.

Split Enz was toured by the New Zealand Students' Arts Council and it was their head honcho, Bruce Kirkland, who arranged the supports for Red Mole. Bruce was a bright boy from Onehunga who'd gone to Auckland University to study law; he graduated but never practised. Instead, he became president of the New Zealand University Students' Association and, from there, the first full-time director of the Students' Arts Council. He saw himself as responsible to an audience and fulfilled that role by giving them half art (e.g. poet Robert Creeley) and half music. In that second capacity he toured bands like southern rockers Little Feat, bluesmen Sonny Terry and Brownie McGhee – and Split Enz.

Most of the rock acts he purchased from Australian promoters like Michael Gudinski of Mushroom Records, for whom he soon went to work. From there, on the back of an antipodean tour by Graham Parker and the Rumour, he was offered a position with Stiff Records in England. They sent him on the road with Reckless Eric, to see if he could handle the chaos. He could. He then became, effectively, Lena Lovich's manager. And thence to New York to act as a conduit into the States for Stiff and for Mute Records acts like Depeche Mode and Erasure. Early, in the 1980s, into the video business, he was general manager at Capitol Records in the 1990s and now runs Tsunami Entertainment out of Los Angeles and is a major player, worldwide, in the music business.

Bruce was large, confident, genial; he had charm and charisma. Like Caterina de Nave, Di Robson, Graeme Nesbitt and other youthful producers and promoters of that era, he understood that artists respond well to challenges and that, to be successful, they also need to be happy. Simple as that sounds, it is by no means universally appreciated. Bruce finalised the tour deal with Split Enz at a meeting with Tim Finn in Los Angeles where he suggested Red Mole as the support. The gig came with restrictions: the opening act could not be more than 30 minutes long and that time limit was non-negotiable; live theatre is notorious for running over. The Red Mole solution was characteristically elegant: they would perform to a pre-recorded tape, exactly half an hour long. Jan composed the music for, and recorded, that tape and played along with it, live, during the show.

There were silences inserted for dialogue: mostly orations from Alan, who played the surrealistic, Janus-faced Knight of the Woeful Countenance. Sal and Deb were the two other performers, the first incarnation of what we would, in later years, come to call, with varying degrees of affection and disaffection, the Gang of Three. When the giant phallus appeared, it was wielded by Deborah on Sally: another precursor, this time of the sexually ambiguous pas de deux they would choreograph for themselves, and dance, in the near future. I wonder now what happened to those four monk's heads and that magnificent cock? They should really be in a museum somewhere, as the Split Enz costumes from that tour, designed by Noel Crombie, are – in Melbourne.

The Moles travelled from Invercargill to Auckland in a rental car; surely it can't have been a Mini? I remember Jan's reiterated complaint about the discomfort of sharing a four-seater with three smokers. 'The puffers are puffing again,' she would say. She had been a smoker herself but, because she was so talkative, her roll-your-owns were always going out and, by the end of the night, she would have contributed more matches than butts to the ashtray. Everyone else, with cheerful abandon, smoked tailor-made Benson and Hedges. Deborah always put the spent matches back into the box and not a few times ended up with a Beehive exploding in her hands. She was a fire-eater, after all. And a Muldoon impersonator.

One of the reviews, much quoted by Red Mole, suggested Split Enz found it difficult to come on after this spectacular opener – or words to that effect. I can't now recall if there were any real tensions between the two groups; I doubt it. Keyboard player Eddie Raynor and Jan became friends, for instance. Most audiences responded to the bill with rapturous enthusiasm. The Red Mole opener was genuinely strange, evocative and, given its vulgarity, stylish too. Split Enz were, in their own way, even stranger, with music that refused to settle into a groove and a show that had its own vaudevillian edge – for example, when Noel Crombie cake-walked across the stage playing the spoons.

I remember a sequence towards the end when the lighting went strobe and you saw on stage a set of weird characters, or caricatures, in stop-motion that revealed images of enigmatic clarity: sometimes they seemed to be imitating the compositions of old master paintings. One Australian punter I know, Damien Minton, swore he saw Rembrandt's *Night Watch*. They were too frantic to be sexy – there were too many time signature changes – but they were lyrically interesting and intellectually rigorous.

Zany, the word so often used to describe them, comes from the character, Zanni, in the commedia dell'arte. He is a servant who parodies the actions of the lordly and august, the more pretentious, among the other characters. Dei Zanni was sometimes used as a generic term for the commedia itself. As for the relationship between Split Enz and Red Mole, it wasn't really clear who might have been parodying whom: perhaps influences transmitted both ways and became mutually beneficial.

~

On March 1977 an anonymous contributor to *Salient* (it was Alan) wrote of Red Mole, 'Last time I came across them they were sitting over the table from me in Veints' tearooms above the main street of Gore laying down some heavy charts about a national tour they were then beginning with the fine art combo Split Enz. They really hauled arse to keep up with Split Enz who were into a very schizo phase. Red Mole did the support act number and just about acted Split Enz out of the tent …' Just about, but not quite? The article wasn't really about that tour, however, but about the future: 'By one of those fortuitous winds that blow across town occasionally bringing in the good with the bad, Carmen, entrepreneur and local mayoral candidate, had been forced to close down her night-club deal at The Balcony … the obliging Carmen offered our intrepid group the premises on Sunday nights for the purposes of knocking a cabaret together.' Carmen, née Trevor Rupe from Taumarunui, was an imperious Māori drag queen who ruled unopposed over Wellington's night life in the 1970s. She ran for mayor, unsuccessfully, in 1977. Her slogan was 'Get in behind!' I voted for her.

Veints' tearooms in Gore became another sacred site in the Red Mole chronology: where *Cabaret Capital Strut* was born. It may be so. I can imagine a conversation that began along the lines of 'What are we going to do when we get back to Wellington?' and ended with a determination to approach Carmen and

Cabaret Capital Strut poster, Joe Wylie, 1977.

ask her about using The Balcony for Sunday night shows. Deborah and Sally had already worked there, dancing a tango, usually to 'Hernando's Hideaway'. They called themselves César and Rosalita. Deborah, in top hat and tails, was César; Sally, in a low-cut red dress, Rosalita. Both were effectively topless.

Jan and I went along to The Balcony one Sunday night in February 1977 to check the place out. It was in Victoria Street, on the corner of Harris Street. A wooden, two-storey building; Carmen had the second floor. You walked up a steep staircase, at the top of which was a reception desk; behind the desk sat the formidable Jeanette McDonald. Jeanette was a large woman with cropped hair and a steely uncompromising gaze; a sweetheart, actually, but only after you got to know her. Maureen Price, one of the strippers, was her girlfriend. Jeanette had ultimate power over who did or did not enter the room, which had a sliding door on a heavy retractable spring; she opened it (or not) with her strong right arm. You underwent scrutiny, you paid (or not) and then she drew back the door and let you in. It always snapped shut, disconcertingly, loudly, behind you. Jeanette stayed on the door for the duration of the Red Mole season.

Inside was all red plush and gold leaf, curtained and mirrored, darkly lit: a rectangular room with the stage at one end and the bar at the other, on your right and left, respectively, when you entered. The stage was small, with two even smaller dressing rooms either side. One of those (stage left) became the exclusive preserve of the Gang of Three while the rest of us squeezed into the other. The stage gave onto a catwalk that extended a third of the way into the room. There were thin tables with thin chairs clustered along the sides of the catwalk and also at its end; behind that, standing room only. The bar, though illegal, was functional: it served spirits – whisky, bourbon, brandy, rum, gin, vodka – with mixers. There was a bulbous red light, the size of a clenched fist, like one of those on the tops of cop cars, concealed beneath the counter. It lit up whenever Jeanette pushed the warning button she had under her desk outside; and then, 'as if by magic', the bottles of spirits would disappear.

In truth, visits by the police were rare and always carefully managed. They knew the set-up and made sure the bar staff had plenty of time to hide the booze so that they could then inspect an obviously innocent operation and give the all clear. This arrangement also continued throughout Red Mole's tenancy. Perhaps someone was being paid or perhaps, more likely, Carmen knew things that ensured people would rather not upset her. In those days she also ran Carmen's International

Coffee Lounge, an Egyptian-themed café at 86 Vivian Street with a brothel upstairs where, it was said, judges, police chiefs, politicians and the like could satisfy desires too outré for their wives or their mistresses to countenance. A charming detail: sexual preferences were telegraphed via a code based upon the position of the teaspoon in the saucer of your (probably fortified) coffee. Carmen remarked, 'Men come with their wives, and then they come back later without them.'

The night we went to The Balcony there were just five other patrons there. They were Korean sailors off a squid boat in the harbour, lounging together at a table on the far side of the catwalk, still in their work clothes, looking up impassively as the queens paraded, to current pop hits played through a tinny sound system, and gradually shed most of their already skimpy clothes. It could not have been duller. Or sadder, for that matter. Maureen, a beautiful young Māori trans woman, was one of the dancers; she had that indefinable something that makes a performer watchable but even she, I could tell, was bored shitless. The place was, in truth, ripe for the plucking.

Alan continued:

So was born Cabaret Capital Strut *a two buck deal of theatrico-musical fun and fare that promises to put Sunday back into the weekend. Two hundred tickets for the hushed up gala opening of this, the latest Red Mole charivari, for March 13, were grabbed up in a couple of days … Fifty people were turned away at the door, at least another fifty tried bootleg invitations to get in but The Balcony is small. With this sort of pressure happening on opening night it looks like* Cabaret Capital Strut *could last a life time.*

Well, seven months, anyway.

And then there was this: 'In the New Year of 1915, Filippo Tommaso Marinetti, Emilio Settimelli and Bruno Corra created the first manifesto for the Futurist Synthetic Theatre, the first conclusion of this manifesto was: TOTALLY ABOLISH THE TECHNIQUE THAT IS KILLING THE PASSEIST THEATRE.' Whatever else it was going to be, *Cabaret Capital Strut* would not be passéist theatre. Its irrepressible vulgarity was replete with examples drawn from contemporary pop culture and from revolutionary, high art cabarets of the past: Paris during La Belle Époque, wartime Dada and Futurism, Weimar Germany; even, perhaps, Pekin 1949. Lubricious and dangerous Wild West saloon entertainments also made a contribution to the mélange.

Alan had a vast knowledge of, particularly European, avant-garde strategies. He had read as much of the Russian futurists as the Italian, as well as the better known French and German practitioners. But his travels in the East also contributed. Not just the India, Nepal and Afghanistan where he wandered as a mendicant in the early 1970s, but the aboriginal cultures of South East Asia he and Sally explored. They knew first hand the hill tribes, like the Hmong, of what was then still called Indo-China; the Batak living around Lake Toba in Sumatra; the Sea Dyaks, or Iban, of Borneo and their cousins the Land Dyaks; the Bugis and the Tana Toraja of Sulawesi. Elements from these disparate cultures flowed into the cabaret and especially into Red Mole's mask-making and story-telling.

Rock'n'roll too. The inaugural poster, by Joe Wylie, emphasised the recently contemporary. It featured a cool cat with a cane dancing in the glare of a spotlight. Above, in a three-part miniature strip, in a set of related moves, that same cat, leaping out of his frame, announced: 'Life could be a dream … sh-boom … sh-boom.' That doo-wop song, sung by the (black) Chords, first came out in 1954 but most people know a slightly later version by the (white) Crew Cuts: 'If I could take you up in paradise up above …' it continues. And the cabaret did indeed become a sort of waking dream, in which the paradisial, mingled with the satiric and the apocalyptic, opened into a fourth space that was profoundly and unapologetically hedonistic.

~

The set list for the first cabaret survives; it's a page long. Alan remarked later that each of the set lists for the cabarets that year fitted onto a single A4 page. This one was in three parts. Doors opened at seven and taped music played as the patrons rolled in. The band, Meantime, performed an overture: jazz and blues. The opening sketch was a satire about the Queen, impersonated by Sally. It was followed by the introduction of the MC, Arthur Baysting, and segued into his number, 'Brazil', with Jenny Stevenson dancing. Chanteuse Kris Klocek, from local band After Midnight, sang 'Falling in Love Again', the song made famous by Marlene Dietrich in the 1930 film *The Blue Angel*. The last act before the first interval was called 'Connection' and starred Sally and Deb with Jan '+ Martin Edmond'. I was shocked when I read that. I have no recollection of it.

There was a musical break, a piano player, New Yorker Jonathan Besser. In the middle section, the first of two Futurist plays was performed: *Dissonance*, by Francesco Cangiullo, a parody of an historical romance. Futurist plays took

Cabaret Capital Strut: Sally Rodwell, Deborah Hunt, Carmen's Balcony, 1977.

the idea of compression to an extreme; entire acts reduced to a few sentences, scenes to a handful of words. No sentiments, no psychological development, no suggestiveness. Common sense was banished, or rather, replaced by non-sense. Another of Cangiullo's plays, *Detonation*, which Red Mole also performed, has a single character, a bullet, a single setting and a single piece of action: 'Road at night, cold, deserted. A minute of silence. A gunshot. CURTAIN.'

89

During the rest of that middle section Jan played Stravinsky (*Circus Polka for a Young Elephant*), Jenny Stevenson performed a gypsy dance, Alan did some satire; nowadays we'd call it stand-up. In the second interval Jonathan Besser again improvised on the keyboards and after that, the other Futurist play, *Towards Victory* (*Verso la Conquista*) by Corra and Settimelli, was performed. It is a mock heroic scene in which a soldier going off to war grandiloquently farewells his beloved; and ends with his sudden death, off stage, when he slips upon a fig skin, falls down some stairs and cracks his skull.

Futurists endorsed vaudeville, music hall and variety shows because those forms lacked a history and, concomitantly, always attempted to involve the audience directly in the performance. Red Mole did that too. You couldn't watch the shows passively or they wouldn't make sense. It is a moot point, however, if anyone at Carmen's actually knew they were seeing Futurist plays. *Towards Victory* was followed by a tap dance, a blues dance, another Kris Klocek song and then Sal and Deb did the tango. After the show was over, Meantime played again and people stayed around to drink and dance.

Lawrence McDonald wrote:

> *The majority of evenings in the theatre do not linger in the memory. They entertain, stimulate, antagonise or bore for a short space of time before slipping into the dustbin of memory. However some evenings last beyond their initial impact and remain with you, joining a small group of touchstones in a personal pantheon of theatrical highpoints which attempt to push beyond the currently accepted limits of theatre. For me the opening night of THE CABARET CAPITAL STRUT is one such occasion.*

Another reviewer suggested that Red Mole had 'overthrown any singular notion of what theatre might be'.

The door was $384, which suggests 192 paying customers. The lights cost $100 and various other expenses – band costumes, laundry, candles, printing, piano tuning – accounted for another $100, which also included rent of $16. Twelve people, including the floor manager, Deb's brother Tim Hunt, and the sound man, Peter Frater, received $10 each. The band got 40 bucks. I'm not on the list of those who were paid, suggesting that I didn't perform after all. Catering was by Peter Fantl. The profit for the evening was $25. It was a full house; for the rest of the time Red Mole played Carmen's, remarkably, the house was never less than full.

~

Cabaret Capital Strut: Sally Rodwell, Arthur Baysting (Neville Purvis), Deborah
Hunt, backstage, Carmen's Balcony, 1977.

Two things people reliably remember about *Cabaret Capital Strut* are concealed in this brief summary of the proceedings. One is item 3 on the set list: 'Arthur Baysting, Emcee + continuity.' This was the first public appearance of Arthur's much loved, much abused alter ego Neville Purvis. 'Neville Purvis, at your service,' he would say. 'That's Neville on the level to you.' Neville was a spiv. He wore white shoes, white trousers, white shirt, white waistcoat, white embroidered jacket, white hat, a black greasepaint pencil-line moustache, dark sunglasses, and carried a white cane. He was from Lower Hutt and he lived with his mum. He drove a Mark II Ford Zephyr and his milieu was one of petty crims who hung around billiard saloons and boarding houses, pubs and burger bars. He was smart but he wasn't: 'I thought fast and, when that didn't work, I thought slow, which is me normal pace.'

Arthur spoke Neville in his own voice: flat, nasal, a bit monotonous. His mode was a mix of the laconic, the satiric and the naïve. In his fiction, he wasn't part of Red Mole: after he'd got out of Mount Crawford Finishing School – jail – they'd asked him to come and lend them a hand. He positioned himself as an outsider and so could refer to the acts he introduced as something a bit beyond his ken. He liked to bait the audience and the audience liked to heckle him back. He had a few standard rejoinders: 'You just keeping taking the tablets, darlin',' was one. 'A saga on the lager' was another.

He told shaggy dog stories and jokes that were funny in a bathetic, low-key kind of way. Asked what the Hutt Valley was like before the Pākehā came, he dead-panned: 'Miles and miles of empty state houses.' Neville was not, not ever, politically correct. In another routine he evoked the famous New Zealand painter, Genghis McCahon. Murray Edmond recalls a third, the tale of the fate of the winner of the annual Silver Plough contest:

As the winner drove home, up the Foxton Straight, in his Zephyr, 'his mind must still have been on ploughing that straight furrow' – and here Neville inserted the only movement in his stand-up comic talk – his right hand went forward to grasp the imagined steering wheel while he turned his left arm, shoulder and his head to look behind him at the disappearing road, in his mind, the straight furrow. The head-on collision did not have to be mimed or named to be imagined by the audience: 'He had ploughed his last furrow.'

Neville was intrinsic to the cabaret. He strung things together, night after night; his thin white thread ran through the outlandish exotica of the rest of the acts. They could consist of anything, but there was one other character who reliably appeared, night after night, the way Neville Purvis did. Called The Pig, s/he was played by Deborah Hunt, with pink papier-mâché ears and a pink papier-mâché snout held in place by black elastic bands; under a long black shirt, a pillow strapped across her belly and chest; black tights; a pink bow tie. She – he – it – resembled, Humpty-Dumpty-like, a bulbous torso with a big head and skinny legs. She was, of course, Muldoon, and in that guise bullied and charmed the audience, jeered and laughed at them, made them the butt of his vanity, his arrogance, his gleeful insolence; and so became a lightning rod for our own anxiety, our fear and our disquiet.

Deb would bound onto the stage and survey the crowd, showing the whites of her eyes; she'd get half a dozen laughs before she even opened her mouth. When she did it might be to coo seductively: 'Yes. It is I ...' and then commence a riff upon whatever absurdities and monstrosities had been perpetrated during the last week in politics. The Pig appeared in the sketch about the Queen. The following week, there was another sketch, a satire about Idi Amin. The Pig was in that one too: a walking contradiction, a visible sign of tyranny that nevertheless allowed, indeed inspired, laughter that was without consequence, apart from the cathartic effect it had upon we who laughed.

Red Mole were not politically correct either. Joe Wylie, shown a Bryan Staff photo of Sally dressed as a cowgirl riding Alan as a horse, remembered when 'Deborah Hunt, in character as Muldoon, requested a Cowboys and Indians bedtime story from a long-suffering minder, Alan and Sally appeared as cartoon Injuns. Alan introduced himself as Chief Running Water or some such, "and this is my daughter, Wandering Star". He then assumed the position as seen in the photo. Sally struck a pose on his back, while Alan sang: "I was born under a wandering star." Tish-boom!'

The second set list (20 March 1977) was almost, but not quite, identical to the first. And that became the pattern over the next seven months. Each night's performance would provide the basis for the next one: with subtle shifts of emphasis, as tired acts were dropped and new ones added, in a process of constant revision that would incorporate any bon mot or breathless coup de théâtre, any lucky accident, improvised the preceding night. Every six weeks or so a new theme would be announced and most of the older acts would be retired. But not Neville, and not the Pig, and not the tango either. I notice, too, in the second set list, that Alan's 'Some Satire' has become 'Poetry'; and that the credit for Happiness goes to Pete Fantl, Jean Clarkson and Richard Turner, who came in and screened films at the cabaret. And kept the bar supplied with booze.

Because he was working at the National Film Unit, Richard was entitled to become a member of the Public Service Association and, as such, qualified for discounts at the PSA store. Every Friday, with a float, he'd go up there and buy the requisite number of bottles of spirits, plus their mixers, for the weekend. Generally Pete brought them in, because he had a car. You'd see him climbing the stairs with the ubiquitous washing basket, full of clinking bottles, held in the crook of the elbow of his amputated arm. These were stashed behind the bar and supplied some of the happiness mentioned in the credits. Carmen's was also full of smoke, both from cigarettes and from the marijuana people inhaled with impunity. There is no accounting for whatever else might have been consumed. Or exchanged. The gamut, probably. It was, in effect, a speakeasy.

The essence of *Cabaret Capital Strut* was its freedom: we had no obligations to anyone or anything else, apart from those due to our own standards and our audiences' proclivities. Any act that didn't work was dropped; any that did, was pushed further, towards outrageousness. Delirium, ribaldry, sexiness, intoxication, hilarity. When we performed a parody of a punk rock band Deborah wore a meat bikini – cuts of sheep's liver or cow's heart over her breasts and her pubes. These would gradually decay until, after protests from other performers, they were thrown out and replacements bought.

The eclecticism of the acts mirrored that of the audience. Up the back at Carmen's you would meet all sorts: from junkie princesses to degenerate artists, from school kids on the lam to jazz musos slumming, from drag queens to future politicians. The cabaret was also innovative in the sense that the shows actually came out of a synergy shared between performers and audience, which created the dazzling multiplicity everyone enjoyed. This was perhaps its greatest achievement. Night of delirium, nights of power. Nights of remembering the forgotten years.

~

Cabaret Capital Strut: (Deborah Hunt?), Carmen's Balcony, 1977.

The six themed shows, in order of appearance, were *Courtney Graffiti, The Arabian Nights, Back to the Fifties, The A & P Show, The Sixties aka Holyoake's Children, Stairway to the Stars*. There was a seventh, the show we took to Auckland, *Red Mole's Golden Hits*, which was an anthology of various acts from the preceding six. However, some of these titles – *Courtney Graffiti*, for instance – were less titular than others. In my recollection only *The Arabian Nights, The A & P Show* and *Stairway to the Stars* were coherent productions; the other three represented musical selections as much as anything else. It's not a coincidence that the former were also the three that had their own posters: a large Turkish-trousered and slippered figure, by Gil Fraser, with turban and bunch of grapes and naked torso, dancing; a cow with swollen udders and the cat ('Sh-boom') on its back; and a masterpiece, by Joe Wylie, to which I will return.

However the season at Carmen's is divided up, it remains a remarkable achievement: from 13 March to 22 May we played Sunday nights; from then until 4 August, Fridays, Saturdays and Sundays; from 4 to 18 August we added Thursday nights; and then from 18 August to 25 September we played every single night of the week. Thirty-seven nights straight, with people queuing round the block to get in and dozens being turned away from every show. Overall, the season at Carmen's, when you count the special nights and the one-offs, included nearly 100 performances, none of which was exactly the same as any other.

A big part of this success was down to the music, and the music came mainly from the Country Flyers, with Midge Marsden on vocals and harmonica, Richard Kennedy on guitar, Neil Hannan on bass and Bud Hooper on drums. The Flyers had a light clean melodic sound and an eclectic repertoire: anything from Chicago blues to Dr John, from Ry Cooder to Jimmy Cliff, from Commander Cody and His Lost Planet Airmen to Little Feat. Midge had been in Bari and the Breakaways; he had his own weekly radio show on the NZBC called *Blues is News*; he owned a legendary record collection. The Country Flyers had a long-standing residency on Thursday nights at the Royal Tiger Tavern and built up a strong following there. Many of those came across to Carmen's. There'd be dancing every night after the show.

Neil 'Scoop' Hannan – Christchurch born, raised in Tawa, the son of a classical violinist – takes up the tale:

My Red Mole journey began in early 1977, at the bar, after one of the Cabaret Capital Strut performances at Carmen's Balcony. Meeting at the bar was to become a consequential part of life with Red Mole, a place to ignore (or not) the great significance of the art. While forever not wanting to over-commercialise, sell out or compromise their performances in any way—the Moles decided to take up my offer to add rock, roots and mid-eastern music to their shows and so began a solid six month period of 'commercial' success. For me, it was always about the show and Alan Brunton's prodigious writing saw to it that there was always a show to be worked on.

Many other musicians came and went: Max Winnie, a guitar-playing folksinger who collaborated with Arthur on a sci-fi country skit; Mike Gubb, son of a shoe shop owner, keyboard player extraordinaire; Andy Anderson; Rockinghorse (Wayne Mason, Barry Saunders, Clinton Brown, Jim Lawrie) who, during *The A & P Show*, stood in for the Flyers while they were on the road; Rick Bryant; Malcolm McNeill. Two stand-out performers were Blerta veteran, the vocalist

Beaver (Beverley Morrison) and a young folksinger from Upper Hutt called Jean McAllister, whom Midge discovered and brought along. Jean had long straight black hair that fell down past her knees, a deft sense of humour, an acute memory and a laugh like the gurgling of water in a drain. She often quoted something her father, a Scotsman, said of her career choice: 'It's a very precarious occupation.'

When we decamped for Auckland, Jean and Beaver accompanied us north and Jean went on to become a Red Mole regular. The Flyers didn't have a keyboardist so Jan became their de facto piano player and learned how to play rock'n'roll. Son et lumière at Carmen's Balcony was provided by the incomparable Peter Frater, whose history with Red Mole is long and complex, extends backwards and forwards in time and includes both miracles and disasters. Frater was a pioneer. In the early 1970s he wired up psychedelic light shows through a series of film and overhead projectors, from which his helpers occasionally got electric shocks, and projected mind-bending light shows straight out of the hippie scene in San Francisco.

One night after the show at Carmen's, when the band was playing and everybody dancing, Richard Kennedy stepped up to the microphone to sing and seemed suddenly to rise into the air for a moment before falling cataleptic to the floor: a near fatal electrocution due to an unearthed PA system. Another time, at the State Opera House, the sound system failed altogether and the show had to go on with only naked voices to accompany the unamplified instruments. That was due, apparently, not to error or incompetence, but an unexpected power surge on the grid. Oddly enough, the lights continued working. Lighting guys are the aesthetes of the techie world; soundmen are more like troglodytes, and much abused. Their successes go largely unremarked while their failures are never forgotten.

Actors joined the cabaret as well. Bill Stalker, TV star and Beaver's partner at the time, did a couple of numbers: a version of 'O Sole Mio' as a disconsolate Neapolitan chef trying to attract patrons to his failing greasy spoon restaurant, and 'Stupid Cupid', the Connie Francis song, replete with mondegreens, in *Back to the Fifties*. Its cousin, *The Sixties Show*, included a parody of the TV soap opera *Close to Home*, called *Close to Shame* ('where no one uses their real name'). The theatre group Chameleon, with Aileen Davidson, came in for one of the themed shows and afterwards their dancer, Ian Prior, initiated a series of intricate moves that led to him joining Red Mole and coming with us to New York. Magician

Timothy Woon, then still a schoolboy, showed how he could produce playing cards and coins out of his own naked torso. Murray Edmond appeared as a juggler, or jongleur, during *The A & P Show*.

Anyone who wished to join Red Mole could do so – as long as they had an act. Aspirants showed their wares to the company early in the week during rehearsals at Carmen's and I don't recall anyone being turned away. If you wanted hard enough, a place would be found for you. In that sense Carmen's became a outlet for any performer – musical, theatrical, dance or word-based – who might have felt constrained on more conventional stages. About 50 people appeared during the seven months. Nor were the queens forgotten. Maureen Price danced as a houri in *The Arabian Nights*, in which Carmen herself graced the stage with her formidable presence. She sang 'Stranger in Paradise': 'That's a danger in paradise/ For mortals who stand beside/An angel like you.' There are people in Wellington who still remember that performance.

~

With a couple of exceptions, I can't now recall any of the roles I played. In *The Arabian Nights*, dressed in purple velvet pantaloons that buttoned at the knee and a red chenille top that Bernadette had given me, I recited a passage from Richard Burton's translation; but what passage was that? Another time, wearing nothing but a loin cloth, dragging a heavy home-made wooden cross on my back, I crawled up the catwalk towards a ringing telephone while the band played Ry Cooder's 'Jesus on the Mainline'. What happened when I picked up the receiver? God spoke, I suppose, but what did he say?

The reason for these lacunae in my memory is straightforward: I didn't really like being an actor. And I wasn't very good at it either. I'd been asked to join the ensemble – 'We'll have to get you into some acting,' Alan said one day – because I was Jan's partner and they wanted to keep her on as their composer. Since the plan was always to go on the road, there had to be something for me to do as well. Ergo, acting. It must have been difficult for the others too, having to carry someone as inhibited as I was then. Once, during a rehearsal at Carmen's, perhaps for *The Arabian Nights*, Alan became so frustrated with my inert yet obdurate presence that he picked me up, by the waist, and swung me around several times. I felt like a rag doll, or a Guy Fawkes figure, or even a scarecrow, but I doubt it freed me up the way it was meant to do.

Cabaret Capital Strut: Sally Rodwell, Carmen's Balcony, 1977.

One role I did enjoy. In mid-1977 The Balcony was booked for a party by the people at Avalon, the TV studios in the Hutt Valley. It was called *An Evening in June* and was a catered, sit-down dinner with a show in three parts. We did *Close to Shame*, of course. Sal and Deb had a new dance, *Cocaine*. Carmen appeared. Neville was the MC and Alan did 'The Elastic Song', which was funny and, well, elastic – in the way of the accommodations politicians make. The Pig performed. Jan played Stravinsky.

My role was barman and for the occasion I bought a short white waiter's jacket and affixed to its back, between the shoulder blades, the hilt of a papier-mâché dagger with the blade presumably buried in my flesh and an impressive-looking blood stain leaking down from the wound. The patrons saw it only when I turned around to make them a drink; it received amused and/or alarmed responses, especially as the evening wore on and people got drunker.

That was me: a sight gag I could handle because it didn't involve the assumption of another personality. My problem with acting was that I could never manage the confusion of identities it posed. Was I somehow implicated in the character I was playing? Or was that a separate entity? If separate, where then was I? And so on. It was a dilemma that arose from uncertainty. When I'd begun to perform, reading from *Genesis* in *Towards Bethlehem*, the question didn't arise because I felt that was certainly me standing up there intoning. But when I played Jesus, who was I? Jesus? Me? Or some combination of the two? Although I did in time become more skilful, as long as I acted with Red Mole I never resolved these questions.

~

Authenticity was an issue for all of us, one that became more acute as the year drew on. The Country Flyers, for example, were a covers band. Rockinghorse too, although, courtesy of Wayne Mason, they had a few originals as well. Red Mole was a kind of covers band: we'd do acts based upon songs the musicians learned to play off records. And, as a troupe which subsisted on parody and satire, a lot of our material was topical and ephemeral. 'Most performances were based on newspaper stories,' remarked Sally in 1993.

And, in time, we became weary of making theatre out of a running commentary on the news. Of course there was more to it than that. One routine was derived from a reading of surveyor Thomas Brunner's accounts of his

100

South Island explorations in the mid-nineteenth century and, in particular, the prodigious amount of native bird life he and his party devoured; another was taken from George Grey's version of the tale of Hinemoa and Tūtānekai. A third enacted a Frank Sargeson story.

Yet this nagging sense of inauthenticity persisted. All of us who thought we were writers, composed lyrics and offered them to musicians to turn into songs. Original songs constituted something of a holy grail then, but they were hard to pull off. It wasn't until we got to Auckland that some decent tunes were written. One reason why Jan was valued so highly in the ensemble was that she could compose original music: she was versatile, fecund in invention and accomplished in execution. Although Arthur's monologues as Neville, Deborah's Pig, Sally's choreography and the poems Alan wrote – such as his 'Chant of Paradise', first performed in *The Arabian Nights* and many times thereafter – did constitute original work, the feeling that we were imitators, like drag queens perhaps, never quite left us.

For example: on 6 March 1977, the week before *Cabaret Capital Strut* began, the number one hit single in New Zealand was J.J. Cale's 'Cocaine'. Sally and Deborah choreographed a dance to the song, which the Flyers learned to play. They both dressed in white, with Deb, as usual, assuming the male role and Sally, the female. Their single prop was a white cube, which they parleyed back and forth between them. The ambience was one of abstract cruelty: an S & M interaction. The song is short, only about three minutes long; so, necessarily, was the dance. It was an instant hit with the punters and remained popular as long as they could bear to keep on doing it. But that, too, was a cover version. 'She don't lie, she don't lie, she don't lie … cocaine.'

In this connection the most interesting of the six themed shows was the final one, *Stairway to the Stars*. It was drawn from a scenario written before the season at Carmen's began. Originally called *Wayzgoose*, it opened thus: 'Out on the tundra an old man dies; his granddaughter at his side grieves silently. To tragic music, the girl departs the wilderness. She is met by two good spirits.' The story was an old one: the provincial who leaves home in search of another life, endures privation, resists (or not) temptation and triumphs in the glitzy world of fortune and fame. It was, in a way, the story of us all; a kind of group self-narration, perhaps, with a hopeful outcome. It was also, in a manner that could not have been foreseen, the story of Red Mole itself.

Stairway to the Stars poster, Joe Wylie, 1977.

Joe Wylie's poster is in three wide horizontal frames, disposed vertically down the page. At the top, a young woman carrying a bunch of flowers, and with a star on the lapel of her jacket, stands beside a country road waiting for the bus looming up behind her. In the second frame she is in some small town of the soul, with a punk haircut, smoking a cigarette, while two hoons in a V8 check her out. She still has the star on her lapel. In the last image she wears a fur coat and a shimmering gown and holds a microphone in her hand. Two lascivious cats in a Rolls Royce convertible have pulled up next to her. In the background, the bright lights of a big city street. Where previously signs read 'Dalgety' and 'Wattie's', now we have the pulsing 'GIRLS'. She still wears a star on her lapel, still maintains that posture of wide-eyed innocence: good spirits accompany her yet. Though nowhere identified as such, she always looks like Sally to me.

Stairway to the Stars was subtitled *A Freak Show*. The original scenario had a quote: 'Life's a ball when you're an underpaid actor.' And it's true that when you enter the carnie world of strip clubs and speakeasies, after-hours low-lit bars, late-night burlesque theatres and band venues you wouldn't want to see by the light of day, you do leave so-called 'normal' life behind. Is this what the subtitle meant? Perhaps. More pertinently, *Stairway to the Stars* represented a larger ambition. A document in the archive, an application for funding, proposes a balletic version with a cast of 16 actors, dancers and musicians, and a pre-production budget of $5000. Such a show was never made, but Red Mole would soon be constructing original works on that scale, with that degree of ambition.

~

Somehow, among the welter of making the cabaret, we published two more issues of *Spleen*. 'Third Year of Publication' was the proud boast on the cover of No. 7, which nearly didn't come out at all. The *Levin Chronicle* declined to print it. A play for three voices, 'Within a Dark Circle', written by Christina Beer (now Conrad) contained several 'cunts', a 'vagina' and a couple of 'cocks', one of which was 'big + red … making the house strong'. I was surprised to learn that the printers actually read the copy; in this case, it was hand-written, which was perhaps why. There was a flurry of phone calls and then, at short notice, the *Wanganui Chronicle* stepped up and agreed to print the issue without any censorship. It was a longer bus trip for the marked-up copy to make, a slower turn-around and they used poorer quality paper, but were in all other respects satisfactory.

I was keen to see that issue come out because in it was a transcription I'd made of a long interview Alan and I did with Len Lye, aka the King of Kinetics. He was in New Plymouth, at the Govett-Brewster Art Gallery, overseeing the installation of sculptural works, discussing further projects with his dedicated engineer, John Matthews, and making the arrangements by which the bulk of his estate would be donated to the repository after his death.

We drove up from Wellington in Sally and Alan's white Bedford van, spent the night camped out above a river somewhere in south Taranaki, and saw Len at the gallery the following morning. He was already ill with the leukaemia that would, in just a few years' time, kill him, but relentlessly upbeat anyway, full of plans. The most grandiose was his notion of turning Pukekura Park, with its grassy pyramidal terraces, into a Temple of Lightning. He had someone in New York composing the music for it: a Symphony of Thunder.

He was endearing in his optimism, a curious mixture of the visionary, the gimcrack and the gee whizz, and seemed to speak a language all of his own, compounded of 1920s antipodean slang – Crikey! – New York street talk and whispers of received pronunciation picked up in his mid-century years in London. Was he a familiar of Robert Graves and Laura Riding? Yes, their Seizen Press published, in 1930, his book, *No Trouble*. I was fascinated by his conviction that he could draw and paint images unmediated by higher consciousness; that he could see into the brain at the cellular level, even scan his own DNA perhaps. I took with me a book to show him, *The Soul of the Ape*, by Eugene Marais, which seemed to have analogies with his own theories, but Len wasn't interested.

Spleen 7 also featured six full-page images of moody, evocative building-in-landscape photographs by Peter Peryer. 'Mars Hotel' arrived unsolicited one day in the PO box and we printed the images without question and without explanation; they looked wonderful. The Splinterview was with Don Terris, all but forgotten now, sometime versifier and painter of Pasifika people. There was an innovative essay on Allen Maddox by Tony Green, reproduced in such a way that the text spilled over the margins on both sides of the page and had to be reconstituted in the mind of an intelligent reader; and the aforementioned play for three voices – Bride, Groom, Woman – by Christina Beer.

One of her graphic works would feature on the fold-out of the next, and last, *Spleen*, No. 8, which contained two notable debuts. The first, Raoul Walsh, was the nom de plume of Redmer Yska, himself recently released from Mount

Crawford Finishing School and 'lying low in Oriental Bay'. The other debut was that of Simon Wilson, in those days a sternly principled Marxist theatre critic. *Art & Life*, it was called, that last *Spleen*. It was laid out at 3 Claremont Grove, the big old mansion in Mount Victoria that had been the German embassy and was now Red Mole HQ. Sally and Alan, Jim and Jenny, Jean and Arthur, all lived there.

The last Splinterview was with painter Jeffrey Harris and I was lucky enough to sit in on that too. It was conducted by Ian Wedde in the sitting room of his ramshackle two-storey house in Roseneath, overlooking Evans Bay, in an intense array of silences that the tape recorder caught but the print version could not. The graphic work of Jean Clarkson, Joy Edwards and Gil Fraser featured. An exhibition space, the Capital Gallery, had been made in a room next door to Carmen's Balcony and these three artists showed there.

My contribution was an essay on Rita Angus. Nick Spill showed me the deplorable condition of her estate, neglected, scattered higgledy-piggledy in the basement vaults of the National Art Gallery. I used that as a starting point for a plea for a reconsideration of her work. Years later I learned that piece had caused some grief for the then director of the NAG, Melvin Day. So it should have. Alan wrote an account of Petrus van der Velden; Ian, a valedictory for Francis Batten's clown, Swede. Hob Nails signed off: 'I am leaving the world of ideas and adopting the axiom, if you can't eat it or fuck it, piss on it. The call of the outback is upon me.' Gerard did go to Western Australia next.

I don't remember anyone shedding tears over *Spleen*'s demise. It had done its job and a future for it had become inconceivable. In Ian Wedde's words, the newly constituted *Art New Zealand* was 'a glossy and more market-savvy inheritor of our useful organ: drumming up advertising revenue, I found myself following in the smooth wake of Peter Webb; a more compelling enhancer of brand values.' Alan said the magazine was only ever meant to last four issues anyway and by some kind of miracle had doubled its run. *Spleen* was a great learning for me, both in terms of the writing I did for it and in the way it advanced my understanding of the processes by which publications are made.

~

At the end of that delirious run of 37 straight dates at Carmen's Balcony we packed up and went to Auckland. We had been offered some shows at promoter Phil Warren's Ace of Clubs, above the Cook Street Market downtown. The initial season was *Red Mole's Golden Hits* but the intent was always to replace it with a new production. I was still teaching in the English Department at Victoria University so couldn't move up immediately. Jan and I commuted by plane for a couple of weekends until the term was over and we were free to move north to join the rest of the Moles.

Why did we leave Wellington? The official story was that the lease on Carmen's Balcony expired, but that was also said to have been the reason we took over the club in the first place. I asked Alan, on several occasions, why we closed Carmen's at the height of our success, with crowds queuing around the block and money rolling in? He was, typically, inclined to give different answers on different occasions; not necessarily false or contradictory, just varying slants on a complex truth. The one I remember best is this: 'It was the toilets. We just got sick of going in every morning and cleaning the toilets.'

I shuddered. I could imagine. The toilets at Carmen's were small and grotty and, after a night of revelry, besmirched in inventive ways that only rock'n'roll patrons seem able to explore to their full potential. Surely, I wondered (but did not say), there was enough in the door-take to hire professional cleaners? But that was not the Red Mole way. Every cent would have been saved and dedicated to future enterprises.

There was more to it than cleaning lavatories, however. The Moles were nothing if not ambitious. Having épated, comprehensively, the bourgeoisie of Wellington, they intended to do the same in Auckland, and beyond. Alan, with his shirt all giddy giddy gout, wanted to sound his barbaric yawp across the rooftops of the world. I think there was a master plan already in operation; it envisaged repeating the Carmen's experience nationwide and then using the finances so accrued to launch ourselves overseas. I think they already had their eyes on the prize: New York, the theatre capital of the galaxy. But they weren't crazy. Contingencies were acknowledged and alternative strategies entertained. Red Mole enjoyed a reputation for burning its bridges, but the flames were frequently retrospectively ignited.

The other matter that intrigues me now is the process by which I decided to join them. The short answer is: without doubt, almost without thought. It was put like this: 'We're going to Auckland to make some more shows. After that, we'll probably go overseas. You can come with us if you want to. Let us know.' There were no inducements. No promises. Not even the expression of a desire that you

Cabaret Capital Strut: Deborah Hunt, Carmen's Balcony, 1977.

might come along. The subtext was: Can you bear to miss out? I couldn't. The only way I wouldn't have gone was if I'd been told I wasn't wanted. In the absence of any such interdiction, then, I just assumed I was going. The same went for Jan: incredible as it sounds, I don't think we even discussed it.

This was life changing. I'd just finished a year as junior lecturer in the English Department. I had my MA. I'd sat in, as a participant observer, on an early iteration (the second I think) of Bill Manhire's creative writing class. I was in a good position to embark upon an academic career. The path ahead was clear. I would choose a topic for a dissertation and enrol somewhere, at a British or American university, to do a PhD. I would be given a scholarship and teach undergraduate classes while I was studying.

And at the conclusion of my studies, properly doctored, I would return to New Zealand and take up a position at one of the universities: Victoria, which awarded me my MA, or Auckland, where I earned my BA. I would be granted tenure and stay there until I retired or died, whichever came first. I would teach and I would publish, though what, I can't imagine. All this I knew, but only in the vaguest part of my mind. I never came up with a PhD topic, never even thought about it. At the ripe old age of 25, all I wanted to do was run away with the circus.

There have been times, mostly penurious, when I have wondered if this was mere foolishness, but I don't think so. I wanted to write and my decisions, whether conscious or not, were made with that in mind. I thought an academic career would ruin my writerly ambitions. That my putative works of literary art would all be still-born. And I think I was right. In those days I lacked confidence; it would have been easy, the path of least resistance in fact, to let my energies run into the necessary, endless work of building an academic career.

~

Something else occurred before we left Wellington: in September, at the registry office next door to the Coal Department in Wakefield Street, Jan and I got married. Why? A folie à deux perhaps, like many marriages. She always said that it was at my instigation, but I recall the idea coming from her and thinking it would have been graceless to refuse. It was not so that we could settle down. Quite the opposite. It was a decision made on the basis that we were going to go away together, perhaps to the ends of the earth. As, in a way, we did.

My parents were there and so were hers, although they arrived late, having driven down from Napier that morning. Jennifer Shennan and Allan Thomas. Sally and Alan, Deb and Pete, with that clothes basket of white and red camellias under his arm. Gaylene, Jan's sister, took photographs that included a number of fortuitous double exposures which she printed, in large format, later. They show the late arrival of Jan's parents, Tui and Ed, at the ceremony over pictures of the wedding party, held at 96 Kelburn Parade afterwards. I was wearing second-hand clothes: dark trousers, a white shirt, a waistcoat, a red and green striped tie I found out later was from Onslow College.

Red Mole's Golden Hits: Sally Rodwell ('I knew the bride when she used to rock 'n' roll'), Ace of Clubs, 1977.

Jan sewed a new green dress for the occasion. She wore it with a grey silk shawl and striped red and white shoes. The ring was made of pounamu. She looked beautiful that day, but there were contrary indications. We did not make love on our wedding night. And, strangely enough, within months, all of that clobber had gone. The ring was broken at Bastion Point when the White Rabbit puppet booth collapsed upon it while being taken down after the show. The dress and shoes were stolen from the dressing room backstage at the Peter Pan Ballroom. I don't know what happened to the grey shawl but it disappeared too.

I don't think anyone else quite understood why we were marrying either. My mother, perhaps cruelly, suggested we'd only done it because Sally and Alan had. I remember Alan's quizzical look during the ceremony: maybe Lauris was right? I thought it was a way of making a commitment that would help us navigate the vicissitudes of life on the road ahead. I don't know what Jan thought, but she soon took to calling me her hubby, which I did not appreciate.

It was as if, having secured me 'for life', she could afford a certain amount of latitude. She could put me in my place. A kind of truce that precluded intimacies.

Both our parents' marriages were like that. I remember remarking to her after the ceremony was over, perhaps in anticipation of our divorce, a decade and half later in Sydney, that the celebrant had not used the words 'till death do us part'. The Bible says it is better to marry than to burn; but some marriages end in fires of no return.

~

We were like babes in the wood, or innocents abroad. When we moved up to Auckland we found a place to rent downstairs in a big old two-storey wooden building in Hepburn Street in Freemans Bay, repainted the flat over the weekend, then, on the Monday morning, moved out. It stank, of mould and bad drains and leaking gas, and we couldn't handle it. On the Sunday night we'd gone for a walk and, on England Street, heard behind us the slap of running shoes on the footpath. It was my old friend Campbell Thompson, who used to hang out with us during our wastrel days at Puka Puka Road back in 1973.

He said he knew of a house nearby that was empty and for rent. We walked around to 19 Costley Street, a cute little two-bedroom cottage with a front door that gave directly onto the street and a back garden falling away into a gully full of paw paw and banana, tree tomato and citrus, swampy taro beds, choko and morning glory vines running wild among the castor oil plants. Next morning, early, I went up to Barfoot and Thompson's on Ponsonby Road and signed the lease.

It was just down the road from the house in Georgina Street where the Moles – Sally and Alan, Deb and, for a while longer, Pete – lived. Further up the street Bud, the drummer in the Flyers, his wife Gabe and their three kids inhabited a mysterious house with a thick hedge of bamboo outside. Bryan Staff was living in Costley Street too: in what he called, in his brassy, amused voice, Costley Heights, while our place below was Costley Downs. It was a colony of Moles.

The house was beautiful: wooden floors, a stained-glass window in the front room with two prisms set into it, which caught the setting sun and sent lozenges of rainbow light around the walls in the afternoon. The other front room I used as a study and workshop. The back bedroom, where we slept, was off a kitchen with a coal range and a wooden table. The bathroom, toilet and shower were outside underneath. Its one drawback was that it was infested with fleas, living in the cracks between the boards on the wooden floors, and even in our bed.

The Moles were worse off: their decaying villa in Georgina Street was swarming

Sally Rodwell, Alan Brunton, Deborah Hunt, Peter Fantl, c. 1977.

with cockroaches of the small brown variety called German. When you switched on the light in the kitchen, the walls moved. One night not long after they moved in they tried to deal with the infestation; the massacre gave Alan the title for the new show at the Ace of Clubs: *Slaughter on Cockroach Avenue.*

It was a detective story, Chandleresque, featuring a private eye called Frank Libra attempting to solve a series of murders that had something to do with the powers-that-be and their attempts to keep the rest of us in thrall to their dream of autocracy and death. Frank Libra was an avatar of a character Alan played at Carmen's: Francis Liberal, a wussy leftie in a cardigan and horn-rimmed spectacles, transformed into a hard-bitten, wise-cracking gumshoe. Libra was also Alan's birth sign.

Barry Linton did the poster. There's Frank, back to the wall, inside a derelict house, with floral wallpaper peeling around him, looking out the window and up a hill towards a version of the Moles' house in Georgina Street. He wears a battered fedora and dark glasses and smokes a cigarette; he's sweating. On his tie is a picture of Rangitoto Island with a yacht in the foreground, a cloud hanging over its summit, seagulls in the sky.

Arthur wrote the lyrics for a beautiful reggae song, 'Rangitoto', which Neil composed. I wrote a set of verses called 'Oh Fat Daddy', which Jan turned into a rock'n'roll stomper; it was a fantasy about Muldoon visiting a brothel. Both tunes came out on vinyl in 1978. 'Crossing the Tracks' was an elegy I wrote for my sister Rachel, recorded one night in Auckland for the NZBC. It was never broadcast, to my knowledge, but somehow became the title of the LP. Midge kept singing those two songs for years and they are the opening tracks on his double album, *The Midge Marsden Collection*. On those recordings you can hear again the rich, layered, beautifully textured voices of Beaver and Jean, sometimes known as the Purvettes, singing backing vocals.

~

Slaughter on Cockroach Avenue had a storyline that didn't cohere and wasn't meant to either. It was a matter of imagery and of tone, a way of moving seamlessly through contemporary milieus. It began with a violent death and ended with a song; hippies, trendies, yokels and yuppies were met along the way. It was melodramatic, satiric, sad and funny. Two members of Limbs Dance Company, Mary Jane O'Reilly and Mark Baldwin, did a number in each half. There were repeating motifs: Jan's Uncle Reg had given her for her birthday a doll, about 45 centimetres tall, wearing a snowy petticoat under a lilac crepe dress, which revolved on a pedestal and played a tinkly tune. This music box sat on the piano and, at points of mystery and danger, played its absurd, heart-breaking melody.

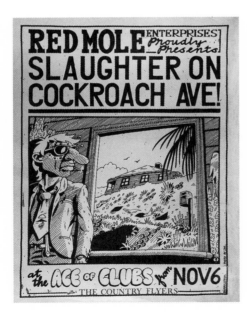

Slaughter on Cockroach Avenue poster, Barry Linton, 1977.

It was the theme for the Blonde, played by Sally. She came in at the beginning to ask for Frank Libra's help in solving the mystery of her brother's murder. We'd seen him, before the show started, one of a group of obnoxious revellers arguing at a table in the audience; he was shot, then ran up onto the stage to die. I was the brother who became the corpse, along with various other inconsequential but not unmemorable roles. The inventor of a bionic lavatory, for instance.

Frank sent his offsider, Sunshine, a pest exterminator, up north to look for clues. There were scenes in a country store, at the Pūhoi pub, on a commune where a group of hippies worshipped a guru called Don Heke. They took ritual doses of tutu berries harvested from the grave of James K. Baxter at Jerusalem. Sunshine, wearing a rat mask, ended up dead, killed by the hippies in a drug-induced frenzy. Frank discovered the body in a nightclub called The Crypt, where he had gone to rendezvous with the Blonde. Maybe she had something to do with the death of her brother after all.

A scene with Polynesian Airlines followed, a non-sequitur. I made a bamboo plane that an old Polynesian woman, an overstayer, wore around her waist like a dress of wings as she flew back home. The plane took off, by magic, during a chant called 'People of the Power'. This was based upon a conversation I had with an old Pasifika man in Hepburn Street, who used that phrase to refer to the bureaucrats of the Electricity Department.

The other part of the magic was a tin god, a free-standing silver tiki one metre tall and large enough for someone to crouch behind unseen while igniting fragments of powdered saltpetre, so that blue flames erupted from its mouth and its eyes. This was the finale of the first half: the tin god spat fire, the plane took off and the band played Leon Russell's 'Back to the Island' while a double set of painted plywood waves swayed back and forth at the rear of the stage. 'I hope you understand/I just had to go back to the island/And watch the sun go down.'

Joe Bleakley, the designer, had come up from Wellington. With his partner in crime, Russell Collins, he made and operated the oscillating waves. He also made, and operated, the tin god. For some reason Joe stored the season's supply of saltpetre in the base of the tiki; one night a spark fell into it and the whole lot blew up in his face. He did his duty, rocking the waves back and forth before the interval, and only then sought help to salve his burns. Luckily the damage was temporary. Joe's masterpiece for *Slaughter* was a mechanical bird that opened the second half by flying across the front of the stage on a wire, carrying a message in its beak from one side to the other. It looked bound to fail; everyone cheered when it made it across.

Part two made even less sense than part one had done. Sal and Deb, dressed as cockroaches, danced to the Mexican folk tune: 'La cucaracha, la cucaracha/ya no puede caminar/por que no tiene, porque le falta /marijuana que fumer.' In some versions the cockroach lacks a sixth leg; in ours she lacked marijuana to smoke. Scientologists came calling and were excoriated for their venality and their pride. Frank went to the gym and on a trip on an expensive yacht to Kawau Island, where he smoked opium and had a vision of a malevolent dwarf and a Chinese giant. Neville Purvis sang a song called 'Money'. The climax occurred in another nightclub, where it became apparent that the Blonde was indeed in cahoots with her brother's murderer: the Shadow, revealed, in silhouette, as Muldoon. After the Blonde also turned up dead in a funeral parlour, the ominous song that opened the show was reprised in a sunny, upbeat version.

Alan asked Leon Narbey to come in and light *Slaughter on Cockroach Avenue*; his wife, Anita, was on follow spot. One unforgettable day, in the Winter Garden in the Domain, Leon made a film with us. *Someday Afternoon* used a technique called stop-motion, analogous to animation, in which the images are captured one by one in a locked-off camera, then run together to make the moving picture. Shot on 16mm black and white stock, it was a retelling of the Adam and Eve temptation in the garden story. Fish levitated from plates, bread broke itself, wine glasses filled (and emptied) autonomously; the Devil, masquerading as a waiter, climbed down a rope and then, ruin accomplished, climbed back up again. The film, which looked like a classic from silent movie days, was projected during the second half of *Slaughter*, between Frank's visit to the gym and his trip to Kawau Island. Joe's mechanical bird featured in it.

At the Ace of Clubs we had to work around the performances of the resident artiste, an expatriate Australian called Marcus Craig, whose character was the drag queen Diamond Lil. S/he kept parties of suburbanites on furlough entertained with efficient if shop-worn routines full of mildly salacious double entendres. The frisson for the audience seemed to arise from contemplation of the possibility of an alternative sexual identity. It was a fully licensed theatre restaurant and the crowds that flocked in on Friday and Saturday nights enjoyed a three-course meal, with apéritifs and nightcaps, while rocking with mirth (or not) to Diamond Lil's antics. We came on afterwards.

The room was twice or three times the size of The Balcony and we had difficulty attracting enough people to fill it for our late-night shows. It was also

Red Mole's Golden Hits: Sally Rodwell, Deborah Hunt ('Sympathy for the Devil'),
Ace of Clubs, 1977.

more genteel and more conservative than Carmen's had been. More hypocritical,
too: that was built into the business. And then we had to deal with the propensity
of Aucklanders to sneer at anything that came out of Wellington, their inability or
refusal to understand that the coherence of *Slaughter* was to be found in its tone
and imagery, not in its narrative. Reviewer and theatre person Adrian Kiernander
got it: 'they found what works best for them is an episodic, picaresque structure
which provides enough plot to tie the show together but is loose enough so that
the varied talents of regular and guest performers can be used to advantage'.

~

The aeroplane I made for *Slaughter on Cockroach Avenue* was built out of lengths
of bamboo secured with knotted green baling twine. The bamboo I cut from
Bud and Gabe's hedge further up the street. One afternoon, in the front room at
Costley Street, I was sawing away at a piece with a Stanley knife when my hand
slipped and the blade sliced into the flesh of my left index finger just below the
second knuckle. An L-shaped cut that bled freely. I didn't say anything. I stuck

my finger in my mouth and walked through the kitchen, which was full of musos nattering and drinking tea, went downstairs, washed the wound under the cold water tap, wrapped a rag around it as a bandage, then went back up again.

In the kitchen a red mist rose unexpectedly before my eyes and I knew I was going to faint. They picked me up, carried me through to the bedroom and laid me on the bed, which is where I was when I came to again – not to the quotidian, but to a vision out of Brueghel: a vast plain upon which fires burned and artisans forged weapons of iron among red flames and drifting black smoke, the barbaric cries of their flesh-eating mounts. I remember lying there contemplating this vista, its strangeness and its power, while Beaver unlaced my boots and scolded me for not taking better care of myself. I probably was a bit run down. Sleep was a precious commodity in those days and, in the lead-up to the opening of a show, as fugitive as grace.

John Davies turned up one night at The Ace of Clubs. He had been overseas for the best part of a year, travelling in Europe, living in England, doing I don't know what. A bio written 12 months later in New York says 'he bicycled from Amsterdam to Marseilles, sleeping in barns and eating chickens after dark. Penny-pinching in London; expenditure on dance lessons with Madame Zesta from Muswell Hill (music hall and Russian ballet); income: from busking in the park and working the West End bars.' He was eager to get back on the boards, as he always called performing. He gave me some acting tips, which I sorely needed. 'If you hold your hands clasped in front of you like that,' he said, 'it makes your character look weak.'

Others were being drawn into the Moles' vortex. Craig Miller, who in 1984 became the pioneer merchant of espresso coffee in Auckland, was a friend of Joe Bleakley. When Joe came up from Wellington he stayed with Craig and his wife Vicky and they began a business making candles and selling them at Cook Street Market, the hippie emporium run by Londoners Brian and Ronni Jones and situated underneath The Ace of Clubs. Craig, who had an entrepreneurial streak, was persuaded, against his better judgement, to become Red Mole's manager. It was the first time we had had such an exalted figure, and the first time that we were forced to contemplate the possibility that Red Mole was, in truth, unmanageable.

Another friend of Joe and Craig and Neil joined the entourage around this time: Modern Johnny Warren, one of the odder and more endearing characters encountered during those years. Johnny was Māori, perhaps deracinated; I don't know where he grew up nor what his affiliations were. He had been a steward on trains and on inter-island ferries; had survived the wreck of the *Wahine* on 10 April 1968. Until a lifeboat rolled on him on the beach at Scorching Bay, crushing his ribs, he was busy saving lives. He and a mate had taken photographs as the stricken ferry went down and returned to the wreck later, surreptitiously, to retrieve the film. The images were sold, he said, to *Life* magazine, but for some reason were never printed.

Johnny was a roller-skater, and a chronic asthmatic. The steroids he had been taking for years caused fluid to gather in his joints and if he fell while skating, as he sometimes did, he was prone to fractures of the wrist or of the ankle. His knees were wrecked as well. He had spent a lot of time in hospitals. He was a small man, with a bulging chest, a long aquiline nose, full lips, rheumy, red-rimmed eyes, a wheezy laugh. And an indomitable wit: never without a comeback line. Like many who have experienced a lot of physical pain, he was an enthusiast for drugs and especially for marijuana and LSD. It was rumoured he shared a birthday with Alan: 14 October 1946. It may have been so. They formed a bond like that between King Lear and the Fool in Shakespeare's play: Johnny became the jester in our court of dusty feet.

His finest moment was the Cook Street Market Christmas Party that year. Brian Jones had hired us to open for Hello Sailor at the old Peter Pan Ballroom, later known as Mainstreet, a room with a square, sprung, wooden dance floor. The revellers from the market crowded on tiered balconies on three sides as the Red Mole ensemble, led by Modern Johnny Warren carrying a New Zealand flag, roller-skated out and completed several circuits of that magnificent floor, while the Country Flyers played the national anthem à la Jimi Hendrix. Johnny had taught us all, in rudimentary fashion, how to skate.

We did other one-off gigs. We were at Bastion Point in late November 1977, where the occupation of a remnant of their ancestral lands by Ngāti Whātua-o-Ōrākei continued for 507 days as they attempted, successfully it turned out, to prevent its redevelopment as housing for the wealthy. We revived *Towards Bethlehem*, under the title *Remember Christmas*, and put it on at the Island of Real in Airedale Street. We went, in January, as White Rabbit Puppet Theatre, to do a mask and pantomime show at the Nambassa Festival of Alternative Culture near Waihī.

After The Ace of Clubs we found another venue – behind the Windsor Castle hotel in Parnell. The Sweet Factory was a long narrow upstairs room in the old

Heard's manufacturing plant, where for 50 years they made the barley sugars, the boiled lollies, the liquorice allsorts, the lifesavers and the rest. The air still redolent of wine gums and pineapple chunks. Sally and Alan and Deb had left Cockroach Avenue and retired for the summer to a rural property in Greenhithe, on the outskirts of the city to the north. Alan was writing a big show for us to do in the New Year.

This move was the beginning of their ménage à trois – 'We were all three lovers,' Deb said – which would continue so long as I was with Red Mole. Pete Fantl went back to live in Wellington, where he married and went on to a stellar career in advertising, using his money to fund documentary and experimental film productions. The devising of the scenario for the cabaret to be performed at the Sweet Factory therefore became the task of Arthur Baysting and the ensemble. Or so the credits say. Sal and Deb were there every day. John Davies had rejoined. Otherwise, it was the same group that performed *Slaughter on Cockroach Avenue*.

~

The show was called *Pacific Nights*: the title came off a T-shirt designed by Barry Linton. He did the poster, a prescient image of an Auckland motorway clogged with traffic, all heading to the Red Mole/Country Flyers/Beaver performances at the Sweet Factory. 'Save the Whales' it says on the back of a packed sheep truck; 'Save Me Jesus' on the freeway wall; and, in a speech bubble hovering over a car at the head of the traffic jam: 'Wasteward Ho!' The poster was also the first appearance, up in the top left-hand corner, of the Red Mole logo, which featured in all future publicity. A mole wearing dark glasses, a cloth cap and a casually knotted scarf jives inside a roundel that has 'Red Mole' written upon its perimeter. The reference to the anarchist 'A' inside a circle is unmistakeable, and apposite.

Barry had contributed gnomic, philosophically astute graphics to literary magazine *Freed* 10 years before. He was an old friend of Alan's, like him born in Christchurch and growing up in Hamilton. When young, unsure as to whether to follow a career in music or in art, he chose art, but continued to play guitar in his own time. He wrote a song for the show: 'Pacific Nites, Pacific Nites/I don't wanna cry, I don't wanna fight/Identify, everything is alright/Pacific Nites, Pacific Nites.' I almost recall the Flyers playing that. I also remember that Midge Marsden, leaving the Windsor Castle after a gig, on his way to the Sweet Factory for the late show, was arrested for non-payment of maintenance, and couldn't make it

Pacific Nights poster, Barry Linton, 1978.

that night. Richard Kennedy had to do his vocals. Next morning there was 'Free Midge!' graffiti on the walls of the city.

There was an act in *Pacific Nights* called 'The Opium'. It was an extension of the Dick's vision on Kawau Island in *Slaughter*: a piece of keyboard music of enigmatic grandeur composed by Jan and accompanied on stage by a three-metre masked and robed figure with round spectacles poised upon its white-painted, Chinese-featured visage. The robes were red, yellow and black. Beneath them, John carried Deborah on his shoulders while she manipulated the long articulated arms of the puppet, its elongated white hands, as it progressed down the central aisle among the massed, silent audience.

What did it mean? It was a kind of dance that mimicked the meditative intoxication caused by smoking opiates. We'd all smoked opium; we still smoked heroin, chasing the dragon, whenever it became available. At Costley Street one time we somehow acquired a bottle of morphine in an alcohol solution – effectively laudanum – and drank it over the course of a night spent making masks and props. I remember seagulls crying over the house as the grey dawn came up out of the Waitematā.

John was all youthful energy and headlong enthusiasm and would tackle anything; it was around this time he learned to walk on stilts. The most memorable survival of *Pacific Nights* was a direct result of his return. One day we improvised a scene based upon 'A Mad Tea Party' in *Alice in Wonderland*. John played the Alice character, a stranger fallen among crazy people. Sally was the March Hare, Alan the Mad Hatter, Deborah the Dormouse, and I a character who isn't in that chapter but was reminiscent of the Cheshire Cat. We each made masks: Sally's long ears and whiskery nose, Alan's tall top hat and parrot on his shoulder, Deb's sleepy mouse-face, my cat. John remained the straight man.

The afternoon of the improvisation was one of enchantment. The puns, non-sequiturs, absurdities and other word play flowed so fast I don't know how we managed to remember what we said long enough to write it all down. Someone must have been taking notes. I have a copy of an early version and could quote from it here, but it might not look so well upon the page as it played upon the stage. 'The Mad Hatter's Tea Party' was cruel and funny, mad and full of mad delight; it concluded with a shaggy dog account of the crucifixion. Audiences loved it and it remained in the repertoire for years, long after I stopped performing with the troupe. I also loved the half-mask I made: yellow and black, with pointy ears and

Pacific Nights: Opium mask.

whiskers made from fibres pulled out of a hearth brush, I felt authentically cat-like when I wore it.

Arthur wrote the publicity for *Pacific Nights*. His brochure was a small triple fold-out on pale ochre paper, typeset, professionally printed: 'Live Theatre with a Vengeance!' it announced. Quite unlike the photocopied sheets of A4 we usually scattered around the place, full of the grandiloquent, preposterous, half-true claims Alan liked to make. Arthur's promo was a pitch to launch our theatre into a new market and at a new venue; it gave equal billing to

Pacific Nights: Deborah Hunt (Dormouse), Sally Rodwell (March Hare), The Sweet Factory, 1978.

the Country Flyers. The humour was understated, wry and might easily have been missed. In his summary of the dramatis personae, for instance, he had a running joke about redheads, which included this about me: 'tall, cricketing barman; would look good as a redhead'. Alan was a natural redhead; Sally, Deb and Jan in those days all hennaed their hair. It was a tilt at my uneasy position, half in, half out of things.

The brochure was a well-made thing but it didn't sound like us and, perhaps not coincidentally, *Pacific Nights* marked Neville's last appearance with Red Mole. He would tour with us as a support act, but he wouldn't be our MC again. There is a longer story here, to do with the troupe's inability to contain divergent personal ambitions. I knew this already. Russell Haley once read a poem of mine and saw that it imitated Alan's work. 'Don't go up against Alan,' he warned. 'Alan's myth is the West. If you go up against him, he'll shoot you down.' I don't think Alan shot Arthur down, but there was no longer room in the shows for the voice of Neville Purvis.

~

We reconvened in the new year, 1978, in a church hall in Herne Bay to begin work on the big show. Each morning Sally and Alan and Deb would drive from Greenhithe over the harbour bridge and up Shelly Beach Road to St Stephen's Presbyterian Church on the corner of Jervois Road; the rest of us would drift in from various inner-city locations. Years later I learned that both church and hall had been built by the siblings of my father's mother Ada, the Trevarthen brothers, one of whom, Alfred, was killed in World War I.

Our liaison there was the caretaker, an Irishman called Pat, who always had a fire burning out the back and a small black and white fox terrier trotting at his heels. He was usually drunk, but cheerful withal, until one day we turned up to find him poking disconsolately with a stick at something charring at the edge of the fire. It was the corpse of his little dog, which he had killed in a fit of rage and was now trying to burn. Things were never quite the same with Pat after that.

We'd begin our sessions by going for a run. In our multi-coloured tights and Red Mole T-shirts with the Barry Linton logo on the front, we'd amble along Jervois Road to Curran Street and then go down the hill, past the Convent of the Little Sisters of the Poor, to Ponsonby Primary School, where we'd do some stretches and other exercises, followed by a few laps of the playground, before puffing back up the hill to St Stephen's. Once we were at the hall again, our warm-up over, we'd pull out our cigarettes and start smoking and working in earnest. The one implied the other. We were turning the scenario Alan had written over the summer into a piece of theatre.

Like some of the others, I was dismayed when he handed out the photocopies. The scenario, 13 single-spaced typed A4 pages long, resembled nothing so much as a piece of narrative prose: 'Galaxies formed in the thin expanding primordial gas,' it began, 'when regions of somewhat greater density contracted gravitationally to form protogalaxies, rotating because of the net effect of gas eddies within them. The protogalaxies continued to contract gravitationally, and then to rotate faster. One of them was our own.'

There was a page and half of this before the first stage direction: 'The Curtain Rises.' Even then, there were mini-essays included. On was on the goliards, wandering students and/or clerics in Medieval Europe, remembered for their satirical Latin verses in praise of drinking and debauchery, and their jeremiads against the corruption of the church. Another concerned the tarantella, the spider dance, an apparent survival into Christian times of a pagan healing ritual. And a long quotation from French dramatist Antonin Artaud.

The work was *Ghost Rite*, both a ritual performed by ghosts and a play ghost-written by channelling the voices of the dead. It recounted a universal history, from the formation of the solar system until now, via recollection of moments of crisis – economic, political, existential or biological, revolutions, plagues, catastrophes, wars. These moments were re-enacted by a group of travelling players. There were seven of us and each assumed a core identity which might then mutate into whatever character we would play in any individual scene. Sally was the Fool, John the Acrobat, Ian the Strongman, Alan the Mountebank, Deborah the Fire Eater, Jean the Minstrel; I was a Pedant called Cornelius.

These identities were provisional and not necessarily apparent to anyone watching the show, with the possible exception of Sally's Fool, who was the central figure and in some ways the star of *Ghost Rite*. Sally, the most versatile among us, the most gracious and loyal and kind, the hardest working, the least egotistical, the still centre around which everything else revolved. The kind of performer who is utterly reliable on stage, and offstage works tirelessly towards the excellence of the next show. Also one who – and this is of course paradoxical – in performance doesn't draw attention to herself but rather to the role she is playing, whatever that might be.

And then I think, who worked harder than Deb? Or was more versatile? More loyal? And, again, more self-effacing, in that sense of giving all to the role? In fact we were a hard-working and multi-talented group, with a messianic sense of the importance of what we were doing. Alan and I were the only ones without some kind of formal training in acting, mask, mime, music or dance; but he made up for it with his imperious grasp of language, by what he could do with words or make words do, and with his magnificent voice.

It turned out to be a fascinating process, converting the prose of the scenario into a drama. It fell into three parts: the Archaic, the Medieval, the Modern. The curtain opened on the primordial scene, when the children of earth and sky separate their parents and begin the fight for supremacy in the sublunary world. The scenario followed the version from Ancient Egypt, in which the sky, Nut, is female and the earth, Geb, male; the analogies with Polynesian myth, where those roles are reversed, were clear enough. This scene was without actors. It was followed by a Palaeolithic drama: a mimed bear hunt, with the players cloaked and carrying big sticks and the bear bodied forth, like the Opium giant, by Deb sitting on John's hessian-shrouded shoulders. Instead of long prehensile fingers, she wore boxing gloves.

'The sun rises as the mime reaches its climax. There is the shriek of agony as the day begins, like that of a jackal. At the back of the acting area appear tall columns, the Stylites. They look remote, like the towers of a city on a hill. The actors have disappeared.' When they return, we are in Ancient Egypt, at Nekhen at the moment when a hunter-gatherer society transforms into one in which a god becomes king. 'He indicates that his victory should be recorded. He is given a staff topped by a phoenix. Enter a Strongman with a crown of two arms bent at the elbow. The Pharaoh is vanquished by the Strongman and, accompanied by Anubis-headed retainers, enters the Boat of Millions of Years. It is a ship of fools navigating by the echoes of Satan's voice. The sea is the sea of instinct. We hear a music perverted to popular taste.'

The third archaic scene was set in tribal times. Deb was obsessed with transformation masks made by Native Americans in Alaska and on the Pacific north-west coast. These wooden constructions depict animals, birds or fish which, when opened out by the wearer, reveal another, usually human face beneath. We made our masks out of papier-mâché, not wood, and the mechanics of such a transformation were beyond me. My helmet mask was a big white-toothed green

Ghost Rite: Deborah Hunt, Alan Brunton, Ian Prior, Maidment Theatre, 1978.

Ghost Rite: transformation masks.

and red bird's head, 'the raven which plucks out men's eyeballs'. Deborah mastered the art of transformation, however, and her character, Hohok, 'a long-beaked bird which splits men's skulls to feast on their brains', pulled strings to reveal the face beneath the face. The scene morphed into a potlatch: a wooden cart piled high with gifts, the disposal of possessions, the sanctification of the ancestors and the proclamation of Cannibal as King.

The three medieval scenes dramatised the Black Plague with its procession of Flagellants, the Tarantella and an heretical account of the Reformation. We passed through the founding of a mercantile economy, the establishment of banks and the instruments of credit, the invention of perspective as a means of representation of the world. 'The essential conflict at this point is between the mad (visionary) truth and the literal truth. The difference between hearing God's voice and reading God's *Word*. The instinctive rituals and songs of the past are now confronted with pedantry ... an event is no longer a repetition of some event from the past but unique, to be investigated as a single point in history.' The Reformation was represented as an attempt to overthrow this pedantry, this single point of view, this tyranny of the objective. It failed.

'There is a cry in the night. Enter characters with burning tapers. A man with a watch in his hand, it goes limp. A locomotive passes in the night, we hear a train whistle. Candles burn in trees. A nude lady walks through a railway station waiting room.' Surrealism is the birth of the modern. This is where the Artaud quote appears. It comes from the opening essay in his 1938 book *The Theatre and its Double*, entitled 'The Theatre and the Plague': 'Over the thick, bloody, noxious streaming gutters, the colour of anguish and opium, spurting from the corpses, strange men clothed in wax, with noses a mile long and glass eyes, mounted on a kind of Japanese sandals made up of a double arrangement of wooden slabs, a horizontal one in the form of a sole, with the uprights isolating them from the infected liquids, pass by chanting absurd litanies.'

Ian, in tails and a leather airman's helmet, danced with a shop-store dummy. I made a head mask in the shape of a green apple and wore it, à la René Magritte, while reading a newspaper: the *Ghost Rite* programme. The Three Graces, Jean, Deborah, Sally, naked except for long wigs made out of strips of white plastic, passed and circled and passed again. A spectral bicycle, which nobody rode, threw coloured shadows upon the cyclorama. The scene culminated in a procession of the blind leading the blind through the streets of pre-war working class Berlin to the filthy rooms of revivalist preacher and self-styled healer Josef Weissenberg, aka the Master.

An historical figure, here he was an analogue of all the twentieth-century dictators and charlatans, including Adolf Hitler; he was attended by a blonde nurse whose job was to fleece the faithful of their possessions. The depredations of the Master and his acolytes were succeeded by a calm, during which the cast, good bourgeois citizens, picnicked in a park on sausages, six-tiered gateaux and sandwiches while waitresses passed with steins of beer. What followed was war. And the finale, the ninth act, an Apocalypse.

Ghost Rite: Ian Prior, Maidment Theatre, 1978.

~

127

Ghost Rite: Sally Rodwell (The Fool), Alan Brunton (Hans Bones),
Maidment Theatre, 1978.

Ghost Rite had three songs and three orations, but apart from cries and whispers, shouts and screams, it was without dialogue. The first song, which Midge sang, was a history of the rise and fall of the tyrant, King Ned; the second was 'Anarchy': 'I have been gathering dust in mountains of ice/Halfway away from the dark side of paradise.' Jean sang it, in her character as the Minstrel, at a medieval fair, while Sally juggled and Deb, shadowed chromatically upon the cyclorama, swung back and forth on a trapeze. Someone ecclesiastical was selling indulgences.

The first oration was Alan as Hans Bones, in a white half unbuttoned waistcoat and wearing a truss over his green tights. The historical moment was 1533, when the Anabaptist Jan of Leyden proclaimed himself King of Munster and instituted a millenarian theocracy, which was bloodily suppressed by a princeling of the Holy Roman Empire.

*My name is Hans Bones and I have come to you from the House of Voluntary
    Poverty.*
I have been transmitted to Eternity.
All things which have been created are held in common by all of us.
Give. Give. Give. Give up your houses, lands, souvenirs.

The second was a paean to the Master, uttered by Sally as the Monotonous
Blonde: 'We hear him move at night through streets where blood reaches to
the hubcaps. His voice makes itself heard on Fridays. He has ordered railway
trains for the foreigners. He is the bottom line.' The Master responds: 'The seat of
government is a toilet seat ... see the birds on fire ... in the long night of paradox
... let's all levitate ... get your feet off the ground ... not to advertise this world
but to find a new ... the proletariat has no fatherland ... take flight for heaven.'

We have entered the last days of mankind. 'Yellow light on a deserted stage.
Someone with a black flag runs across stage. Tension builds as more figures run
with flags.' Bob Marley and the Wailers' ninth studio album, *Exodus*, came out in
June 1977. It was recorded in London, where Marley fled following the attempt

Ghost Rite: The ensemble, Maidment Theatre, 1978.

129

upon his life in Kingston, Jamaica, during the lead-up to a general election in December the previous year. Prime Minister Michael Manley's election slogan was the phrase, 'We know where we're going', and Marley reiterated these words in the title track, nearly eight minutes long, the last on side one: 'We know where we're going/We know where we're from/We're leaving Babylon/We're going to our Father's land.'

Red Mole co-opted that riff, used an alternative set of lyrics and made the song the finale of *Ghost Rite*: 'Good morning driver/Can I go home with you?/Yes I am anxious/To catch that Liberty Bus.' There are references to millenarianism and to cargo cults; we're all going to go to another place now. A cart transforms into an aeroplane, the Fool is the pilot. We are masked in strange styles: I have on a fencing mask that makes me look like an insect. Just before take-off we remove our masks and, in unison, blow fire.

~

The *Auckland Star*, on 12 April 1978, said *Ghost Rite* took two months to prepare, cost $27,000 to stage and that the performers received $200 each in wages. The time frame is right and the latter figure may well be correct, but the former is preposterous. Where would we have got an amount like that from? The QEII Arts Council? They might have made a contribution but not nearly so much. Money accrued during the seven months at Carmen's? Possible but unlikely. Perhaps the real figure was $2700, but that seems too small. A lot of cash was spent, however, on four big, custom-made props: the inflatable, the wheel, the cart and the cubes.

The cubes were a set of modular open metal constructions, nine in all, which were intended to be broken down and reset in different combinations. With them we would build pyramids, towers, palaces, forts; we would also clamber over them. But they were, for some unknown reason, made not of light-weight aluminium but of steel and were too heavy to do much with, beyond lugging them on and off stage. And they weren't stable. They rocked. Lethal for shins and ankles, elbows and knees. And heads. During one of the shows, making a change in the wings, I bent over to lace up my shoe and smashed my face into a cube concealed behind the blacks. I did the final number, 'Liberty Bus', with blood from a gashed eyebrow streaming down my cheek.

The cart was a splendid artefact, with two high spoked wheels, a flatbed in between, two shafts with which it could be pulled around. It was made out of

Ghost Rite: Sally Rodwell (on cart), John Davies, Martin Edmond,
Maidment Theatre, 1978.

pine, sanded and varnished, highly finished. However, like the cubes, it was
unwieldy, heavy and unstable. You couldn't easily climb upon it or load it up with
smaller props. The idea that it would somehow transform into an aeroplane for
the finale turned out to be fanciful. Both cart and cubes were made to a standard
of durability inappropriate for theatrical props, which are best when they are
light, ephemeral and multi-purpose: like the smaller props and masks we made
ourselves.

No account of *Ghost Rite* is complete without mention of the wheel. This had
been custom-machined, at some expense, at a place on the North Shore, and was
a double-rimmed tubular aluminium structure large enough for a person to stand
inside, braced, like Leonardo da Vinci's drawing of Vitruvian Man. Between the
acts of the drama, this wheel, an actor spreadeagled within, passed from one side
of the stage to the other. It was skittish to ride, especially on a raked stage: you
couldn't afford to get the trajectory wrong. Someone had to launch it in the wings
at one side of the stage; someone else waited to catch it on the other. That it never
once ran away into the audience is one of the wonders of that short tour. It made

a compelling image, though. And it was, after the first few times, exhilarating to ride.

The fourth of the major props was a thing of beauty. It was Joe Bleakley's version of the beginning of the world, the cracking of the egg of creation, the separation of earth and sky. The curtains opened on a bare stage. The light was blue; you heard a hiss of air. Gradually you became aware of something there, something large and round, something translucent. The inflatable took on the shape of a sea anemone, a round of tentacles facing inwards and pointing down towards the heart of the circle they enclosed. Like the light it was bluish-grey, and retained a cloudy translucency, as if the dim shapes you saw drifting within were made up of all the forms of life on earth. Because we actors entered from the back of the auditorium I saw this wondrous apparition each time it manifested.

One of the peculiarities of being in a show is that you don't actually see it. You're either on stage, looking out at the audience, or you're off stage preparing to come back on again. It isn't until you see photographs that you know what the production looked like. These arrived eventually and they were spectacular. *Ghost Rite* was lit by an expatriate American living in Herne Bay, a man by the name of Jay McCoy. He was softly spoken, unassuming, from the West Coast, and an immaculate light worker. Washes of red, yellow, green, blue, purple came and went on the cyclorama behind the players. Jay used it to paint sunrise effects,

Ghost Rite: The ensemble (finale), Maidment Theatre, 1978.

moon glow, the sombre darkness of impending war, the brightness of departure. In the photos even the cart, even the cubes, with their tracery of thin, prehensile lines, looked good. They had the semblance of antiquity, and the medieval, that the scenario anticipated. You could detect an overall movement from the dim, blue-grey of the beginnings to the incendiary reds and yellows of the finale, during which the ensemble blew fire and then took off into the beyond.

Ghost Rite was also a musical tour de force. Jan assembled a five-piece band and composed a 90-minute score. The musicians were Spencer Probet on drums and Tony McMaster on bass, Wayne Laird on percussion, Edwina Thorne on trumpet, Jan on keyboards and Jean and Midge on vocals, where appropriate. The band was called The Methylated Spirits and this brief tour their only outing, but Tony and Jean would go on to become perennial, and excellent, musicians and composers for Red Mole. It is a case for profound regret that *Ghost Rite*, like so much from those far-off times, was neither filmed nor recorded.

~

Or is it better thus? Maybe memories are more resonant than actual documentation would have been; film footage and tape recordings may have disclosed things better not recalled. Inexperience, ineptitude, a lack of finesse, a paucity of skills? Some of the critics, while praising the visual spectacle and extolling the musical score, complained of imprecision in the actors' performances. Simon Wilson in *Salient* scolded us for our 'bourgeois aestheticism'. Others were more apposite: '*Ghost Rite* is by D.W. Griffiths and Salvador Dali delivered out of Egypt,' wrote John Ghent in the *Auckland Star*. A few people were blown away by the scale of the spectacle, its ambition and by the marvellous visions revealed.

We did the show only five times: twice at the Maidment Theatre in Auckland, once at the Founders Theatre in Hamilton and twice at the State Opera House in Wellington. There was to be a sixth gig in Palmerston North but it was cancelled at the last moment. Because I had experience with heavy vehicles, it was my job to drive the rental truck with the major props inside. After the last show in Wellington, and a few vodkas, while attempting to back the loaded vehicle out of the narrow alley beside the Opera House, I collided with the front veranda of the building and nearly ripped it off. Everyone, including the Opera House staff, was remarkably understanding, but there was still the damage to the truck to repair. Johnny Warren, who was taking over from Craig Miller as our manager, knew a panel beater on the North Shore of Auckland. We drove all night back up the island and arrived with six hours to spare. Johnny's mate repaired the damage and we returned the truck to the rental company on time and apparently none the worse for wear.

~

The eight-page *Ghost Rite* programme was tabloid style, folded, like *Spleen*, but printed on thicker, whiter paper. The cover featured the Red Mole logo and the advice 'Some Day All Theatre Will Be Like This!' It was meant to provoke and it did. Those who did not like the show objected to the implication that *Ghost Rite* was the future of theatre. Even those who liked the show were perplexed. Who did we think we were? Murray Edmond remarked: 'The phrase has a wonderfully paradoxical life in that it is both hopelessly grandiose and yet teasingly prophetic – what if they are right, what if this is the theatre of the future?'

When you first unfolded the programme, there was the *Ghost Rite* poster, drawn by Joe Bleakley and featuring the seven core characters sailing a Ship of Fools upon an Egyptian sea. Inside, in lieu of individual biographies, a square of space was given to each performer to fill as he or she wished. The results veered from the eccentric to the incoherent to the informative: Deborah announced a five-year plan that included crossing the Empty Quarter, Rub' al Khali Desert, by camel. In the centrefold, under the heading 'More About Your Mole', was a history of the group thus far. This was the first of many histories which, over the next 25 years, proliferated alongside the shows to constitute what might be called an alternative narrative.

Was it the first? Or just the first published? Another history came out as a press release:

In the blind palace of the Dutch king next to the rotunda, a whisper was reported. It was said that Lord Saturday had discovered a new continent beyond the land of Prester John. The Lord of the Market offered the king a jacket made of sheepskins which cost six roubles in Bokhara and as he passed it over he reported the whisper from Addis Ababa. Drunken armies were fighting in the lost acres claimed by Lord Saturday; people were talking in rumours and as they entered the gates they called out: <u>Red Mole! If you should come again, we would give it all away and follow you!</u>

In all of the many Red Mole histories – including, perhaps, this one – the mythological exists alongside, and in a symbiotic relationship with, the actual. They are not the same thing, but one is always crossing over and becoming the other, so how can we know each from each? The history in the *Ghost Rite* programme is chronologically precise but contains inventions and exaggerations; the press release is mythological, and yet includes exhortations which may be read as real: 'I listen to voices on the paths of freedom. It is necessary to tear open the prisons. At night there is a whisper from the telegraph station five steps from the dark side of hell which is broadcast on all frequencies all through the lonely night. Keep the good faith and chant of paradise and Red Mole shall return.'

The histories are best understood in terms of the shows. If each show was unique, unrepeatable and therefore ephemeral, the histories try to give longevity to their transience. The exaggerations, the grandiosity, the myth-making in the histories attempt to reproduce those special qualities of live theatre, the moments of extreme emotion, of ineffability, of beauty and terror, of cataleptic laughter, which cannot by their nature endure. The histories do in prose what the shows did in theatre, though with a half-humorous, half-despairing recognition that the attempt must always fail.

Ghost Rite's history revisited Luang Prabang, where a prophecy was spoken by Lord Saturday: 'You are now initiated into the mysteries. It is your doom to travel the world as a group of barefoot players. You will be called thin surrealists. You will be accused of shoddy workmanship. You will remain poor. You will yearn for paradise and never reach it. You will call yourself Red Mole and forever you will kick walls.' This was more than a prophecy; it was an agenda. On the back of the programme was a bikini-clad woman searching her body for moles in a hand mirror. Around about her were a series of destinations we were, allegedly, soon to play; of those mentioned, only Ethiopia and, possibly, the Levin shopping mall, were not visited in the next few months. Our doom – to travel the world – had begun.

~

Red Mole's first post-*Ghost Rite* gig was two weeks at the Auckland Easter Show in Epsom. We were one of the acts on the John Maybury Showtime Stage, along with singer Toni Williams, the Society Jazzmen and the Fly North Quiz. The Chaplinesque *Hard Luck, Harold Bigsby* was written by the ensemble and performed half a dozen times a day. Sally played an out-of-work optimist who was perpetually disappointed, disparaged and persecuted in the quest for gainful employment. 'Get a job,' we sang. 'Get a job if you can get a job.' That song morphed into a parallel version called 'Chop a Tree': there was an ecological as well as a political subtext, and a romance. In the end Harold got the girl and they lived happily ever after. Or something.

It was the *Ghost Rite* ensemble, with the exception of Alan, who was out at Greenhithe writing another script. The Red Mole chronology says he did the lights but there were no lights that I recall, or at least only those rudimentary illuminations required for the infrequent evening performances. Otherwise we played in the glare of daylight, in the odour of candy floss and hot dogs, to the tinny music of the merry-go-round and the carousel organ, the bang and crash of the dodgems, the blague of carnie voices spruiking impossible entertainments. 'Step right up' – if I had wanted to run away to join a circus, here it was.

The new show, *Crazy in the Streets*, also had a carnival feel. Loosely based upon Alan's growing up in Hamilton, it was the nearest he came to a piece of autobiographical writing for the theatre. A soldier (Soldier) returns home from World War II with souvenirs: a carved wooden dog and a spent shell case. They belonged to his mate, who is dead, and they are consigned to his mate's girlfriend. She – Jocasta, later Aster – takes on Soldier in lieu of her lost lover and they have a child, a boy, called Boy. Soldier leaves; he returns an indeterminate time later with another child, Finn, a stutterer. Aster looks after both boys for a while, then gives them into the care of a church-loving couple. Who sunder when the wife, in the midst of a torrid affair with the preacher, goes with him on a pilgrimage to the Holy Land. The kids are set adrift again.

Boy and Finn, but mostly Boy, go through rites of passage. He meets a half-man half-woman. A fairground somnambulist who lives in a coffin prophesies futures; he falls in love with a girl called Abigail Robertson, who does not reciprocate; Ivor Fisher and the Satellites play the Starlight Ballroom. In the penultimate scene Boy, now a postman delivering packages for the World Record Club, meets his mother and father again; they are a hooker and a pimp in a suburban brothel. Finn goes for a jockey; Boy leaves town, heading for the Big Smoke.

All this is told in retrospect. The play opens and closes on a bench outside an old men's home where Boy and Finn have ended up, prey to the melancholy reminiscence brings. Finn is blind and neither he nor Boy knows quite what has happened, so that the drama circles around the uncertainty of the past and the

Crazy in the Streets: Left to right: Ian Prior (Cousin Finn), Sally Rodwell (Jocasta), and Deborah Hunt (Abigail Robinson), Ngaio Marsh Theatre, 1978.

way we are haunted by images of dubious provenance, which are all the more powerful for their ambiguity. The language is sometimes poetic: 'The sky is blue as the inside of a miracle. The moon goes down on the far side of midnight and the sun makes a run for the gap. It's always time to move on.' And sometimes comic: 'How f-f-f-far did you g-g-get with old rodent f-f-f-features?' Finn asks after Boy's first date with Abigail.

Finn was played, brilliantly, by Ian Prior. John Davies was just as good as Boy. Sally and Alan were Aster and Soldier. Deb did a star turn as the Somnambulist, Christine. She was Abigail too. The charismatic preacher, Father Devine, dressed in pink taffeta robes, be-wigged, arrogant, entirely corrupt, berates his congregation: 'I have seen you coming in from the darkness/with your armpits wet/& your overconfident nostrils on fire/like gardarene swine marching in the street/falling over your clichés/up to your necks in platitudes.'

We loved doing *Crazy in the Streets*. It was nostalgic, absurd, funny, delicate and joyful. Audiences loved it too. Anyone who grew up in a small town, as most of us had, could relate. We'd all gone to the A & P show; we'd all wanted to get away to another place; we'd all found that, when we got there, we were still

Crazy in the Streets: Deborah Hunt (Fortune Teller), Ngaio Marsh Theatre, 1978.

ourselves: 'Go away, Boy, and break somebody's heart.' The play was related to the collection of poems Alan prepared at Greenhithe and published, under the Red Mole imprint, with drawings by Jean Clarkson, as *Oh, Ravachol* (1978). In A3 format, on the same white paper as the *Ghost Rite* programme, it selected from work written during his European and South East Asian travels and from the Wellington years.

Cousin Finn appears in 'Self Portrait', about a boy growing up and leaving home: 'there's the widow's son/he is going out of town with his cardboard valise:/ the same one that came back/with his father's suit inside'. Some of the poems from *Spleen* reappear revised; there are acknowledgements, mainly in the titles, to members of the Red Mole troupe. There's this: 'cousin finn has gone for a soldier/fate tumbles dice/between his lashes,/the relative moon shatters'. Jockey or soldier? Ravachol the clown appears in 'Beggars Cat & Widow's Dog', about a threadbare circus. He was a real person, an anarchist who earned his living playing the accordion at high society balls in Paris during La Belle Époque. He was guillotined in 1892.

~

While we were rehearsing *Ghost Rite* Alan gave me the poems that became *Oh, Ravachol* to read. I responded enthusiastically but without insight. I didn't know what to make of them. I even gave them back to him in a disordered state. In return, I offered him the folder of poems I carried around with me at the time, called 'Stills from a Vagabond Cinema'. He didn't know what to make of them either; or perhaps he did. He said one day he might as well just throw them back at me. He probably thought it better not to comment. He might have been appalled at my imitations of his style and tone. Or amused. None of those poems has ever been published.

Alan was more kindly than I have perhaps indicated, especially to those most vulnerable. He valued innocence, because he was a kind of innocent himself. He'd come up through a system – church, primary school, high school, the universities – that automatically disparaged people like himself – poor, working class, isolate, oddly configured, red-haired – and developed ferocious defence mechanisms. He had a sharp tongue; could skewer a pretender in a phrase. He didn't see why anyone else should have it easier than he did, and he'd had it tough. Many people never forgave him for some off-the-cuff remark he made to or about them or just in their hearing.

On the other hand, if you were within the circle, in the Red Mole family, he would stand by you through thick and thin. But that didn't mean he'd tolerate pretension, mediocrity or bad faith. And then there was his gift, the luxuriousness and beauty and strangeness of what he was able to write. He wasn't exclusive either; he always offered me, and others, chances to come up with our own routines, and patiently nurtured the results.

He liked to parody authority figures – art professionals, dentists, doctors, generals, preachers, poets, professors – with a glee that never quite obscured a presence, like some Old Testament prophet, waiting in the wings to pronounce some doom. Offstage he was just as funny, rasping away at the differences between what was happening, what people thought was happening and what was being said about what was happening. An ironist of the first order. Like Modern Johnny, never without a comeback line.

~

Oh Ravachol: Alan Brunton (back cover image), 1978.

There was a problem with *Crazy in the Streets*: its running time of about 45 minutes made it too short to stage by itself. So we joined it to another piece of about the same length, *Our World* (sometimes *Our Whirled*), and called them a double feature. *Our World*, which always played second, was more cabaret than drama but it did have a spine. The narrative, which combined elements of *Hard Luck, Harold Bigsby* with *Stairway to the Stars*, was about a girl going to the city in search of work but focused less upon the prospects (or not) of employment than on the potential for corruption in the metropolis.

Denise Thrupp was the innocent abroad. Her love interest, also the antagonist, was the handsome and devious Herb Charming. The city was Wellington; some of the digressions they stumbled into went as far back as the *Cabaret Capital Strut*. 'The Family', for instance, a dysfunctional group on an outing to the beach. Deborah, as Joy, the mother, had a routine in which she tried, and failed, to set up a fold-out deckchair. Alan was an overgrown kid called Lyall who had just one stentorian line: 'Gimme something to eat!' I was Dad, a detestable martinet called

Goin' to Djibouti: Ian Prior, Alan Brunton, Modern Johnny Warren and
Martin Edmond.

Our World: The Labour Caucus: Martin Edmond, Ian Prior, Alan Brunton, Ziggy's, 1978.

Denis. And so on. We usually managed to fit in a dance to 'Lying in the Sand', the Hello Sailor hit song: 'I just wanna lie, lie, lie, lie in the sand.'

It was for *Our World* that we improvised a sketch based upon Muldoon's probably false allegation that former Labour minister for agriculture and leadership aspirant, Colin Moyle, had been questioned by police after being detained while cruising a gay beat behind the Wellington Town Hall in 1977. The target of its satire was the ineptitude of politicians and their attempts to solicit public approval for their mendacity. Four of us, in drag, each impersonated a member of the Labour caucus. Sally, for instance, was Tizard McLizard, a woman dressed as a man dressed as a woman. When Sir Basil Arthur constantly attempted to promote the interests of his constituents, the rest of the caucus would turn on him: 'Bugger the people of Timaru!'

We took *Crazy in the Streets* and *Our World* to Wellington, Christchurch and Whanganui, and revived *Hard Luck, Harold Bigsby* at the Wellington Trades Fair in the May holidays. At some point *Our World*, never really a distinct entity, mutated into *Goin' to Djibouti*, and this was the show that toured through both islands before we decamped, in stages, for Mexico and the United States of America towards the middle of the year.

~

We bought the car off Midge: a 1965 EH Holden station wagon known as the Green Shark. A big, solid, heavy vehicle, it was ideal for moving band equipment around. After I'd paid for it but before I went around to his place in Herne Bay to pick it up, Midge and his girlfriend had a fight and she slammed the front driver's side door so hard the window glass shattered. We were going to the movies that night – *Looking for Mr Goodbar* – and, as usual, I parked up behind the cinemas in Lorne Street. When we came out the car was gone. The police found it three days later in Paraparaumu, where the thieving joy-riders had abandoned it.

According to the cops it was still driveable so Jan's sister Gaylene and her boyfriend Barry Saunders, who were on their way up to Auckland, offered to bring it back. They soon wished they hadn't: the clutch was burnt out, the gearbox shredded, the muffler gone and the inside had been trashed. Squashed meat pies on the floor. The stink of spilled beer and cigarette butts. Broken glass. They arrived at Costley Street dazed and confused, headachy from the exhaust fumes and psychically afflicted by the miasma of chaos and violence hanging over the vehicle.

It wasn't irreparable, however, and after I'd had it fixed up, by another of Johnny Warren's mates on the North Shore, we took the Green Shark on the *Goin' to Djibouti* tour, along with the Mole's white Bedford van and Tony McMaster's immaculate Rambler Classic, also white, also a station wagon. 'We' were the seven actors from *Ghost Rite*, along with Jan and Tony as musicians. Johnny was our manager. We'd established a relationship with Gareth Jones, director at the Four Seasons Theatre in Whanganui, an elegant young man who drove a powder-blue sports car, so we played there on our way down to Wellington. I remember staying in the Alwyn Motel at Castlecliff, with views out over the grey sand, scattered with tree branches whitening like bones, to the cold winter sea.

In Wellington we appeared at Ziggy's, a short-lived nightclub near the Trades Hall in Marion Street: a large, square, upstairs room with a diagonal stage in one corner and barely adequate dressing rooms behind. It was more suited to bands than to theatre and we did the season there with Rockinghorse. Barry didn't seem

Our World: Soldiers: Martin Edmond, Ian Prior, Alan Brunton, Ziggy's, 1978.

to have suffered any lasting effects from that nightmare drive to Auckland. We improvised an act to the current Rod Stewart hit, 'Sailing'. We were naval officers on patrol, out of Gisborne, on our way to Moruroa Atoll to observe the latest French nuclear test, when a neutron bomb went off and everything descended into silence. Well, we thought it was funny. More pertinent, perhaps, was a cover we did of the Grateful Dead's 'Ship of Fools', with the ensemble heading off beyond the edge of the known world.

Barry Linton did the poster for *Goin' to Djibouti*. A procession moves away from us into a desert landscape. Their leader blows a slug horn; the second player, with rabbit's ears, pulls the cart from *Ghost Rite*; there's another sitting under the canopy, looking back at us. A single escort. A fish dangles from a string. The fifth player, walking behind the cart, is long-nosed, robed and holds an umbrella against the sun. Last of all, also looking back, in close-up, is a lizard-faced figure

A Red Mole blows fire.

Siddhartha poster, Alan Brunton, c. 1975.

Cabaret Paris Spleen: Sally Rodwell, Frances Edmond, Alan Brunton,
The Performers Theatre, 1975.

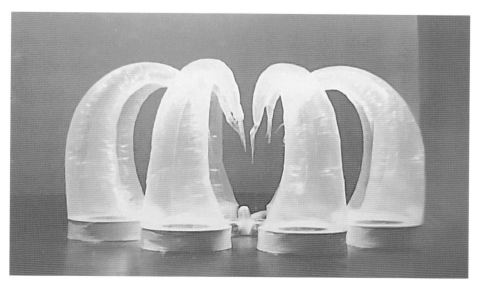

Ghost Rite: The Inflatable, Maidment Theatre, 1978.

Ghost Rite: The Cart, Maidment Theatre, 1978.

His Majesty's Theatre, Queen Street, Auckland, 1978.

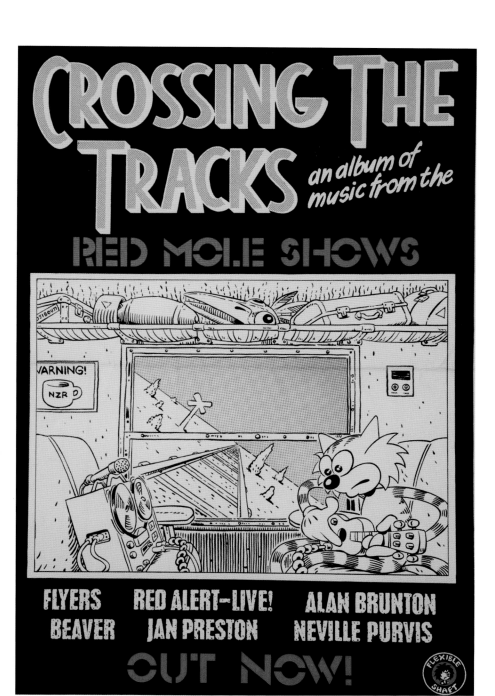

Crossing the Tracks poster, Joe Wylie, 1978.

Jan Preston and Martin Edmond, Halloween, San Francisco, 1978.

ABOVE: *The Last Days of Mankind*:
Alan Brunton as The Ordinary Vernon,
Theater for the New City, 1979.

RIGHT: *The Last Days of Mankind*:
Sally Rodwell as Agent Orange,
Theater for the New City, 1979.

The Last Days of Mankind: John Davies, Theater for the New City, 1979.

RIGHT: *The Last Days of Mankind*:
Apocalypse Blues (ensemble),
Theater for the New City, 1979.

RIGHT: *The Last Days of Mankind*: a Madman at the Gate (John Davies), Theater for the New City, 1979.

Deborah Hunt, Alan Brunton, Ian Prior visit New Zealand House, London.

Back in New York, 1979: Martin Edmond, Jan Preston, Sally Rodwell, John Davies, Neil Hannan, Alan Brunton, Deborah Hunt.

Dead Fingers Walk: Alan Brunton and friend, Theater for the New City, 1979.

Dead Fingers Walk: Palm Tree puppets, Theater for the New City, 1979.

Numbered Days in Paradise poster, Alan Brunton, 1979.

Numbered Days in Paradise: Crucifixion, St Peter's Hall, New York, 1979.

Numbered Days in Paradise: Maiden (Sally Rodwell) and Coyote (Deborah Hunt),
St Peter's Hall, New York, 1979.

Team talk New York, 1979.

The 1969 Pontiac Le Mans SW: Martin Edmond, Jan Preston, Neil Hannan.

The Excursion: The weighing of the heart on the scales,
Theater for the New City, 1982.

in a gleaming top hat. There's a big bird, an eagle or a vulture, hovering overhead and music in the air. We're committed, enthusiastic, insouciant; we're on the road to nowhere.

Some say the French colony at Djibouti was founded by poète manqué Arthur Rimbaud during his adult career as a trader and gunrunner; it may be so. Alan remarked later that he became interested in the place after learning that its sole viable industry was a soft-drink factory. There was the Ethiopian connection as well, the millennialism of Rastafarians leaving Babylon and going to the fatherland. The finale of *Goin' to Djibouti* was the same as that of *Ghost Rite*, a fiery

Goin' to Djibouti: poster, Barry Linton, 1978.

conclusion played out to the riff from *Exodus* reconfigured as 'Liberty Bus': 'We can have a lot of fun/Calling out to John Frum/Rock this buggy, make it roll/ Echoes coming in from the lost patrol.'

Although *Goin' to Djibouti* was a compendium, an anthology, incorporating bits and pieces from many other shows, it had a coherence of tone and theme: a meaner, sharper edge than *Our World*, a stronger sense of impending doom. Some picked up on this: 'The most refreshing thing about the show is its lack of logic,' wrote Howard McNaughton in the *Press*. When Sal and Deb danced 'Cocaine', it felt terminal: those must have been among its last performances. 'The Family' degenerated into sneering viciousness, relieved only by the blackest of humour.

We'd all been asked to come up with individual acts. Ian's involved something he called 'virus likus' although, rather than speak, he did it mostly as mime. Alan played a bent doctor, an abortionist, with a black patch that he shifted randomly from one eye to the other. In the course of his spiel, he investigated the insides of his ear with a knitting needle and inspected the results: herpes, perhaps, in the wax deposits. John, remote, otherworldly, walked by on three-metre stilts, as if he

Goin' to Djibouti: Deborah Hunt, Sally Rodwell, His Majesty's, 1978.

were already in Djibouti. Sally's turn was a pill-addicted housewife, a precursor of Rhonda Gonne, the loner from Berhampore South in her 2000 collection, *Gonne, Strange, Charity*. Deb's Pig had its final outing.

I gave voice to my sense of a diseased polity through a character called the Undertaker. 'I'm the Feel of the Times/And I'm knocking on your gate/With a question from the Church/And an answer from the State.' He wore black, apart from a purple-lined cape someone had given me in my hippie days. And a battered top hat, so old it had begun to turn green, which Deborah found. He was conducting the funeral of democracy – an extravagant conceit, but one in accord with the way things were then, or the way we felt they were. This was my swan song as an actor.

~

In Christchurch we were joined at the Ngaio Marsh Theatre by a crew from the National Film Unit in Wellington who were shooting the hour-long documentary which became *Red Mole on the Road* (1979). It was a small, four-man unit: director Sam Neill, a cameraman, a soundman and a gaffer. John Reid, from Wellington, had a co-scriptwriting credit with Sam. At that point Sam had done as much directing as acting, and his acting was as likely to have been on stage as on screen, with *Landfall* and *Sleeping Dogs* the exceptions. What I mainly recall about him as a director, however, was his uncertainty. He seemed never to know quite what to do next.

This was understandable because, throughout the shoot, he was struggling with Alan for control of the film. If Sam didn't know what he wanted, Alan certainly did. But Sam wasn't going to be dictated to by Alan, so he resisted. And thus it went: a battle of wills that played out over weeks, from Christchurch up to Auckland. Alan's idea was that, as performers, we existed in three incarnations: the characters we played on stage, our real-life selves and an indeterminate third, a kind of ur-self, in white face, mostly encountered on the road: as desperados, ghosts, hitch-hikers, vagabonds. While driving through the landscape as ourselves, then, we encounter others who both are and are not ourselves. Sometimes, when interviewed, we speak as these ur-selves; generally they appear in mime. They are never commented upon.

Alan and Sam's arm-wrestle had consequences for me. Sam decided that I was a good interview subject, no doubt because I was non-threatening: both articulate and compliant. But his decision to spend time with me soon led to mutterings: 'Why's he talking to him? He doesn't know what's going on. He's not even really an actor.' Or so, in my paranoia, I imagined. In a way I agreed, but I was still flattered by the attention. I negotiated the dilemma as best I could, and in the film, judiciously edited by Judy Rymer, there's no sense of conflict in the group, nor of any favouritism. We're all given our due, as it were, as performers, as people and as revenants. The documentary ends with a nod to *Close Encounters of the Third Kind*: the aliens we meet coming out of the swirling mist of the spacecraft's exit shaft are ourselves.

There are star turns. In the box office of the Theatre Royal in Nelson, Alan, as Uncle Al, the Kiddie's Pal, in a scarf, a red bowler hat and a red jacket, is interviewed while selling tickets and stashing the night's takings into a shoebox: one-, two- and five-dollar bills. He chuckles as he folds the money away, comparing us to evangelists bringing a message to the unconverted – as I suppose we were. In a school hall on the West Coast, perhaps in Murchison, Sal and Deb do an act for a group of young kids sitting on the floor. They start out as bird puppets, peering around the corners of a curtain, singing a song. In the reprise they step out as

From left, back row: Martin Edmond, Tony McMaster, Unknown (Mouse), Ian Prior, Unknown (mask and wig); front row: Jan Preston, Modern Johnny Warren, Jean McAllister, Deborah Hunt, 1978.

glamorous swimsuit-clad puppeteers in high-heeled shoes: 'Oh we are little birds/ And we fly around the store/We poop on the windows/And we poop on the floor/ We poop on the butter/And we poop on the jam/And we poop poop poop/On the grocery man.' The kids go wild.

The narrative thread of the film is our progress north to the culmination of the tour, two nights at His Majesty's Theatre, now demolished, in Auckland. We're ambivalent; no one really believes we'll sell out the show but we all still hope we might. There's that strange combination of the earnest and the nonchalant, so characteristic of those years.

The crunch moment for me comes from a sequence filmed backstage at His Majesty's. Deb and Sal are changing for their next routine and Deb is worried she won't be ready in time. Alan reassures her. He says the gravedigger is next and, if necessary, he'll go out and do something. He puts on Uncle Al's red bowler hat and red jacket. Johnny Warren is in the background, hopping from one foot to the other, purple with anxiety, wheezing, actively distressed: implicated in a drama

White Rabbit Puppet Theatre set, c. 1978.

from which he is forever excluded. He's said the show must go on, but now it has there's nothing he can do.

Alan counting the takings in Nelson raises another question. We must have made quite a bit of money on that tour: there were full houses in Whanganui and a 70/30 split our way on the door. The fee for Ziggy's was $850. The Arts Council gave us a $1000 grant to tour both the South and North Islands, with a back-up guarantee of another grand, which I'm sure we would have found a way to claim. The payment from the National Film Unit was $4000, with an additional $1000 in expenses. That's 10 grand, not counting the door takes from Nelson, Auckland and elsewhere, and whatever we might have made from T-shirt sales. We were all paid the same, irregular disbursements, always in cash, in sums I no longer recall.

Alan was meticulous with accounts. I imagine a portion of those unspent funds went towards the travels he and Sally and Deborah were about to embark upon. After that finale at His Majesty's, after we all blew fire for the last time and marched off into the empyrean, an eerie silence fell. It was July 1978, and within days, it seemed, the Gang of Three had gone, via Los Angeles to Mexico City. John followed a few weeks later, aiming to rendezvous with them there, though he didn't actually catch up with them until Thanksgiving Day in Washington DC. Deb proposed we all meet again in New York on New Year's Eve. Or was it 1 December? Whichever it was, I was determined to be there.

Jan's new five-piece band, Red Alert, aka the Red Mole Orchestra, gigged around Auckland for a few more weeks until, in spring, all six of us, in stages – three, two, one – flew out for the States. I don't remember how we paid for our fares. Maybe we had some savings. Money was different then, easier to come by and of lesser import. I do recollect thinking we were taking a step into the unknown. I don't believe any of us had left New Zealand before. None of us knew what we were getting into. Or what we were trying to do – apart, that is, from going on an adventure.

IV

Unnumbered Days

1

The Barbary Coast

Tony picked us up at Los Angeles airport in a small blue compact hatchback, a Ford Pinto; their petrol tanks had a propensity to explode if the vehicle was rear-ended. We drove through the Inglewood Oil Field, where pump jacks like primeval birds bent and fed upon the blasted earth; past Culver City, Miracle Mile and La Brea Pits; on towards Hollywood, where we were staying at Howard's Weekly Apartments just off the Boulevard on North Whitley Avenue. Tony seemed to know his way around already. With drummer Stanley John Mitchell and singer Jean McAllister, he was already living in the apartments. Guitarist Richard Kennedy was going to meet us in San Francisco in a few weeks' time.

Tony was, like Jan, from Greymouth. He worked four years behind the counter of the local BNZ before embarking upon a career as a musician. Like many bass players, he was interested in sound and made himself responsible for putting together the PA the band would be singing through. Tony was astute, with a confidential manner that always suggested some entertaining intrigue might be afoot, as it usually was. Stan, from Palmerston North, had the simplicity and directness a lot of drummers possess, along with a sense of being away in a world of rhythm. He was well experienced at touring and recording.

Howard's Weekly Apartments was nondescript, rundown, a warren full of dubious itinerant types like us, but affordable and good enough for now. Our room faced south but there were impediments to the view. An ancient air-conditioning unit was fitted into the window, which meant it couldn't be opened. It wheezed and laboured night and day to produce, not cold air, but a smooth slab of white encrusted ice, against which you could lean your hot forehead. The other obstruction was the atmos itself.

When you looked towards Hollywood Boulevard you saw dim shapes moving through a wavering yellow-brown oily haze, a noxious petro-chemical smog produced by the concentration of automobile engine emissions under an inversion layer. It was ever thus. In 1542 Spanish adventurers called this place La Baya de los Fumos after the smoke from the cooking fires of the local Tongva Indians, or from wild fires in the chaparral, which had become trapped beneath a layer of cool maritime air that was itself caught between the sierra and a higher band of warmer air.

Hollywood Boulevard didn't have the glamour I expected. It was grubby and sad, populated by small-time drug dealers, hookers and pimps, grifters and hustlers, who spent their time passing back and forth looking for a mark, a john or a score. If you went east, the porn shops, the head shops, the liquor stores and the general air of dissolute abandonment and threat increased; the Museum of Death is down there now. If you went west, there were Grauman's Egyptian and Chinese Theatres, the expensive restaurants, the Walk of Fame with the stars set in the pavement, a classier sort of people perhaps. Or not. Angelinos, like Americans everywhere, had a voracious appetite to enter into proximity with celebrity. The first time we walked down the Boulevard, Jan, with her short red hair and her silver trousers, was asked who she might be? David Bowie's sister?

Once away from the main drag, however, you walked along quiet, leafy, elegant streets of red-tile-roofed, white stucco apartment buildings, with plantings of palm and hibiscus, hedges of flowering pink and white oleander. I remember the sweet smell of gardenias, which I'd never met before, on the balmy night air as I went around to the 24-hour supermarket to buy ridiculously cheap, high-quality fresh fruit and vegetables: cantaloupes, to me then the height of luxury, could be had for 17 cents a pound.

Stan and Tony, both jazz aficionados, were amazed to learn that players they'd idolised on record could be seen live and free at cafés or bars where you might sit at a table all evening so long as you had a drink in front of you. By the same token, acts we thought must be huge turned out to be hard-working musicians with a modest following, just like the bands we knew in New Zealand. After a gig at the Palomino in North Hollywood, Commander Cody, but not His Lost Planet Airmen, stood at the entrance and, as we left, shook the hand of each and every punter who had come to see him play.

There were rites of passage. One night Tony and I went to buy some dope in the car park behind a fast food outlet – was it a Wendy's? – on Sunset Boulevard. The guy in the passenger seat took our cash, then the driver accelerated away, leaving us bereft of both money and drugs. Marijuana was accounted a necessity in those days; we soon found a better source. Then, at Brentwood, we bought a bronze 1972 Buick Estate Wagon with a Hebrew (perhaps Zionist?) sticker on the rear window and a knock in the big end. It was capacious enough to seat all six of us, three in the front and three in the back, with room behind for the guitars, the amps, the keyboards and the drums. We joined the other large cars cruising the wide boulevards, all travelling at the same speed, accentuating their resemblance to schools of predatory fish, with their grilles gleaming like bared teeth. We began to make our own contribution to the oily, petro-chemical smell that was always in the air.

We bought the car because we were going to go north to San Francisco. I no longer remember why. Perhaps we thought a smaller city might prove more manageable than the vastnesses of Los Angeles; perhaps because we knew someone living there. The plan to join the Moles in New York seemed to have fallen into abeyance. On the other hand, it was still only September and they weren't even there yet. There were times of confusion: turning the car the wrong direction into a one-way street and finding three lanes of traffic bearing down upon us. Cries of alarm from the musos while I wrestled with the wheel, trying to ignore the thump in the diff, always worse in reverse, and the horns of other drivers as I backed around the corner again.

Somewhere in LA, at a skating rink, we saw Alastair Riddell (ex-Space Waltz) and his band Decade Decade play. It was one of the strangest gigs I've been to. Alastair is very tall and so, it seemed, were his band. They were set up in the centre of the rink, remote and far away as Norns. It was hard to hear them above the metallic sound of the skaters going around and around; they looked like stick figures playing upon a wheezing calliope in the middle of an oblivious merry-go-round. Afterwards Alastair was rueful, apologetic. It was as if he had done something shameful.

Another day we drove into the Hollywood Hills to visit Hello Sailor, who were living in a rented house in one of the canyons. Tony had been their bass player in an earlier incarnation; I'd known Dave McArtney and Graham Brazier since we'd been 20-year-olds knocking around Auckland in the early 1970s. There were five saloon cars parked on the road outside and, up some steep stone steps, five proto-rock stars were lounging, some with, some without, bikini-clad girlfriends, around a blue swimming pool. In the gloom of the mansion David Gapes, their manager, ex-Radio Hauraki DJ, was on the phone. He looked frantic, as if his mop of curly hair might be about to stand straight up on end, but the Sailor boys seemed pretty relaxed.

They were discussing the recent proposition by Ray Manzarek, keyboard player and founder member of The Doors, to reform the band with Graham instead of Jim Morrison, who had died in 1971, as lead singer. Ray had seen Hello Sailor play one night at the Whisky a Go Go on Sunset Boulevard and thought Brazier might like to join them as vocalist on a revival tour. Graham wasn't into it. 'I'm my own man,' he said. 'I wouldn't desert my band-mates.' I remember leaving feeling abashed, as if we were poor copies of the real thing, but Hello Sailor was already in disarray and would soon retreat in confusion to Auckland and thence to a disastrous sojourn in Australia. Perhaps that was another reason why we wanted to go to San Francisco: no other New Zealand band we knew of, with the possible exception of Mother Goose, had played there before.

~

We drove north up Highway 1 through Santa Barbara and Pismo Beach and San Luis Obispo, small seaside towns with Spanish names and remnants, or revivals, of mission architecture. Pismo called itself the Clam Capital of the World, even though clams were extinct there and had to be flown in from the East Coast. Then Big Sur, Monterey and Santa Cruz. The Pacific boomed on our left as we negotiated cliffside roads, some of which have since fallen into the sea, with the sierra on our right, its fragrant slopes growing mesquite and sagebrush and pine. I remembered the sense of freedom that comes from being on the road, along with that other excitement, risk, and the consequent anxiety about what might go wrong.

Nothing did and we arrived in San Francisco and drove into the city and pulled up at the intersection of Haight and Ashbury, ground zero of the hippie movement, the HQ of the Summer of Love. Not out of any sense of pilgrimage but because Jean's friend Rachel Stace lived in an apartment on Ashbury Street, just a few yards up from the famous corner, where flower children begged on the pavements and barefoot dreadlocked criminals cruised the passing crowds looking for victims. It was a hippie skid row. I knew Rachel only slightly; she had been one of those running Macavity's restaurant in Wellington when I used to go there in 1974.

She was living with a guy called Rick, who later emigrated to New Zealand. There was another fellow around, Perry, and I got to know both of them during the next few months. Perry because I used to work for him, selling sweaters allegedly knitted out of Guatemalan wool – actually Mexican synthetics – down at Fisherman's Wharf. I liked Rick and we got on. I still remember the piece of admonitory wisdom he imparted to me one day while cooking hamburgers in the backyard: 'Morton,' he said, 'there are some things you only learn chronologically.' It's true, there are. Needless to say, Rick was older than me.

We left Jean at Rachel's place and carried on downtown, looking for somewhere to stay. I remember checking out a cheap hotel in the Tenderloin, on Turk Street, where a desk clerk gave us a key and we went upstairs to look at a room. It had a lime green candlewick bedspread over a thin mattress on a double bed; and the stench of urine was so rank we never even crossed the threshold. They were asking $24 a night to lie between those piss-stained sheets.

I don't recall anything else about our first night in San Francisco: Where did we sleep? Where eat? What about Stan and Tony? My next memory is of the place we ended staying for the duration, a flat above a Chinese laundry near the corner of Greenwich and Gough streets in Cow Hollow, just a couple of blocks from Highway 101, where Van Ness Avenue turns into Lombard Street along the approaches to the Golden Gate bridge.

Tina, who invited us to come and share her flat, was a student of anthropology from Connecticut. In her early twenties, a sweet-natured, naïve, outgoing young woman, full of cheerful optimism, yet ignorant and occluded in her views. She told me, seriously, that the bums down in the Tenderloin or on Mission were there because it was their choice, as Americans, to live that way. If they wanted a different kind of life all they needed to do was change their mind and it would be theirs. I was too astonished to argue. She also thought that Māori in New Zealand lived in grass huts, went naked and practised cannibalism. The advent of a group of Kiwis into her life prompted her to begin to specialise in the anthropological study of the tribal people of Aotearoa.

Meanwhile Tony and Stan went to live in the basement of a grand old house on Steiner Street in the Fillmore District; Richard, when he arrived, joined them there. They were the premises of the Center for Postural Integration, run by a guy called Jack Painter. He was Tennessee-born, a former professor of philosophy and psychology at the University of Miami and a body/mind therapy specialist. At the Steiner Center, among much else, they practised Rolfing, a deep tissue massage technique which is supposed to realign the body's energy with that of the earth's gravitational field.

It is also meant to banish accumulated trauma by separating muscle from bone, so that bad choices encoded in your 'armour' cease to guide your actions in the future. The sound of someone being Rolfed was horrifying: screams and yells and moans, as if they were undergoing systematic torture; as perhaps they were. On the other hand, patients were encouraged to self-express. After the required dozen sessions, the flesh of those who had been Rolfed seemed to hang more loosely from their bones, and they became vague to the point of distraction, if not actual idiocy. Perhaps it was PTSD.

Other weird stuff went on at the Steiner Center: sessions where groups of people would take mescaline, brought up from Mexico by a guy called Raphael, then undergo video therapy which involved being filmed, tripping, naked, while watching themselves, in real time, naked, tripping. This was to encourage self-awareness. Richard recalled coming upstairs one day to make a cup of tea and finding the big sitting room on the ground floor full of unclothed people of all sexes. 'Hair,' he wrote. 'Lots of hair.'

There was an orgone box in a corner of the room where you could go to sit, with the door closed, in order to recover the lost 'esoteric energy' whose deficit lies at the root of so many diseases and neuroses. Or so Wilhelm Reich theorised. I sat in it once but felt nothing at all. On the other hand, I didn't have the patience to spend the many hours it was supposed to take to reabsorb the orgones that gathered, through some cosmic honey trap in the insulation, in that tiny, claustrophobic space.

Years later Jean told me how half the band ended up living at Steiner Street. Jan, who had an instinct for such things, memorised the telephone number of a rehearsal room for hire she saw on a sheet of paper someone was showing someone else, in confidence, in a music shop on Haight Street, and rang the Steiner Center, which did indeed double as a rehearsal space. Stan and Tony and Richard slept in it when the band were not rehearsing; stowed their mattresses and bedding and clothes away when it was. There was a hot tub next door, which they could use at any time. It kept them warm in the winter months the way the clothes dryers in the Chinese laundry underneath our room in the flat at Greenwich and Gough did us.

The dryers would whirr away until 11pm, sending warm, soap-scented air up through the floorboards. Jan bought some remaindered pieces of taffeta and sewed patchwork curtains for the windows of our room, which otherwise looked directly into the living room of our landlord, Roosevelt Chung, on the opposite side of the street. Always when I think of that time now, I see dragon shapes gathering in the milky winter light falling through those pale pinks and soft ambers and transparent blues and greens and lavenders, while foghorns sound at the Golden Gate and mist from the Pacific Ocean rolls in past the Presidio and pools about the houses in the lee of Russian Hill, where the jazz clubs and the red light district used to be on the Barbary Coast.

~

The first gig we went to in San Francisco was Pearl Harbor & the Explosions at the Palms in Polk Street. They were a three-piece – guitar, bass and drums – with Pearl E. Gates as their lead singer. She'd been part of a local glam rock act called Leila & the Snakes; she was feral, magnetic, theatrical. She wore a T-shirt that said 'Here Comes Trouble' and later married Paul Simonon, the bass player with the Clash. More new wave than punk, the Explosions had a hit the following year with a song called 'Drivin''. But we were more taken with the venue. It was small, a 100-seater, with a high stage at the back of the room, decorated with faux palm trees lit up all orange and green. There was a fashion then for fern bars – Henry Africa's, in nearby Mason Street, with its hanging plants, antiques and tiffany lamps, was the exemplar – and this was a kind of palm bar. We wanted to play there, so we went backstage and asked who booked the acts.

Red Alert poster, Barry Linton, 1978.

It turned out to be an agency called Fat Cat Promotions; the two principals were a couple, Stephen and Michelle, with an office in North Beach. I called them up, they requested a tape and some publicity material, then came along to hear the band play; after which they decided to take us on and began booking gigs. Supports rather than headliners, because who would come to see us? We were complete unknowns. By this time Tony had bought a white 1969 Dodge van and individual band members were getting their gear together. You didn't have to lug around a PA and lights like you did in New Zealand. You just turned up with your instruments and your amps and plugged into the venue's systems.

Nevertheless it was disconcerting playing around the Bay Area. Many of the gigs were out of town, in one or other of the satellite cities that surround San Francisco: over the other side of the Bay Bridge, in Berkeley or Richmond or Vallejo; north across the Golden Gate in Marin County or further up at Santa Rosa; south down the coast. Because traffic was so heavy we'd have to leave in daylight, long before show time, and spend hours inching along the car-clogged freeways. When we did reach the venue we'd often find ourselves in some hard-core dive supporting a guitar band with a local reputation but without other credentials. There seemed to be any number of these acts, usually with a front man after whom they were named and a long-haired hero on lead guitar – if those two weren't the same person.

The thing that astonished me, though perhaps it shouldn't have, was the number of old hippie bands still playing around the traps. We supported Country Joe McDonald and, yes, he sang 'One, two, three, what are we fighting for?'. And his former band-mate, Barry Melton, usually known as The Fish, a plausible blond-haired multi-instrumentalist who later became an attorney. Terry and the Pirates were another act we opened for, in Richard's recall 'a kind of all-star band with John Cipollina from Quicksilver Messenger Service and other luminaries. We got a very positive review in the BAM (Bay Area Music) for that gig.' And then there was violinist David LaFlamme's band, formerly called It's a Beautiful Day, which had, in fealty to the passing of an era, changed its name: It Was a Beautiful Day.

There was an absolute contrast between these acts and the punk scene that clustered in the inner city – at the Deaf Club on Mission and at the Mabuhay Gardens, a former Filipino restaurant, on Broadway at North Beach. On the Barbary Coast you'd hear bands like the Mutants or the Dils, Tuxedomoon or

Red Alert publicity shot: Richard Kennedy, Jean McAllister, Stanley John Mitchell, Jan Preston, Tony McMaster, Auckland, 1978.

Romeo Void. San Francisco punks, mostly alienated middle-class kids, dressed in black and, to go with their moon tans, had bleached white hair. They were super cool, laid back. The last thing they wanted to be seen doing was reacting to anything at all. The world was doomed and the way to deal with it was by leaning against a wall in a darkened room somewhere, broadcasting your hip despair to anyone who might notice. I remember a particular band we ran into several times at a rehearsal studio: three men and a woman, white-haired, fantastically tall, pale as ghosts, in Bible black, who regarded us with unconcealed contempt.

They didn't know who we were, but did we? We were Red Alert, a name most Americans misheard. 'Read a lot?' they'd ask, puzzled. It was a punky kind of name but our music was not. Stan and Tony could play anything but their first love was jazz. Richard, a southpaw who, like Jimi Hendrix, held his guitar upside down and back to front, was a virtuoso with roots in country rock and the New Orleans sound. Jean was a beautiful singer but, at this point in her life, preferred doing backing vocals. And Jan was … Jan. An electrifying piano player, a skilled vocalist, a big stage personality who nevertheless caused some people to feel a strange disquiet. She had a sort of reserve, a withholding, that was at odds with the rampant sexiness Americans expected of rock'n'roll women.

Red Alert's repertoire was eclectic: covers of the Neville Brothers and Dr John ('Iko Iko', 'Such a Night'); Warren Zevon ('Nighttime in the Switching Yard'); Chuck Berry ('Too Much Monkey Business'); Bob Marley and Jimmy Cliff ('Get Up, Stand Up', 'You Can Get It If You Really Want'). These were mixed in with originals that ranged in style from jazz rock to progressive rock to our own attempts at country or reggae or soul songs. The cover versions were always popular with knowledgeable American audiences and everyone admitted the band were accomplished musicians, could play and had a good sound; but what were we about? Nobody, least of all us, really knew.

It took me a while to realise that Stephen and Michelle were in it for the long haul. They could see the band had potential and set themselves to realising it. Michelle was usually in the office, working the phones; it was Stephen (I can't remember his surname) who took us in hand. He tried to encourage a unitary sound, suggesting we rewrite some of the originals in a consistent style; drop the more anomalous among the covers; and offered up a list of alternative tunes we might like to play. They included Martha and the Vandellas' 'Nowhere to Run' and 'Work to Make it Work' by Robert Palmer, both songs that became staples of the set.

We were also writing originals. There was one, reggae inflected, an attempt at a manifesto, called 'Pacific Rock'; I'm too ashamed to quote from the lyrics. Another was 'Red Sky', a recasting of 'Liberty Bus' from *Ghost Rite*; that earned me a rebuke from Alan Brunton when he heard it. A third was 'Dr Sanctify', which Jan composed to lyrics Alan had written before we left New Zealand. Then there was the single, 'Hysteria', produced by Rick Nowels and Ray Starr, recorded in their home studio. We had 100 copies pressed before we left San Francisco. It was a fast rock'n'roll song with punkoid lyrics:

Civilisation is a strange disease
You have to empty your pockets
And get down on your knees
In a three piece suit God sits on his throne
He'll answer your prayers
When he gets off the phone …

As the only non-playing member of the band – I operated lights, shifted gear, drove, and talked to whoever needed talking to – I used to spend a lot of time with Stephen. I'd go round to the office about 11 o'clock most mornings. Michelle would be on the phone and he would be making the first joint of the day, using an album cover to 'clean' the dope of seeds, setting them rolling down the tilted laminated surface onto the desktop before discarding them. Later, stoned, we'd go out to one of the cafés or bars he frequented in North Beach and sit with a coffee or a beer, watching the world go by. Stephen had been around the music scene a long time and knew everyone. Somebody was always stopping for a chat.

Though he was well intentioned and companionable, there was something about Stephen that made him difficult to like. In his world, everything was for sale; there was no respect beyond that engendered by money and power. You let yourself be fucked over by those more powerful than you, you fucked those less powerful – that was how things worked. This aspect to his personality, old and corrupt and venal, was expressed for me by his mouth, a gaping black, red-rimmed hole. I'd look at that wet orifice, talking, and shudder. It seemed like a maw from which the stench of the world arose. And yet he was not a bad-looking man, quite handsome really. And his wife, full name Michelle Marie Bourgeois, was an attractive woman. Nevertheless, they gave me the creeps.

The problem wasn't just that we were confused; it was also that they were old school. Their name, Fat Cat, said it all. This was made painfully obvious one day when Stephen exploded with rage after a band called the Dead Kennedys called him up and asked for representation. 'How dare they!' he fulminated. 'How dare they take a name like that!' He refused to book them so we never played with them, but we did see them one night at a hall in Santa Rosa, entertaining a room full of college kids. Jello Biafra was spraying the crowd with foam from a shook-up can of Budweiser while sing/shouting 'Gonna kill kill kill kill kill the poor'. Or was it 'California Über Alles'?

Obviously we were not going to become a hard-core punk band like that; nor were we going to be hippies or dinosaurs or guitar heroes. Perhaps, in some alternative future, we could have become a new wave band of unknown import. The ability was there but, as graffiti on a dressing room wall in a Berkeley dive we sometimes played observed, 'It takes more than talent.' This was written below a picture of a long-haired male muso fingering an ejaculating guitar.

~

The hardest thing was keeping the band together. People were beginning to get homesick and one day Stan announced he was returning to Palmerston North. No sooner had we persuaded him to wait a bit, to give it a little more time, than Richard decided that he, too, was going home. Many years later, he explained that 'it was really the unhappiest year of my life. After all the anticipation of going to the USA with a band (a dream come true scenario) to find myself in the depths of misery after a month was utterly unexpected, and a complete shock. Severe homesickness, love-sickness put me lower than I have been before or since. A very unhappy band situation didn't help, and geographical escape seemed to make sense.'

It was a fraught time in San Francisco. Just a block away from the Steiner Center was a compound with a large building on the north side and, on the south, a yard full of stacked up shipping containers which, we learned, held the personal possessions of those thousand or so pilgrims who had gone to live on the Peoples Temple Agricultural Project, aka Jonestown, in Guyana in South America. Jim Jones' church was under intense scrutiny at the time. He was being courted by political figures, mostly from the left, because of his influence on electoral politics; he was also being investigated for corruption, especially human rights violations. A group called Concerned Relatives, those who had 'lost' family members to the 'church', were the most vociferous: their loved ones, they said, had been brainwashed, bullied, coerced, even kidnapped. They wanted them back.

On 14 November 1978 Democratic Congressman Leo Ryan, a campaigner on rights issues from seal culling to the need for more oversight of the CIA, flew from Washington DC to Georgetown, Guyana, accompanied by staff, journalists and representatives of Concerned Relatives. Over the next few days he visited Jonestown and attempted to negotiate releases with Jim Jones and his cabal; some among the pilgrims ('defectors') decided to leave anyway. When Ryan and his party, including 15 defectors, were about to fly out from nearby Kaituna airport, a pretender among them, one Larry Layton, pulled out a gun and opened fire. It was an ambush: others in the escort were also armed and they started shooting too. Ryan, three journalists and one defector were killed; nine people were injured. The murder of Ryan was brutal: after his body had been riddled with bullets, Layton shot him in the face.

It was 18 November 1978. When, next morning, units of the Guyanese army, alerted by those who had escaped the ambush, cut their way through the jungle to the settlement of Jonestown, they found the bodies of 909 people, including hundreds of children, lying dead about the camp. They had, allegedly voluntarily, drunk soft drink laced with cyanide, though some of the victims had also been shot and others injected with hypodermics. There were several suicide notes. One, from Jim Jones' wife Marceline, disinherited her daughter and left all her assets to the Communist Party of the USSR. Another proclaimed: 'We died because you would not let us live in peace.' Not all the pilgrims perished; some ran away into the jungle. It turned out that the people of Jonestown had, at least twice before, lined up to drink a lethal cocktail, only to find the liquid innocuous and the exercise 'a test of loyalty'.

Jonestown was a San Francisco story. In the aftermath of the massacre there were banner headlines in both newspapers, the *Examiner* and the *Chronicle*, with the numbers of the deceased printed in big black letters; these numbers increased day by day as more information came to light. There were photographs, too, and endless commentary. When we made the bus trip to the Steiner Center for a band rehearsal, there would be news vehicles and journalists, sometimes choppers overhead, at the Peoples Temple. And crowds of weeping relatives, mostly African Americans, who had lost family members. It was one of those stories which was impossible to ignore, even if you wanted to. It went on unremittingly for 10 days and then, suddenly, was superseded by another, in its way even more shocking, and much closer to home.

One morning early I went down the stairs to answer a knock on the door of the flat at Greenwich and Gough. It was Richard. 'The mayor's been shot,' he said. 'And I'm going home.' Mayor George Moscone and Supervisor Harvey Milk had been murdered by one Dan White, also a member of the San Francisco Board of Supervisors – essentially, the city council. He was a first termer, a Irish

American Catholic representing District 8. He had grown up there, in Portola, a poor neighbourhood to the south of the city. He'd been in Vietnam as a volunteer with the 101st Airborne Division; he'd been a cop and a fireman too. Struggling financially on the diminished wage he received as a supervisor, he had, in an attempt to earn extra income, opened up a fast food stall selling potato bakes on Pier 39; it wasn't going well.

In his early days as a supervisor, White worked closely and amicably with Harvey Milk, the first gay man elected to high office in the city and a national leader of the Gay Liberation movement, but they had fallen out when Milk declined to support an initiative White promoted. It was an edict aimed at preventing the Catholic church from building a detention centre for high-offending juveniles in District 8. White subsequently resigned from the Board of Supervisors and then, after taking advice, tried to rescind his resignation. Moscone, an Italian American, at first agreed to allow White back on the board; then, after also taking advice, from Harvey Milk among others, decided the resignation must stand.

On the morning of 27 November, after he heard this news, Dan White went down to city hall and climbed in through a basement window. He was carrying a loaded .38 pistol and 10 rounds of ammunition and used the window because he wanted to avoid going through the newly installed metal detectors at the front entrance. He went up the stairs to the second floor, entered Moscone's office and, after his plea for reinstatement was again declined, shot him dead. Then he crossed the landing to Harvey Milk's office, reloaded, and killed him too: five shots, two point blank to the head. Afterwards he drove to the Northern Police Station, where he had been a serving officer, and gave himself up.

White pleaded diminished responsibility due to depression caused by, among other things, eating too much junk food – the so-called Twinkie defence – and got seven years for manslaughter, of which he served just five, in Soledad Prison. He committed suicide not long after his release, at his home in Portola in 1985. It seems unlikely that homophobia was a motive for the killings. White's own campaign manager, political consultant Ray Sloan, was gay, and Milk had attended the baptism of White's son. Rather, he seems to have felt he had been betrayed, that he was the victim of a conspiracy and wanted revenge. He was quoted as saying: 'I was on a mission. I wanted four of them.' It was summary justice administered by an aggrieved and paranoid man, like something out of the Wild West.

I don't know how much the air of crisis that hung over the city in those November days had to do with Richard's decision. Perhaps not as much as the personal factors involved. As with Stan, we managed to talk him out of going. 'I didn't actually change my mind about following through and going back,' he wrote. 'I got cajoled into staying and was unhappy about it, but it was only the notion of doing something extreme and regretting it that kept me there.' It's curious, then, that of the six of us, Richard and Stan are the ones who never returned to New Zealand to live. Stan's in New York City, in Brooklyn, where he has his own band and a flourishing career as a musician. He also makes ceramics. Richard, who eventually reunited, albeit temporarily, with the lover he missed so badly, lives in England and, likewise, has a thriving career as a musician and tours frequently in Europe.

~

San Francisco seemed death-obsessed, and I don't just mean with respect to Jonestown and the Moscone/Milk assassinations. In the constellation of American cities, Frisco, 'Everybody's Favourite City', is the last chance saloon. Here people who have tried and failed elsewhere wash up. Here, if they fail again, they can always go out to the Golden Gate bridge and jump off, as hundreds have and continue to do. The number of suicides off the Golden Gate was, until 1995, counted officially, the way the deaths at Jonestown were; the count was discontinued just three jumps before it reached 1000; by 2018 it stood at around 1600. This sense of confronting last things gave the city its eclectic, alternative, free-spirited ambience; but it also gave it that doomed edge. And, after all, it is the home of the Grateful Dead. I came to dislike the place, but I didn't want to go home. I wanted to go to New York to rejoin the Moles.

We must have been in touch with them again by then. In December Modern Johnny Warren turned up on his way over to the East Coast. He'd seen the Sailor boys in LA and after checking in with us for a few days flew on to resume his managerial duties on the eve of the show the Moles were going to open at the Westbeth Centre in New York in January 1979. Alas, it was not to be: Johnny was mugged on the Lower East Side on Christmas Day, the bread and milk he'd just bought were stolen and the mace his attackers used caused him serious health problems, exacerbating the breathing problems he already had because of his asthma. He returned to New Zealand for treatment, his dream of taking Red

Mole into the arms of the Robert Stigwood Organisation unrealised. He also caused future problems for me, telling Alan that I was running my own little Red Mole over there in San Francisco.

~

There were other dramas. Tina invited a couple she'd met to rent the spare room in the flat at Greenwich and Gough. Andreas was Chilean, a fiery redhead who worked as an omelette cook at a restaurant in nearby Union Street. His girlfriend, Marcia, was the daughter of the Guatemalan ambassador; though whether he was the US ambassador to Guatemala or the Guatemalan ambassador to Washington, I was never quite sure; probably the latter. She was a Spanish speaker too. Marcia was petite, blonde, beautiful and utterly devoted to Andreas, whom she sometimes called the Red Man. They met on China Beach one day when he was suffering from a severe case of sunburn on his usually milk-white skin.

They were going to be moving in with an Israeli couple over at the Mission but the room wasn't ready yet. The Israeli guy, Moshe, worked for El Al and when I asked him what he actually did he said, portentously, 'My job is to die.' He was a marshal, ostensibly a passenger, whose real role was to take on any terrorist who might attempt to hi-jack the flight, even if it cost him his life. He would of course be armed. His girlfriend Tzilla worked on a TV show called *What's Cooking* and was making a jacket sewn entirely out of clothing labels. They told me what the Hebrew on the bumper sticker on the Buick said: 'The land of Israel for the people of Israel.' Yes, a Zionist slogan.

It was a while before Andreas learned to trust me but when he did he told me his story. He was a fugitive from justice; there was a warrant out for his arrest upon a charge of mayhem. Mayhem? What was that? One Sunday afternoon when they were living over in the Avenues, a drunken sailor from the Merchant Marine started harassing them. They had been partying at the front of their house, with all the windows wide open, when this guy, a stranger passing by, invited himself in to join them and then tried to hit on Marcia. Andreas told him to back off but he would not. After the second warning had no effect, Andreas went to the kitchen for a knife, came back and administered a ritual punishment called widening the smile. It's a horizontal cut about half an inch long made at each corner of the miscreant's mouth.

The sailor ran bleeding away but was, unfortunately, well connected, with an older brother in the military. The family pursued the matter, Andreas was identified as the perpetrator and charges were laid against him. Rather than go to court, and thence to jail, he'd gone on the run. So here he was, about nine months after the event, generous, volatile, passionate and more than a little crazed. He considered himself a political exile and was inclined to see his crime, which he acknowledged without guilt or shame, that flashing knife, as a blow against his oppressors. Once, when the police came around to our house looking for him, he disappeared for three days.

It was what had happened to his country that made him mad: the CIA-backed coup against Salvador Allende on 11 September 1973, which led, directly or indirectly, to Andreas living in the country that had destroyed the democratically elected government of his own. Some of his grudges were personal. His commanding officer during his military service, a man he considered a mentor and a friend, Orlando Letelier, had been assassinated by a car bomb in Washington DC in September 1976.

The hit was ordered at the highest levels and carried out by Cuban exiles working with the DINA (Dirección de Inteligencia Nacional), the Chilean secret police, set up with the advice of an exiled Nazi SS operative, Walter Rauff. US agencies, and Henry Kissinger himself, had prior knowledge of the impending assassination and allowed it go ahead. Letelier had been Allende's ambassador to the US; post-coup, he became a prominent opponent of the Pinochet regime, co-ordinating international efforts to isolate and bring down the dictatorship. His death only exacerbated Andreas' rage.

By now it was January 1979 and we had a regular gig at a place called the Miramar Beach Inn south of the city at Half Moon Bay. We were headlining, doing two or three sets a night at the elegant seaside venue with views out over the Pacific Ocean. They fed us seafood chowder or French onion soup; their house red was excellent. The locals would turn out, there'd be dancing and other convivialities, like joints of strong dope smoked with happy punters out the back of the inn between sets.

We had a small following by then, which included a lonely young millionaire called Glen, whose fortune was based upon selling advertising to community newspapers in the expanding real estate precincts in the hills behind San Mateo and Redwood City and Palo Alto. Glen would drive his Lamborghini to Miramar Beach, garage it nearby and then catch a cab to the inn. On one of these nights Marcia and Andreas rode along with us too.

It was a good gig and we were happy as we drove back to town in the wee small hours. Our habit was to go in convoy, the Buick and the Dodge, to the Steiner Center in the Fillmore to unload the gear before heading home. We were bumping the black boxes down the chute into the basement when some cops pulled up. This wasn't unusual: we were always having to deal with police and usually avoided trouble because a bunch of Kiwi musicians seemed so improbable, even to cops.

Andreas and Marcia were sleeping in the back of the van. Maybe he'd had a bit too much to drink, maybe he was disoriented, because when an officer shone a high-powered torch beam in Andreas' face and asked him who he was, he gave his real name. It was startling how quickly they came up with the information that he was a wanted man, distressing to see him manacled and hauled away, horrible to witness the cops' gleeful brutality. I remember Marcia's desolate cries.

He got two years. I visited him in the city jail where he was awaiting trial before we left San Francisco. We talked on telephones through a smeared plastic screen. His pride and his anger were intact; it did not seem he would be deported to Pinochet's Chile. Marcia had gone, in the interim, to live with her parents; there was no doubt, whatever happened, that she would stick by him. I called Andreas up about a year later from Los Angeles. He was out of jail but sounded diminished, as if the rage that fuelled him had burned out and left a hollow shell behind. He was like a character from a Roberto Bolaño novel, and his fate, too, was Bolaño-esque. I have no idea what happened to him.

~

Andreas liked to tease me about my attitude to living, which he called 'proper'. He meant I believed in doing the right thing, whatever that was, and that I was too anxious about the future to be really alive in the present. He used to say, 'Martin, can you *waste* time?' And once his friend Moshe, the Israeli whose job it was to die, said to me, sotto voce, in case someone overheard him. 'California is a police state.' This was true. The cops were ubiquitous, fearsome, a law unto themselves and entirely unpredictable. We were always being pulled over for some reason or other and had to be careful what we said to them because we'd overstayed our three-month tourist visas and were, technically, illegal aliens. Hence, after the shock of Andreas' arrest and incarceration, we decided to try to regularise our status. Stephen referred us to a migration agent he knew.

It was one of those emblematic encounters, like something out of a private eye novel: Dashiell Hammett rather than Raymond Chandler. After all, we were in San Francisco. The guy's office was on Post Street, further up towards the Embarcadero from Sam Spade's place at 891, on the border of Nob Hill and the Tenderloin, where Hammett lived in apartment 401 while he wrote *The Maltese Falcon* and *The Glass Key* and *The Thin Man*.

It was upstairs in a warren of rooms painted a dingy green colour with walls flimsy as cardboard. We went through a door with his name on the glass – call him McCoy – to a small waiting room with cheap furniture and old magazines. There was a smell of gas and formaldehyde. After a while we were joined by a fellow who worked as an Elvis impersonator and was trying to sort out some inter-state matter so he could continue to appear in Las Vegas, Nevada. He told us how many sequins he had sewn onto his white Elvis costume. The number was in the thousands.

McCoy was overweight, confidential, wearing a brown linen suit with a pale orange shirt and a short, wide, colourful tie loosened at the collar. He said he could us get green cards, no problem, it'd just take time. And money. He wanted an advance of $1500, though whether that was just for Jan and me or for all of us I don't recall. It didn't matter because it was out of our price range. We couldn't find that much cash and, even if we could have, I wouldn't have given it to him. The whole encounter was somehow fictional, right down to the insincere handshake and the wheezy goodbyes when it was over. I don't think Mr McCoy expected ever to see us again and he didn't.

One night we went to a toga party at a fraternity house in Berkeley. It was astonishing to see, on the wall in the kitchen, the residues of food that had been thrown up there and left. Gobbets of sour cream; peanut butter and jelly; strings of spaghetti in reddish dribbles of tomato sauce. Food throwing, one of the frat boys told me, was a time-honoured ritual desecration of the communal home and no one would dream of cleaning it up. It looked like the art-directed wall in the 1978 John Belushi movie, *Animal House*, and gave me the same feeling the encounter with McCoy had done: of straying into a zone where the real and the fictional were not entirely distinct from one another, or where the fictional was always morphing into the real and vice versa.

Had we gone to play at a private party? Were we invited there after a gig? Most people were wearing togas and garlands but we were not. We fell in with a guy named Plato and his friend Brad and spent the evening with them. Plato's toga was a rich dark green embroidered with gold trimmings and he was indeed Greek, a dark, curly-haired, rotund, cheerful man in his forties. A physicist who worked at Livermore, the famous laboratory where research into the design of nuclear weapons like Polaris missiles had been done. He was also gay. His boyfriend, Brad, in a white toga, was a thin, pale young man with a long nose and rodent-like features. Jan must have misheard his name when they were introduced and spent the evening calling him 'Rat'. I didn't correct her. Nobody else seemed to notice or, if they did, to mind.

San Francisco was a gay town. If you went down to the Castro, any night of the week, you would enter crowds of men dressed identically – plaid shirts, blue jeans held up by braces, black or tan lace-up ankle-high boots, moustaches – engaged in the preliminaries, the aftermath or the commission of an orgy of sexual indulgence that was without restraint. The jam-packed street was itself the theatre of this celebration under a sky that was yellow with an impending apocalypse no one was aware of yet. Aids was not then a word on anyone's lips; people spoke of clones and breeders and imagined a future in which one would dominate and then supersede the other. This, too, seemed fictional, though more along the lines of an invention by William Burroughs.

I heard Burroughs one night in Berkeley in a lecture hall at the university. He was dry, cadaverous, abrasive and very funny as he read a piece about standing for office as the inspector of drains in a Kansas municipality; I remember his reiteration of the phrase 'the purple-assed baboons of the Board of Control'. His power arose from his disenchantment and his refusal to subscribe to the norms of civilisation; along with his excoriation of those whose pretended fidelity to those same norms was an hypocrisy concealing a rapacious solipsism.

I also saw Tom Waits in Berkeley, at the Zellerbach Auditorium. Leon Redbone opened for him. I already had *Blue Valentine*, his latest album, recorded in Los Angeles a few months before. Tom performed in front of an Edward Hopper-like set that evoked the forecourt of a gas station by night, with the red tail-lights of a 1957 Chevrolet Bel Air set up between a couple of bowsers. He sang from inside a cloud of cigarette fumes and was like a column of twisted smoke himself. His band was all stripped down: tenor sax, electric guitar, acoustic bass, drums and piano. He played 'Somewhere' (from *West Side Story*), 'Whistlin' Past the Graveyard', 'Romeo is Bleeding' and 'Kentucky Avenue', his ode to a disabled boy he knew as kid growing up in Whittier, California.

I saw a sweetly optimistic Jimmy Cliff in the same venue about the same time. A greater contrast can hardly be imagined, unless it was with a third act we caught at a jam-packed San Francisco Ballroom where Dr John, Mac Rebennack, in a big hat and sitting sideways to the audience, was apparently able to make the upright piano jump up and down upon the stage. The Boomtown Rats at the Japan Center Theatre lived up to their name as they wove back and forth on a tiny stage and theirs was a gig I would rather not have seen. The Ramones at Winterland, the old skating rink, just two days before it closed forever at the end of 1978, were majestic, sublime, with perhaps the best light show I have ever seen.

~

These were just distractions. I was, as Andreas intuited, wasting time; I was sick to death of living in death-obsessed San Francisco. Also I missed the magic of the theatre. So that, when a message arrived from the Moles in New York, asking if we might like to come over and do the music for their new show, I knew at once that it was the right thing to do and set myself to persuading the others that this was so. This proved unnecessary: at the meeting, it turned out we were unanimous in our desire to go.

I'm not sure why. Maybe Richard and Stan and Tony were tired of sleeping on mattresses on the floor in the rehearsal room in the basement of the Steiner Center. I would have been. Meanwhile, because Rachel Stace had left town, Jean had moved in with us at Greenwich and Gough, in the room Andreas and Marcia had vacated. I think we all felt we might gig around the Bay Area for another year and still find ourselves in the same situation.

In a coincidence no one could have foreseen, Fat Cat booked us into the Palms the week we decided to leave, closing the circle and fulfilling the desire to play there we had expressed six months before. We did the gig and afterwards I told Stephen and Michelle we were going to New York. Stephen went white. Michelle was tight-lipped, furious. 'You're going to have stop somewhere, Morton,' she said, bitterly. Even though we had not signed any agreement with them, they threatened legal action. I had underestimated the extent of their commitment and the hopes they had for us. One day they got A & R man Paul Wexler, son of the legendary Jerry Wexler, to come and listen to the band audition at the Steiner Center: Maybe our chances of getting a record deal were better than I thought? Maybe it was going to happen after all?

171

Something odd happened while we were promoting the Palms gig. We were pasting up posters down the dark end of the street in Polk Gully, its walls festooned with bills and flyers, when, returning to the car, we came across a fellow taking down one of the posters we'd just put up. He said he souvenired band posters because you never knew which act might become famous and thus whose memorabilia might turn out to be valuable in years to come. He'd been doing it for a decade and had some posters that were worth a mint now. We suggested he leave up the one he'd been taking down and offered him a pristine copy instead but he said no. They were worth more if they had been used. It was a strange valedictory: there was a guy in San Francisco with a Red Alert poster, waiting for us to get famous.

~

Tony and Richard took the Dodge van across country. 'What a trip!' wrote Richard.

> *I remember driving across the Bay Bridge at 9 pm. I guess we had a busy day. We wanted to take the southern route to avoid snow, so we drove south all night to pick up Route 40. It was a mega drive, and we hadn't even turned east! I seem to recall getting a repair job done in the desert (Needles?) but aside from that it was a surprisingly straight run. There were the bald tyres, but when you consider what could have gone awry … any police attention would have shut the whole thing down. We chain-smoked dope all the way. We had a mattress spread over the band equipment in the back and took turns driving/sleeping. I don't think we checked in anywhere. We rolled into New York, pretty road weary, navigated our way to the Theatre for the New City, parked and waited. We had plainly arrived on another planet.*

I sold the Buick and signed up with an agency that assigned drive-away cars: they found travellers who, for the price of the gas, would return vehicles to people who'd left them behind and flown home instead. They told me of a car in Fresno that had been abandoned by its previous drivers, an English couple: Did we want to take that one? Why did they abandon it? I asked. They said it was haunted, the agency replied. Really? A haunted car? It seemed absurd. The vehicle belonged to a podiatrist on Staten Island in New York. It was another Buick, a sedan, with ample room for four bodies and our scatter of possessions. I said yes.

The agency flew me down to pick it up. About 300 kilometres south and east from San Francisco, Fresno was a big sprawling railway town built on flat valley land along the banks of the San Joaquin River, where the ash trees grew that gave the place its Spanish name. Not that I had time to look around. The car was at the airport and I started back immediately. There were two snow tyres lashed to the roof rack – the podiatrist must have been out west on a skiing holiday – but it was otherwise unremarkable.

It was a long time since I'd been behind the wheel of a powerful vehicle on the open road. The highway undulated through a hilly wide brown land the colour of gingerbread. There was no traffic. On a long straight rise I let her rip. It was beautiful accelerating up the hill until, near the top, too late, I saw a Dodge Monaco with the black and white livery of the Highway Patrol half concealed at the side of the road. He pulled me over.

'Remain in your vehicle!' he shouted as he slid along the passenger side. He asked to see my licence. I was wearing a blue pinstripe jacket and my wallet was in the inside breast pocket. Over my heart. As I reached for it he pulled his gun, the muzzle pointing over the lip of the window while he crouched down behind. Christ. I told him why I was reaching into my pocket. He said to hold my jacket open so that he could see if there was a weapon there. When he looked at my international driver's licence he changed his tune. 'Hey!' he said. 'Noo Zeeland! Hey!' He didn't write out a citation, just sent me on my way with the advice that I should henceforth observe the speed limit. You may be sure that I did.

~

Before we left San Francisco, early on a cold March morning, we drove over to Stephen and Michelle's house, where I pushed an envelope containing 100 dollars under their door. Guilt money. I wrote 'S & M' on the sealed envelope and wondered if they would get the joke. I don't know. I never heard of them again. After that we set off in Richard and Tony's tyre-tracks across the country. Four of us, two in the back and two in the front. Jan and Jean, Stan and me. Stan and I shared the driving. We didn't intend to check in anywhere along the way; we had some speed to keep us going all the way to New York City. It took three days and three nights.

We went east to Sacramento and through the mountains to Reno, Nevada, and then took the straight road to Ely, intending to pick up Route 70, a southerly crossing, at Salina and follow it to Washington DC before turning north. We soon found out what spooked the English couple. As you approached 100 kilometres per hour the shell of the Buick began to vibrate, causing a hum that increased in volume until it became a scream that was distressing and, to the musicians with their sensitive ears, painful. You had to slow down but after a while I discovered you could drive through the barrier as well: around 110 kph, the noise faded out again. So we carried on, travelling just above or just below that hazardous frequency, rolling down the wide and beautiful highways of America.

In the badlands of Utah we came through a landscape of red and white snow-capped and snow-banded mesas, like a set made in the far past for the cowboy movies that would one day be shot there. The mesas showed a delicate fringe of white where the fall had gathered in the skirts of rubble they wore. They passed and repassed behind one another, shifting the view, as the car arrowed through the empty land. At a place called Green River we stopped for coffee and, after buying cigarettes at a machine at the rear of the café, I left my wallet sitting on the top of it. It contained my driver's licence and a few hundred dollars in cash. By the time I realised it was too late to go back. Curiously, I had in mind a vivid image of just where that wallet was and what it looked like sitting there.

Curiously, too, as the journey went on, that haunted car sound diminished and by the time we reached Kansas troubled us no more. We had to cross the Rockies first. There was a storm raging. In the gloom of the night, shadowy drifts piled either side of the road, taller than we were, as we toiled upwards amidst skirling clouds and veils of falling snow. There was no question of breaking the speed limit here; you had to be hyper-alert lest the car go into a skid and end up in one of those drifts. We spun out a couple of times but nothing serious occurred and eventually we made the summit.

The ride down to Denver was worse. There were trucks abroad; several times we saw big rigs, jack-knifed and moribund, beside the road, and on one occasion heard a klaxon blare behind us. Stan managed to wrestle the car off the road before a semi-trailer, its headlamps like great eyes glaring in the night, howled past and disappeared into the white-out. His brakes must have failed. Next morning out on the plains we saw many other wrecked trucks and trailers stranded on the shoulders of the blacktop like dinosaurs crippled in some catastrophe. It seemed a profligate waste of resources typical of this alien, rich, incomprehensible land we were driving through.

In Kansas City we paused again and I got on the phone. I was looking for the number of the café in Green River, Utah. A woman at the exchange in Atlanta, Georgia, out of the goodness of her heart, decided to help me. She said there were 11 places in Green River that fitted my description and she was going to call each one of them in turn. 'You just hold the line, honey. I'm going to find your wallet.' At the second café she rang the fellow said he'd go and take a look, and came back and said my wallet was still sitting there in the dust on the top of the cigarette machine, just as I had imagined it to be.

I asked him to send it to the New Zealand Consulate in New York and gave him the address. I said he should take some money for the postage and in exchange for his trouble but he said he would not do that. When I picked the package up in New York it was addressed to 'Sweet' not 'Suite' 6 and everything within was just as it had been before. This was another, civic America, distinct from that of the pimps and grifters, the crooked attorneys and the agents on the make. An honest Mormon in Green River, Utah, and a kindly black woman in Atlanta, Georgia, restored my belongings to me and all they asked in return was a thank you.

Past Kansas a news story we'd been hearing about since we left California got bigger and bigger until it was all over the radio. One of the reactors at a nuclear power generating plant at Three Mile Island near Harrisburg in southern Pennsylvania was melting down. There was a chance that a cloud of radioactive hydrogen gathered therein would explode like a bomb; talk of evacuating the Tri-State Area – the metropolitan area of New York, New Jersey and Connecticut, precisely where we were headed. But how do you evacuate 13 million people? One of the disquieting things, which soon became obvious, was that such an evacuation is not possible. There is nowhere else to go.

Route 70 would have taken us through Indianapolis, Indiana, Columbus, Ohio, south of Pittsburgh, Pennsylvania and thence to Washington – too close for comfort to the drama unfolding at Harrisburg. We bent south, going through Louisville and Lexington in Kentucky, across the Appalachians to Route 64 so as to intersect with Route 81 and come up to DC that way. I don't remember much past Kansas City. Reactor TMI2 continued to melt down and we hurtled on, it seemed, into the heart of the maelstrom. We'd seen *The China Syndrome* before setting out. In another eerie confabulation of the fictional and the real, the nuclear power industry asserted that such an accident was impossible just 10 days before one occurred.

In Washington DC we stayed with Jim and Jenny Stevenson. Jim was First Secretary, Commercial and Trade Commissioner at the New Zealand Embassy, involved in negotiations for meat, dairy and wool trade access to the Americas. They gave us a five-kilogram block of Mainland cheese – it kept us going for weeks – and we carried on north to New York. The tail end of the storm we'd driven through in the Rockies was still about and it was sleeting as we slid through the slushy streets of downtown Manhattan to the Theater for the New City at 10th Street and 2nd Avenue. It was April Fool's Day, a Sunday; Red Mole were rehearsing a show called *The Last Days of Mankind*.

2

The Abyss of Cities

The first of April 1979 was the day Ayatollah Khomeini declared an Islamic Republic in Iran. When we went inside the Moles, in a startling act of prescience, were rehearsing a piece called 'The Universal Light Sketch Company Presents: The Madmen at the Gate Imitate the Loyal Burghers of Isfahan Lamenting the Passing of the Shah of Iran'. All five characters carried masks on sticks that they could hold, or not, before their faces, depending upon whether they were playing a Madman or a Burgher. Or themselves. There was a repeated refrain, spoken by John Davies' character: 'Who is this Ayatollah Khomeini? Who is this mad Mullah?' At that point, nobody really knew.

They broke off rehearsal to greet us. When Jan gave Alan a hug he said, 'Careful, I'm fragile.' It was a joke but he meant it. This was in a small dressing room backstage. Sal and Deb were cool and watchful, their eyes bright with suspicion. John and Ian Prior, newly arrived from New Zealand, seemed neutral. Or were they just unsure? Clearly something was wrong but I didn't know what it was. Later I learned what Modern Johnny had said: that I had been running my own Red Mole out there in California. He was wrong but it wasn't something I could address directly; you can't disprove a false allegation. Better to show loyalty in action. I could do that.

The Moles were living midtown, at 49th and Broadway, on the edge of Hell's Kitchen, in a hotel called the Consulate; they suggested we might stay there as well. We drove up and booked in to Room 1011 on the tenth floor. They were in

The Last Days of Mankind: The Madmen at the Gate: Deborah Hunt, Alan Brunton, Ian Prior, Sally Rodwell, Theater for the New City, 1979.

John Davies, New York, 1979.

1215 on the twelfth. The Gang of Three, I mean. Quite a few of us ended up living there. We infested it like a plague – of moles. The Consulate was quiet, hushed, sepulchral. A residential hotel rather than a place for itinerants. You had to be buzzed in by the desk clerk, who sat along a side wall halfway down the lobby, between the street door and the lifts.

The one I remember best is Alex, a big, kindly, weary, black man in his sixties who mostly worked the night shift. He was never less than welcoming but always gave me a sense that he was living in the midst of an unfolding catastrophe there was no point in elucidating and no possibility of escaping. It was a New York kind of feeling, very different from the hysteria and febrile paranoia of San Francisco. The Consulate was staffed around the clock and its residents, who were mostly clandestine like us, came and went at all hours. Its colours were yellow, dark brown and a muted, shadowy red.

Next morning, Monday, as the musicians and actors convened to work out what they were going to do in the show, I set out to return the Buick to the podiatrist on Staten Island. At the toll booth at the other end of the Brooklyn–Battery Tunnel I found the only cash I carried was a $100 bill; when I tendered it all hell broke loose. Officers of the Triborough Bridge and Tunnel Authority requested me to pull over and get out of the vehicle while they interrogated me. They were armed. The fact that it wasn't my car only made matters worse. It was extraordinary how volatile everybody wearing a uniform seemed to be; bizarre the way suspicion of unlawful intent could so easily translate into actual crime, actual punishment.

There were problems with the podiatrist too. The two snow tyres lashed to the roof-rack of the Buick when I picked it up in Fresno were still there. We hadn't touched them. But the podiatrist – greying, Jewish, in his fifties – said there had originally been four. Where were the other two? I didn't know: they might have been lost or stolen when the 'haunted' car was abandoned in Fresno. It took a while but, like the TBTA men, in the end he believed me. I rode the Staten Island Ferry back to Battery Park in Manhattan, looking quizzically up at the Statue of Liberty, the Mother of Exiles, standing out there in the water.

~

The Moles had bought a 1969 Buick Le Sabre in LA – dark blue with a black vinyl roof – and driven it to Mexico. I don't know what they did there. Ate lots of peyote, probably. And mushrooms. In Alan's 1991 collection *Slow Passes* there's

John Davies, Alan Brunton, Sally Rodwell, Deborah Hunt, New York, 1978.

a long poem called 'Introductions All Round', in two parts, the second of which is an opera buffa set in the small town of Puerto Angel on the Pacific coast of Oaxaca and involving, among much else, protracted and hilarious attempts to have a car repaired by the local mechanic, a man known only as L. He has to make a new bomba – a petrol tank – from the metal of melted down saucepans. It takes several him Domingos (Sundays).

Hence, when John Davies arrived at the appointed hour and at a pre-ordained spot for the rendezvous in Mexico City, the Moles weren't there; they were still in Puerto Angel. He waited, spent all his money, was arrested, secured his release then headed for San Antonio, Texas, where he found a job on a building site. They drove north later in the year; he finally caught up with them at Jim and Jenny's place in Washington DC, where Red Mole put on a show at the New Zealand Embassy on Thanksgiving Day which, in 1978, fell on 23 November. After that they continued on to the Big Apple. In the photo taken just after they arrived, they look like gangstas. All four of them, standing on a street corner in Manhattan, are wearing knee-high leather boots and extravagant coats and hats.

Sally wrote:

On December 15, through meeting Jack Micheline, we performed at a poetry reading in the Village with Ted Berrigan, a show we called 'goin' to New York'. We needed a theatre that would take us, not that we had a show, just ideas and a title, Goin' to Djibouti. *A Belgian company called Le Plan K was advertised at a theatre called Westbeth. Maybe Westbeth was a venue for foreigners? We went to that address (it was still snowing) and rang the bell. The Artistic Director was on some other planet, although he came originally from Cleveland, Ohio. He said we could do the show there in January if we had a part for his girlfriend Yolande. It was the old Bell-RCA studios where hi-fi had been invented. There were two usable spaces, we would be down, Le Plan K up.*

Alan said that they chose the title *Goin' to Djibouti* (the title of the New York version was always printed in scare quotes and with a small 'g') because they wanted to reuse Barry Linton's poster. In the New Zealand show of that name 'Djibouti' was equivalent to 'Nowhere', but this iteration was in fact set in the Horn of Africa. Its heroine was a Cuban soldier who went to join the freedom fighters in Eritrea. She fell in love with an African man but, in the ensuing complexities, caused by big power rivalries, they ended up on opposing sides of the conflict. Cuba did send troops to help Eritrea against the Ethiopian Empire, but when Haile Selassie was deposed by communists, Castro abandoned Eritrea and instead ordered his troops to defend the dictatorship that had taken over the country.

The Moles had nowhere to live so they moved into the theatre itself. Sally again:

We made masks from the junk on the streets, waste-paper baskets and pieces of arm-chairs; costumes from Mexican cloth; shadow puppets from forks and spoons. We bought $3.00 lights on Canal Street and used them for the shades for soldiers' helmets. We slept wrapped in coats jammed up to the radiators; when we woke, we rehearsed. I remember the speed. We taped incredible Ethiopian music from records we found in the Lincoln Center's Performing Arts Library. John wrote the tune for 'Birds of Paradise' and practised crawling in a lizard mask along the ventilator pipes at Westbeth. We hired two musicians,

Goin' to Djibouti (NY version): Fidel Castro mask, Westbeth Theater Center, 1979.

Goin' to Djibouti (NY version): Mad Hatters (John Davies, Yolande Ruggier, Deborah Hunt, Alan Brunton, Sally Rodwell), Westbeth Theater Center, 1979.

Lenny and Neil. We initiated Yolande into our dance routines as Deborah and I recreated acts from Carmen's – 'The Tango' and 'Moon over Bavaria'.

I never saw that show – the only major Red Mole production in seven years that I missed. However, the script of *Goin' to Djibouti* was published by Bumper Books in Wellington in 1996 and when, years later, I did read it, I was astonished to find that one of the bases for the action was 'The Mad Hatter's Tea Party' sketch we'd improvised for *Pacific Nights* the year before. The four characters had morphed into Boy, Hare, Mouse and Teacher; the feeling was the same – anarchic, barely coherent mayhem – and the sketch had been extended structurally so as to last the length of the play. There were other survivals. The narrator was a development of Alan's corrupt doctor from the first Djibouti, here introduced, mobile eye patch and all, as The Ordinary Vernon.

Noel Carroll in the *Soho Weekly News* wrote:

Red Mole specializes in a brand of fierce, comic nihilism articulated through a mixture of popular forms drawn from the carnival and the music hall.

Goin' to Djibouti (NY version): Mouse (Deborah Hunt?), Westbeth Theater Center, 1979.

Part Mardi Gras, part vaudeville – masquerade, mime, tap dancing, Jesus-jumping, mumming, calypsos, tangos, shadow puppetry and one liners combine in a relentless series of satires and parodies expressive of a lively cynicism towards virtually everything. The performance is a revue and a festival on the one hand, and a fragmentary melodrama that we understand mostly from the program notes.

Goin' to Djibouti *is rich in its quotations of theatrical forms. The pole fighting, for instance, alludes to the canboulay. These references to Third World carnivals, with their anti-colonial elements, does establish a generic opposition to oppression as part of Red Mole's aims. The most arresting festival elements are the masquerades. Actors sporting outsized papier-mâché heads mime lizards, turtles, chicken, leopards etc. Parading around the stage, they joyously celebrate the obliteration of the distinction between animal and man that is essential to fertility imagery.*

Carroll said Sal and Deb were 'the best comediennes I have seen in years' and added: 'The level of performance is exceptional. The stagecraft and props are superior. The evening, on the whole, is exhilarating.'

Let the last word on *Djibouti* be Sally's:

It was one of those magic nights in your life, our first NY performance, a crazy, surreal, philosophical/political cabaret made out of visions and junk and unbelievable bravado; they liked it, we liked it, there was no going back. We had reached this place, this mecca, this city where you could construct a theatre on any street corner, out of every dumpster, where every inhabitant was on stage, where you could talk to perfect strangers and invite them to your show and they would sail on in like they were just the biggest thing, this city where performers could occupy their very dressing room and call up the New York Times *and say, 'Look, we're from New Zealand and we're opening next week. Oh yes it's a great little piece we did ourselves and it's called …'*

Not all the reviews were as laudatory as Noel Carroll's. Erika Munk later complained, in the same paper, that the *Village Voice's* notice was 'irritatingly dismissive'. Nevertheless it was a dream start in the Big Apple and on the basis of the response to *Goin' to Djibouti*, Red Mole secured a three-week season at the Theater for the New City. The TNC originated in the Westbeth Artists Community, which was more than just a theatre: it provided, and provides, affordable living and working space for artists and arts organisations in New York. The old Bell Laboratories building was converted in 1968–70 as a low- to moderate-income rental housing and commercial real estate project, developed with the assistance of the J.M. Kaplan Fund and with money from the National Endowment for the Arts.

Crystal Field and George Bartenieff founded the TNC in 1971 in order to make 'poetic work that would also encompass a community ideal'. They'd moved several

Goin' to Djibouti (NY version): Sally and Ensemble, Westbeth Theater Center, 1979.

times before, in 1977, going over to the East Village and converting a former Tabernacle Baptist church at 156 2nd Avenue, near East 10th Street, into a theatre complex with a rehearsal room and three performing spaces. George, Berlin-born in 1933, was a stage and a film actor; Crystal was a dancer. My sense was that she made the decisions and he acquiesced. Like many old lefties, they seemed able to combine an impeccably correct public profile with a crepuscular and manipulative approach to the politics of the personal. I didn't warm to them.

Not that it mattered. I was just a minor player in a larger enterprise. What, in fact, was my role? At the Consulate we rarely visited each

The Last Days of Mankind: Deborah Hunt, New York, 1979.

other's rooms, preferring to communicate by telephone. But early in our sojourn there – possibly the night we arrived – Deborah came down from the twelfth floor to talk. She seemed stressed, but was never one to beat about the bush. She sat down on the bed, took a deep breath, looked me in the eye and said, 'We don't need another actor.'

I knew this conversation was coming and I was ready for it. 'That's good,' I said, 'because I don't want to act any more.' And all the tension just blew away. It turned out that they did, however, need a lighting operator. Although I'd never done theatre lighting before, I'd lit plenty of band gigs by then and I knew I could do it. I was more experienced as an operator than as a designer, but in theatre the design is usually worked out with the director anyway. So it was decided. I would light *The Last Days of Mankind*.

The Theater for the New City was old, dilapidated, the auditorium we played a basement room that held maybe 60 people. Unusually the lighting box, so called, was not at the back but in a kind of alcove stage left, where you sat before a set of antiquated mechanical levers that had to be pulled down or pushed up

The Last Days of Mankind: Alan Brunton (The Ordinary Vernon), Theater for the New City, 1979.

to make a lighting change. It took the strength of your whole arm to do this as, with a grinding noise and showers of blue sparks flying, connections were activated somewhere inside the grim arcana of that ancient rig. The advantage was that I was close to the actors, and because I knew them so well I could anticipate pending changes of action or mood and thus synchronise my lighting – something that would have been more difficult to do from the back of the room. After that first, fraught, magical performance, Deb came up to me, her eyes shining, and said they could *feel* my changes.

The Last Days of Mankind, like many Red Mole shows, had a vestigial plot that an audience might not construe without associated reading material. The title came from Viennese satirist Karl Kraus, whose 1918 master work of the same name was 15 hours long and written to be performed on Mars – because audiences on earth would not be able to stand it. It was 'the tragedy of mankind played out by figures in an operetta, fragmented and without heroes, in which the most glaring inventions are quotations'. Alan's references in his scenario were mostly Germanic: August Sanders, the early twentieth-century documentary photographer; filmmaker Werner Herzog; his compatriot Rainer Maria Fassbinder; plus American minimalist composer John Cage. Alan was rewriting Karl Kraus for performance in contemporary Manhattan.

The show happened within a series of frames. The audience was greeted outside in the foyer by five actors, travelling players 'with a vaudevillian air of some day long ago'. An acrobat, a clown, a cowboy, a mesmerist, a ventriloquist. Inside, the show began with an overture, followed by a song – 'There's nothing like a look at the past/It trips around your brain like a spider in a glass' – that

The Last Days of Mankind: The Kids (Ian Prior, Sally Rodwell, John Davies, Deborah Hunt, Alan Brunton), Theater for the New City, 1979.

segued into vulgar contention among a group of five ungovernable, and armed, children.

These were, of course, the players met outside and they continued to appear, in different guises, until the drama concluded with the same five, adult, crippled, dressed all in white, hobbling across the stage to the attenuated chant: 'Ra ra ra/ For Miss Enola Gay.' 'Enola Gay' was the name of the Boeing B-29 Super fortress that dropped the bomb on Hiroshima on 6 August 1945; the pilot called the plane after his mother. One of the players, a man, was left sitting alone with a telephone beside him. It rang and rang but he did not pick up.

In between there were big production numbers like 'Apocalypse Blues', a sexually ambivalent grand guignol set in a topless bar in Amsterdam; 'Give Me A Dollar Stranger', a song John performed while shadow puppets accomplished a solemn burial: 'My brother's at the gate, pulling in the flag/The doctor turns and closes his bag.' In the consciously Brechtian 'The Madmen at the Gate', because of the masks, there were three levels of identity in play: Actor, Burgher, Madman.

The Last Days of Mankind: Sally Rodwell (Sister Mercy), Theater for the New City, 1979.

Then there were satirical excursions into Manhattan's demi-monde – adult personals, strip clubs, fancy restaurants. Alan recited a version of 'Cripple Cockroach' while Ian impersonated the dead man walking. After he gave the dollar in his hatband to Sister Mercy and disappeared into a black hole in Times Square, she discarded her nurse's uniform and transformed into Agent Orange: Sally as the incarnation of that toxic hormone spray, referencing the recent revelation of severe chemical contamination at a place near Niagara Falls called Love Canal. Meanwhile Deborah did a turn as a mutant child gleefully exploring the landscapes of dissolution and decay: 'little bitty Apocalypse, little bitty Armageddon'.

It was the thematics of *Ghost Rite* married to the serendipitous form of the cabaret. Clare Fergusson, a performance artist from New Zealand, appeared twice, first with a self-portrait painted upon the torso of her naked body and then, after the catastrophe, painting herself white all over except for a black band across her eyes. Leon Narbey's movie, *Someday Afternoon*, screened in an otherwise silent auditorium so that all you heard was the hum of the projector and the flick-flick-flick of the film running through the gate. Although the message was one of impending doom, the ensemble were all still singing and dancing and cracking jokes. I thought it was wonderful and so did those New Yorkers who came along; we sold out the season. Yet I have not been able to find a single review.

Recently I heard a sound recording of one of those performances. It was made by bass player Neil Hannan, formerly of the Country Flyers, who arrived in New York during *Last Days* and became, with Jan, the main composer and performer of Red Mole music during the rest of our sojourn overseas. Some of the faults of the ensemble are obvious: a tendency to shout, to talk over one another, to upstage; a penchant for clumsy action over the subtlety of disclosure; a kind of gawky, unapologetic amateurism. At the same time, the actors' virtues are displayed: barbarous energy; humour that does not hold back from breaking any taboo; the ability to move at will from the ridiculous to the sublime; moments of ghostly revelation.

~

After *The Last Days of Mankind* was over a meeting was called, attended by everyone who had participated in the show plus a few others, like Neil Hannan and Joe Bleakley, who'd turned up in New York. The plan

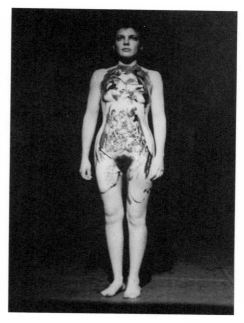

The Last Days of Mankind: Claire Fergusson, Theater for the New City, 1979.

was to go over to England for the summer and then, all going well, to attend, in August, the Edinburgh Festival Fringe, the largest arts festival in the world. There are no selection criteria for Edinburgh; anyone can go. On the other hand, you have to get yourself there, find a venue and some way to pay for it. Our season at the TNC was successful but made us only the derisory sum of $125. About six times that was taken at the door but various costs, mostly to do with publicity, had to be deducted. It was the beginning of May and we were broke again.

This, too, was brought up at the meeting. Anyone who wanted to go to England would have find their own airfare. We'd all have to get jobs. Sal and Deb were already working at a couple of mid-town strip clubs, the Wild West and the Adam and Eve, as topless dancers. Jan found a job, as a waitress, at one or both of these establishments as well. Alan and John used to carpenter together, though that might have happened later. I don't know what Ian did. As for me, I answered an advertisement in the *Village Voice* for a writer of adult fiction and went down to a place on 3rd Avenue for an interview.

Neil Hannan, New York, 1979.

Florence, the proprietor, said, 'Write us a sample.' On my way back to the Consulate, in a sex shop on 42nd Street, I bought a cheap paperback with a lurid cover and took it home to read. When I'd absorbed enough of the style I threw it out the window, where it fell open, cover side up, among the bizarre assemblage of trash lying on a roof down there, and for the rest of our time at the hotel lay, swelling in the rain, browning in the sun, on a soggy mattress next to a headless doll, a life-size pink panther and a dead pigeon. My audition was successful and I began work immediately.

Meanwhile, for a while, Red Alert continued to play around the traps. There were a couple of gigs at CBGBs down in the Bowery and at one or two other places in town. CBGBs was a long, narrow room with PA and lights already extant so you could just turn up with instruments and amplifiers and plug in. The band's sets were received with a mixture of mild interest and polite indifference, which was better than the raging contempt often shown acts there.

The scene in New York was different; it was larger and more diverse though, paradoxically, more unitary than that in San Francisco. You didn't come across dinosaur bands, nor relics from the sixties; everything was new and real: punk, new wave, no wave. Bands like Nervus Rex, Suicide and Richard Hell & the Voidoids didn't seem to carry any baggage from the past; nor to have, or want, much of a future either. One night, at an undisclosed location, I heard Pere Ubu play.

We also scored a gig, through a guy from Tennessee called Moonshine, with the Yippies (Youth International Party) at their clubhouse on Bleecker Street in the East Village, where they had on the wall a poster showing the crossed out faces of politicians they had thus far pied, and the uncrossed out ones of those they hadn't got to yet. These beautifully appointed rooms were still under construction when we arrived. Before we could start setting up, members of the local branch of the New York Fire Department came and closed the place down because they had thus far refused to issue the requisite permit. The Yippies took it on the chin, cheerfully abusing the firemen and telling us we could play instead at their old club rooms across the street. The stage was on a mezzanine in the sitting room of a grimy terrace house full of scarred couches and decaying armchairs.

While we were getting our gear organised a battered white saloon car with District of Columbia plates pulled up outside and five young black men got out and came in and said they were playing tonight too. A former jazz-fusion band from Washington called Mind Power who'd reinvented themselves as punks and changed their name to the Bad Brains, they'd been banned from playing in DC and were moving to New York City. In fact, they'd driven up that very day and come straight to the venue. Their bassist was so tall he had to play with his body bent almost double under the low ceiling of the mezzanine. Within a fast and furious set they performed one startlingly beautiful reggae number that has remained in my head ever since: 'Oh the man there/He was a lawyer/But he couldn't get across.'

The other venue we longed to get into was Max's Kansas City on Park Avenue, where Blondie and Talking Heads used to play and where a degree of glam rock theatricality was mixed in with the sterner punk ethos. Here the thin, tired, terminally cool booker, a man dressed entirely in black, solved the problem of the band's identity once and for all. He listened closely to 'Hysteria', shook his head sadly and pronounced. 'You are,' he said, as if it were some kind of affliction, 'a rock'n'roll band.'

It was such a relief that Red Alert broke up soon afterwards. Stan and Tony and Jean took to calling themselves Stanley Slumber & the Rude Awakenings and began busking on the streets in the theatre district. Richard decided to come with us to London but rejoined the others once we were back in New York again. That foursome became the Flying Sheep and, later, the Drongos; a much better band than Red Alert ever was.

~

Something that didn't concern me then intrigues me now: the master plan. I was never part of the inner circle of Red Mole, never privy to the decision-making. Not that I minded. I was in a state of acquiescence that was part passivity, part lack of confidence, part simple curiosity. I didn't consider myself put upon, manipulated or exploited; I was more likely to suffer from a sense that I wasn't contributing as much to the enterprise as I could. I already knew I wanted to become a writer and, since I didn't know how to do that yet, it made sense to drift along in the wake of a group of people who seemed to know what they were doing and how to go about doing it.

In an interview given before we left New Zealand Sally suggested that Red Mole was going to go overseas for a year or two and then return home: which is exactly what happened. A year later, in New York, in February 1979, negotiations began with the Queen Elizabeth II Arts Council regarding funding for the next stage of the journey. Director Michael Volkerling was in Manhattan and he advised the Moles to make two applications: one for an immediate grant of $2000 to cover current expenses; another for $10,000 with which to go to Edinburgh for the festival. Both applications were made, in the usual way – a last-minute frenzy. John and Ian took the completed forms around to the Sheraton Hotel on 7th Avenue between 52nd and 53rd Streets and slipped them under the door of Volkerling's room at 4am on the morning he was leaving town. We heard nothing more about the short-term grant. The story about the other one unfolded in London.

Hamish Keith, then chairman of the Arts Council, also discussed with Red Mole the possibility that they might be part of the New Zealand delegation to the Third South Pacific Festival of Arts in Port Moresby, from 30 June to 12 July 1980. A follow-up letter from Volkerling, dated 1 October 1979, confirms this, 'subject to Cabinet approval'. Red Mole were planning to go on afterwards to another festival in Tokyo, appearing there with avant-garde Japanese theatre group, Black Tent. This, then, was the master plan: a trip to London; an appearance at the Edinburgh Festival; a return to New York; a cross-country tour of the United States; another tour of New Zealand; the festival in Port Moresby; the festival in Japan. All of the trips and the tours happened; none of the festivals did.

~

It was in New York that I finally began to figure out how to become the writer I wanted to be. There were two lessons. One, paradoxical as it sounds, was the discipline imposed upon me by the writing of pornography. I had to go in to the office on the top floor of a six-storey building on 3rd Avenue and, in order to write, sit at a machine – a vast and unwieldy early incarnation of a word processor. You typed onto a tape that was then taken across town and inserted into another machine, which printed out the words in page format. Corrections were made manually, using scalpel, glue and white-out, before the pages went away again to be bound. A book was a hundred or so pages long. Novella rather than novel size; cheap pulp fiction in an A5 format. I had to complete each one before I was paid for it: $128 per book. About a dollar a page. I worked in that place for six weeks and in that time wrote six books.

There was no way I could indulge the luxury of wondering what I wanted to say. I just had to write. And I had to write to a specific demand. Generally speaking, the fantasy to be indulged was the sole instruction given. My boss, Florence, a large and kindly lesbian, would heave herself down next to me in the chair and say: 'Morton, this one is for men who like …' The other requirement was a lubricious scene of some sort every few pages. Longer than that and it was assumed your reader's attention, or his erection, would flag. Otherwise, I was free to invent whatever I wanted. I wrote one set in ancient Rome; one where the action took place among a group of anthropologists in New Guinea; a sci-fi fantasy unfolding in a mirror version of Manhattan. And so forth. In the absolute requirement to write, along with the (almost) absolute freedom about what to write, I discovered a fluency that, on better days, I still possess.

I could also come and go as I pleased. If I decided to work I used to walk over in the morning, through Times Square, down 42nd Street, right onto 3rd Avenue. Every day I saw things along the way that I could fit into the current book. That was illuminating, too. I'd spend maybe five or six hours tapping away, then return to the hotel. Those walks home were as dreamy as the morning ones, but in a different way: satiation rather than anticipation. I felt liberated, not just from the demand to write but from the need to worry, to pretend, to strive. Until then, writing for me had always been an effort. Finding something to say, finding a way to say it – both seemed excruciatingly difficult. The results, paltry as they were, always showed the exertion that had gone into their making. Now, suddenly, I didn't care. And it was in that mood of not caring that the second lesson came.

Among the pieces in the manila folder of things I kept from that time, called 'Some Wheres in the West', is a single page of writing called 'The Abyss of Cities'. It was typed on the old Imperial portable I used then. I suppose it's a prose poem. I don't actually remember writing it but was clearly pleased with myself for doing so because I dated it: 'June 9, N.Y.C.' it says at the bottom of the page. I've never tried to publish it and wouldn't do so now either. Its significance lies, not so much in what it says but in the voice in which it is written. It is my own – by which I mean, the voice of my prose. Once it was found, I could immediately channel the multifarious voices of others – the living, the dead, the revenant, the unborn.

I think I must have been aware of the breakthrough as soon as it was made. 'The Abyss of Cities' had come unbidden out of the dreaminess of post-porn composition; I knew enough by now not to try to replicate the process, not to force the issue the way I usually did. A few weeks later, in London, in a similarly dreamy state, though not in a post-porn reverie, I wrote an untitled companion piece, part two of 'The Abyss of Cities'. Then that mode went dormant until after my return to New Zealand in 1980. It didn't matter. I'd found something that would remain with me until such time as I was willing and able to explore it further. So I suppose there was a third lesson, beyond discipline and 'inspiration', that mysterious quality called confidence.

~

Walter Benjamin once speculated upon the revolutionary potential of a reality determined by the popular song last on everybody's lips. That spring in New York it was Anita Ward's 'Ring My Bell'. It seemed to come out of every doorway, every car stereo, every boombox: 'You can ring my be-e-ell, ring my bell, ring my bell.' There was a warp in the song: Ma Bell was the common name for the Bell Telephone Company, which carried so many calls daily. It seemed that Anita Ward was not just longing for someone to ring her bell; she was also imploring the rest of us to get on the phone – at once, to anyone.

A few weeks later the song was 'Miss You' by the Rolling Stones, off their *Some Girls* album (1978). It was that unitary thing again, perhaps because Manhattan is, after all, an island. It could be unexpectedly kindly too: at the Consulate, they refunded our sales tax because, as Alex explained, after three months in New York you were considered a resident of the city and residents didn't pay tax. It amounted to a week's free rent and was a nice counterpoint to our continuing status as illegals. By now, the black hooker who stood nightly on the stoop outside Tin Pan Alley, the club next door to the Consulate, had ceased to ask, plaintively, 'You want to go with me, sugar?' and, when I passed, just said hello and gave me a sweet and somehow complicit smile.

New York could be startling in other ways. After we'd decided to accompany the Moles across to London for the summer, Jan and I tried again to regularise our immigration status. We stood in line for half a day at an office downtown, in a shuffling crowd – 'your tired, your poor/Your huddled masses yearning to breathe free' – from all parts of the globe. At the head of the queue we explained our predicament to another weary black man with more than a passing resemblance to Alex the night clerk. He looked disbelievingly at us through the thick lenses of his spectacles. 'We have people here with *real* problems,' he said. 'You two go along now.' We went along.

New York could be sinister too. A power blackout one night was like an intimation of apocalypse: Where would we go? What would we do? The descent into barbarism seemed just hours away. Another night, after a big sports event in Queens, as rogue and drunken males poured into Hell's Kitchen and the air filled up with a golden brown haze made as much of pheromones and cordite as exhaust fumes, it felt as if an atrocity were about to happen around any street corner. The progress of King Tut – an exhibition of the treasures of Tutankhamen – through the land suggested, not just a city, but an entire country in the grip of death obsession. Every night we went to sleep to the sound of breaking glass: at the back of the clubs on 48th Street, around 3 or 4am, they smashed all the empty bottles of beer consumed that evening into a metal bin. It generally took about 20 minutes.

In Times Square, at any hour of the day or night, among the ceaseless masses of people passing in the street, the dealers sidled up to you and whispered in your ear: 'Coke, smoke, bo, bo, wanna buy some bo? 'Bo' was short for Columbian but if you did buy a joint off one of these guys you might find, as Richard once did, that it contained not marijuana but five single rice grains laid end to end and rolled inside half a dozen cigarette papers. One night a couple of the musos went two blocks east of the Theater for the New City to buy some dope and came back ashen-faced: they'd found a pool of blood on the stoop where their contact, a young Puerto Rican called Juan, usually stood. He'd been stabbed to death – or had he stabbed somebody to death? – in a turf war with dealers further down the street. I wrote a lyric about the incident called 'Forbidden City'. Jan and Neil set it to music, coming up with a deep, dark, rolling, soulful blues song.

~

195

In an interview given in 1994 Sally remarked, 'Red Mole isn't a group of people – it's a philosophy.' The journalist who wrote the piece, Jane Bowron, added: 'They believe they are part of a world-wide clan.' She was right. Something like the Ummah, perhaps, the Arab word for community; but, if so, it was a community of the faithful that did not necessarily know of its own existence, or had yet to be disclosed in its fullness. This is not unusual. Any rock group's fan base conforms to that model. The contention that Red Mole was a philosophy is harder to elucidate. What kind of philosophy? Some essential components: a commitment to performance; a refusal to adopt any a priori position; a love of personal freedom.

In fact I don't need to say more because we have the Red Mole manifesto, itself the distillation of a number of propositions, written down in 1974, into five core principles:

to keep [the] romance alive
to escape programmed behaviour by remaining erratic
to preserve the unclear and inexplicit idioms of everyday speech
to abhor the domination of any person over any other person
to expend energy.

The processes by which members of the clan found each other are endlessly fascinating. Let me give two examples. There was a Kiwi guy called Austin Trevett and his American partner, Tracy Smith. Neil Hannan, before he came to New York, asked his friend Ug if he knew anyone there. Ug, real name Ian Whipp, had been at Nelson College with Austin and still had his contact details. Neil got in touch and Austin and Tracy became, over a period of years, Red Mole people. He was a good photographer; she performed with them during the Mole's second stint in New York in the 1980s. They had other resources. Austin worked as fleet transport manager for an American airline and Tracy was a flight attendant. This became useful to us later on.

Austin was an enigmatic character. He was quiet and mannerly, with a sardonic undercurrent to his watchfulness, as if he had seen and done a lot of different things and, along the way, learned the virtues of observation and detachment. This was indeed the case. He spent some years in India in the late 1960s and early 1970s and had been part of a group importing goods from the East into the West. Malcolm McSporran remembered, in London, about 1971, asking Austin

Nance Shatzkin, New York, c. 1981.

for a character reference after he had been arrested for possession of hashish. Austin complied, but his appearance in a canary yellow suit made an unfortunate impression upon the presiding magistrate. In late 1970s New York, however, when he wasn't wearing a business suit, he dressed in jeans, T-shirt, sneakers and a leather jacket.

The other person we met at that time was Nancy Shatzkin, who became Red Mole's longest serving, best and perhaps only professionally competent manager. Nance's parents were book people who worked from their home at Croton-on-Hudson, north of the city. Their firm, Two Continents, was a trade books distributor for smaller publishers or for foreign publishers doing the occasional title in the US. At the time she met the Moles, Nance was at a loose end and responded enthusiastically when asked to help out at the TNC. The meeting happened at the house of a New Zealander she was dating at the time; he had invited the Moles around for a meal. Nance is energetic, engaged, dedicated, with reserves of emotion and intellect she is prepared to devote to any cause she feels worthy of her attention. She is exactly the kind of person you would want to advance your interests in a town like New York.

When we did fly across the Atlantic to London for the summer, Nance began to plan a cross-country tour for us when we returned to the States in the fall. I recall her telling me that she mailed out something in the order of 220 promotional packages to theatres in cities and towns across the land. Her efforts actually led to two tours: the first through the cities of the eastern seaboard – Philadelphia, Washington, Baltimore, New York – and the second across country. There were also an indeterminate number of ancillary dates for White Rabbit Puppet Theatre.

Meanwhile my immediate fate was to undertake managerial duties in Britain. It was something I was ill-equipped to do; I approached it with the trepidation formerly reserved for my appearances on stage as an actor. On the other hand I'd had plenty of experience booking gigs for the band, and that's really all the Moles were asking me to do. Over the ensuing months, then, I did very little lighting, stage management or writing, and a whole lot of talking to many different kinds of people.

~

We caught up with Bruce Kirkland just before we left New York. One evening he outlined a possible future scenario. He said he could see Red Mole as high-rolling gangstas, in black hats, long coats and high leather boots, with big jewelled rings on their fingers, touring the eastern seaboard in a convoy of large automobiles. Or flying out to Las Vegas and then on to Los Angeles to do gypsy shows before returning via New Orleans to the Big Apple. What he envisaged resembled in some respects a darker, more recent hallucination, the one in the Bob Dylan song 'Early Roman Kings' off the 2012 album, *Tempest*.

The reality was less romantic. We ended up camped out at JFK Airport with thousands of others trying to catch a flight to London. It was the middle of June 1979, and on the 6th of that month, after a crash during take-off killed 271 people in Chicago, the Federal Aviation Administration grounded all DC10 aircraft in the US. The planes were to stay out of the air until their manufacturer, McDonnell Douglas, addressed the safety issues.

We had been planning to fly across the Atlantic on Freddy Laker's Skytrain, but his DC10s were grounded too. Skytrain was a walk-on, walk-off operation which didn't require advance reservations. You could buy tickets at the airport on a first-come, first-served basis. Fortunately other airlines had been forced to offer similar deals and we were lucky enough, after not very long, to secure some seats on British Airways. I remember the price of a ticket was about what I was paid for a single volume of pornography.

~

By the time the DC10 ban was lifted on 13 July, we were already in London. My sister Katherine was living in Shepherds Bush and we stayed with her. On the night we arrived, 17 June, Dire Straits were playing the Hammersmith Odeon: Would we like to go? Of course we would. We didn't have tickets but in those days, if you walked towards a venue, you inevitably encountered scalpers along the way. The first fellow to approach us asked for an outrageous amount of money; we knew that prices became cheaper the closer you got to the door, so we turned him down. I was astonished when he put his face right up to mine and snarled: 'Fucking colonial!' In nine months in the States no American had insulted me because of my nationality or my affiliations; they tended to see our exoticism as augmenting their own status. 'Hey, Noo Zeeland!'

Many people despise Dire Straits for what they became, but these were early days, they were hot, and 'The Sultans of Swing' was a song on everyone's lips. And it was in fact one of the most beautiful concerts I have seen. It was the lighting: washes of shell pink and pale blue, of jasmine yellow and soft purple mixed in with lavish swathes of a creamy white that seemed almost solid when dry ice clouded the stage. The changes were painted through the transitions in the music, the washes altering as subtly as pigments in a Whistler painting.

It was gorgeous in an amorphous, nerveless way, the kind of lighting that surrounds and permeates rather than shows things in hard outline. Mark Knopfler played extended guitar solos on most of the songs, picking at his red Fender Stratocaster as if he were rehearsing a minimalist composition written by Messiaen. Time stretched and receded and then came back again, in waves. It felt like riding around a Möebius strip, or drinking from a Klein bottle.

That light show remains exemplary in my mind and, in intensity and beauty, was comparable only to the one which the Ramones put on at Winterland at the dead end of 1978. They used deep reds, blues and greens, stark white, pouring down apocalyptic radiance from a very high rig, while the changes were keyed to the chord progressions with a precision that was uncanny. Those four lank black-clad figures, even the drummer, seemed immobile amidst the deep, saturated washes as their enormous sound roared from the Marshall stacks. The Dire Straits set-up, by contrast, was impressionistic, as if emotion itself had become visible. They represented two extremes of what you could do with lighting and I wanted to be able to command both styles: industrial-scale, expressionistic Blitzkrieg bop and the dreamy nocturnes of 'Down to the Waterline' or 'Wild West End'.

~

It's odd that a London pub band should have had a worldwide hit with a song about another London pub band, but the scene was wide open then, mostly because of the ascendancy of the punk ethos of anything goes. London was full of opportunities. Yet a sense of violent threat lay over the city too. Now that Margaret Thatcher was in power – she had been elected prime minister on 3 May with a 43-seat majority – it was as if the skinheads and the bovver boys, the aficionados of white riot, once part of the decaying punk scene, had a kind of victory.

Rock Against Racism gigs were still a thing: there was a huge rally with the Anti-Nazi League in September 1979, at Brockwell Park in Brixton. The Clash were down at Vanilla Studios in Chelsea in an old factory refurbished as an auto repair shop, writing the songs they would release later in the year on *London Calling*. As good a gig as Dire Straits was the Specials at the Hammersmith Palais, where the mixed race audience bounced up and down to the same rhythm as the mixed race band on stage. Ian Dury and the Blockheads, over at the Odeon, gave us plenty of reasons to be cheerful.

We couldn't stay with my sister indefinitely so we moved across town to a place called Intergalactic Art in the Elephant and Castle. Alan had found its address in a listings magazine in New York. There were four permanent residents in the old six-storey hotel at 31 Morecombe Street in a bombed out neighbourhood two blocks behind the Walworth Road: Roland, a tall redhead with a stammer who was building a light synthesiser in the basement; his girlfriend Mandy, a frail, delicate, neurotic English beauty who spent most of her time in bed; Steve, a sallow-faced wide boy and drug dealer; and Nick, a reserved Englishman who worked as a professional underwater photographer.

Neil Hannan recalls:

The place was run by Roland, who seemed to be the brains and Steve, a black Liverpudlian, who seemed to be the rent collector. Alan decided the place was really a squat and wondered why we'd pay rent. Alan's tongue, being his weapon of choice, got Steve riled, he knew he was being insulted, didn't know

how but he knew he was, so he went upstairs, put on his steel capped boots,
stuck a blade in his back pocket and came back down to confront the smart
arse Brunton. Luckily, the Moles had found a real squat in Hackney and were
able to announce they were leaving before Alan 'got his'.

This must have happened before we moved over from Shepherds Bush. I
remember, later, going up to Patchwork Squatters in Hackney and there was Alan,
with hammer and nails, turning a door into a desk. I wondered if this presaged
a longer stay. At Intergalactic Art we paid £11 a week, with food included in the
tariff. It was invariable: porridge for breakfast; for lunch and dinner, a home-baked
dark, dry, sour, crumbly loaf and a stew made of bacon bones, potatoes, carrots,

Alan Brunton, New York, 1979.

split peas and onions. This started out thick and then thinned, as water was added, until it became a grey, disgusting gruel; at which point, usually after about a week, it would be poured away and another, identical, batch made. Any complaints about the dreariness of this fare brought forth commiserations from Roland et al., because they were eating it too. After a while most of us started eating out, which only meant, of course, that their vile stew lasted even longer. If you didn't finish your serving, Steve would pour the left-over portion back into the pot.

The internal economy at Intergalactic Art was micro-managed: there was a phone in the lobby and I used it to look for work for both the theatre and the band. I had to log every call I made (about a hundred in all) and pay for each one individually. When we negotiated the use of Nick's green Bedford van to carry the band's gear to and from gigs, he charged by the mile, writing down what was on the speedometer before and after the gig. Apart from anything else, this discouraged joy-riding. The hotel was useful as a rehearsal space, but we were being exploited, if not actually bled dry. Even the blond Lebanese hash Steve sold us was useless. It just gave you a headache.

The question of work was complex and unsatisfactory. We were still hoping to go to Edinburgh; we thought we had a commitment for Arts Council funding. We found someone who'd hire us a circus tent to perform in, but the fellow required a deposit to secure the deal. His deadline was in mid-July: Where was the money? Another theatre group from New Zealand, the Heartache and Sorrow Company, were in London that summer. They, too, were planning to go to Edinburgh. Their manager, Di Robson, had been associated with Red Mole in Wellington and said she was willing to work with us again. But where were her priorities? Surely they lay with her own group?

Heartache and Sorrow had a repertoire: *Songs for Uncle Scrim* by Mervyn Thompson, a play about Katherine Mansfield and Jennifer Compton's *Crossfire*, which won an Edinburgh Fringe First Award (in a production designed by Joe Bleakley). The only piece of theirs I remember seeing, however, was their eponymous song and dance show, which reprised sentimental pop tunes from the 1950s and 1960s and appealed primarily to baby boomer nostalgia. Perhaps unfairly, we tended to regard them as unoriginal, promulgating a soft form of traditional, passéist theatre. We, of course, were boldly going where no group had gone before. It seemed unlikely that both of us would end up attending the Fringe in Edinburgh, and so it proved.

The deadline for the hire of the tent passed before the Arts Council fiat came down. Yes, there was $10,000 available for New Zealand theatre groups to attend the festival but the money would be paid to Heartache and Sorrow who might then, if they wished, pass some of it on to Red Mole. We were furious. It was insult added to injury. It seemed unbelievable that a government funding body would behave in such a duplicitous fashion. What was really going on? Probably Red Mole were seen as too radical, too untrustworthy, to receive state funds and go as official ambassadors to a prestigious festival. When Heartache and Sorrow did give us some money – it was less than the cost of the deposit for the tent hire – we used it to buy airfares back to New York.

Meanwhile we scraped around looking for other work. Di Robson booked us a gig at Sheffield where, in July, there was the UandU Commonwealth Youth Conference; UandU stood for Unite and Understand. We played a season at Theatre Space near St Martin-in-the-Fields just off Trafalgar Square. I had nothing to do with the organising of that one either, but subsequent Red Mole gigs at the Albany Empire in Deptford came on the back of a band gig I booked there. There were performances at Oval House in Lambeth, at the London New Zealand Rugby Club at Aorangi Park in Wimbledon and at the tenth Annual Surrey Free Arts Festival in Guildford where Red Mould (sic) shared the bill with Mungo Jerry. Somehow all of these gigs were done on the run, as it were; none were especially memorable.

Mind you, I wasn't always around. Before the Sheffield trip, for instance, I went over to Amsterdam to see if I could pick up any work there. I came back without any solid dates – at the Milkweg they said autumn, maybe – but with a bag of dope in my shoe. When I went to Intergalactic Art to pick up my suitcase I found Roland, Mandy, Steve and Nick sitting down to a feast of gargantuan proportions made up of assorted delicacies they had purchased with money they'd gouged from us. Their guilt was written all over their mercenary faces and I hope my apparition ruined their digestions.

I arrived in Sheffield in time to attend a mayoral reception at the town hall. There were delegates from all over the Commonwealth but, on closer examination, they turned out to be drawn from communities already living in Britain. The Indians were from Leeds, for instance, the Jamaicans from Bristol and the Kenyans from South London. Sheffield was a working-class town but that didn't mean the mayor wasn't dripping with finery, wearing ermine-fringed and satin-lined robes and, around his neck, a huge gold chain with a medallion. We were billeted by an hospitable couple called John and Maureen Fair. We did *The Last Days of Mankind* at the Crucible Theatre, as well as puppet shows and outdoor parades and other improvisations. The band, now called the Shakey Islanders ('infinitely more promising than their name', said *Time Out*), also played.

Last Days had already, and ineluctably, decayed from its New York iteration. This always happened. Partly as a result of the need to replace specific references – 'candlelight dinners at Sweet Basil's' – with a local equivalent. Also we were missing, for example, nude body-painter Clare Fergusson. But the thought that went into a show evolved as we travelled. In New York at the end of *Last Days* the telephone rang but the man in white huddled next to it did not pick up. In Sheffield he waited beside a telephone that did not ring. A local reviewer assumed it was God (or Godot) not calling.

In London, a weary, patient, good-hearted woman called Ann Fenn was running a summer festival at Theatre Space, 48 William IV Street, WC2. She had three performance areas available and we ended up in the one called the Crypt. It was in the basement of the old Charing Cross Hospital. You descended to an auditorium that seemed to be without walls, extending forever into the gloomy catacombs beneath the piles of London. The stage, too, was unbounded and, when it rained, stormwater gushed down open drains just behind the performing area, spraying those in the wings and drowning out the actors' voices. There was an old sign outside the room: 'Fractures and Splints', it read.

For the Crypt we put together a cabaret show called *Blood in the Cracks*. It had elements drawn from other, older shows. Sally did Agent Orange. Deb reprised her topless fire-eating act, a counterpoint perhaps to the damp, hoary, darkening venue. John wrote a song, lyrics by Alan: 'Ancient lights at the Palais de Dance/Long-legged schoolgirls taking a chance.' Alan performed a rap in the person of Denis Thatcher: 'I'm the man/I'm the man/I'm the man/Who gives the Iron Lady/Her monthly oil and grease.' The stand-out piece was 'The Operation', inspired by the locale. From the belly of a patient on a table, who was starving and cried out constantly for food, a demented doctor wielding a monstrous saw, and assistants armed with knives and hypodermics, drew out a bizarre series of items including a string of sausages and a banana, which was peeled and eaten. We were always hungry.

By now Jan and I were living in the East End, in Deal Street, Whitechapel, not far from Spitalfields, in the flat of a secondary school teacher who was

Sally Rodwell, New York, 1979.

away for the summer. I remember scanning his shelves one day looking for something to read, but the books were hard-core, hard left, hard yakka: Marxist theoretical texts; documentary reports of atrocities at home and abroad. I returned to the abridged *My Life and Loves* by Frank Harris I'd carried to and from Amsterdam. When I went walking in the street, crowds of skinny under-nourished kids with Scots accents crowded behind me crying out: 'Legs! Hey, Legs! Give us a shilling! Give us a pound!' They advised me to go up to the West End: 'You see some real people up there'. In the suffocating London summer slabs of meat hanging up in the back of Pakistani butchers' shops became encrusted with jewelled flies.

The band had come over from New York without a drummer and we needed one. Bud Hooper, from the Country Flyers, was in town, living with Gabe and their kids in Clapham. We went out to see him one night but he couldn't be persuaded. Spencer Probet, the drummer with the Methylated Spirits, was also around but he didn't have a kit. Through pianist Dave MacRae, Neil found a young musician from Leeds called Chris Whitten; we offered him one of his first 'professional' gigs. Chris was just 20 years old, a tall gangly young man, intensely rhythmic, with an easy high action and a startlingly good sound. He was into jazz-rock but was nothing if not adaptable. It was he who laid down the beats for Alan's Denis Thatcher rap.

Chris hitched a ride with us to New York where he advertised his wares in the *Village Voice*, hung out in the Blondie scene and auditioned, unsuccessfully, for James Chance & the Contortions. He went on to have a stellar career, playing and recording with acts as diverse as Julian Cope ('World Shut Your Mouth'); the Waterboys ('The Whole of the Moon'); Paul McCartney (his 1989 album *Flowers in the Dirt*); and, yes, Dire Straits (their final world tour of 1991–92). After a sojourn in country New South Wales he's back in the northern hemisphere, still playing, a highly respected session drummer.

It wasn't easy finding work but there were compensations. One day I was invited to meet a promoter at a venue in the city and walked in on a Joe Jackson gig. It was lunchtime and he was spruiking his upcoming album *I'm the Man* (1979) for an invited audience of press and hangers on. I joined about 50 other people eating canapés and drinking champagne while listening to an excellent half-hour set that included the soon-to-be hit single '(Don't you know that) It's

Different for Girls'. Joe appeared on the album cover as a spiv holding his jacket open to show the dodgy merchandise suspended from the lining: just like John Davies did in *Ace Follies*.

Another day I ended up meeting some people in a pub in New Cross, south of the river. They were two brothers with big wide pale moon faces, expansive shirt fronts and a confidential, vaguely threatening manner. When it was time for the afternoon closing imposed upon all English pubs in those days they pulled the curtains and kept on drinking. They were crims who also managed a band. It was called the Craze and they performed in front of a huge Union Jack. Mods not rockers. I didn't realise at first that their name was a pun upon the Kray Brothers. Anyway, the bruvvers offered us a support with the Craze at a famous venue in south London called the Albany Empire. Dire Straits had played there too. It seemed we couldn't get away from them.

The Empire was a big, old, elegant room in Deptford. It was packed when the band came out to play: a deep floor of massed punters standing shoulder to shoulder, crowded galleries around the walls, hundreds of people. The Shakey Islanders went down pretty well, considering our diverse origins and eclectic material. We got an encore and there was one man in the crowd, a tall long-haired hippie, who was especially enthusiastic. Unfortunately this fellow didn't know when to stop and continued to heckle throughout the Craze's set, which was primitive, intense, short on musicianship but long on energy and commitment. Their singer climbed up onto the speakers where he rode, precariously, the swaying three-high Marshall stack while continuing to belt out the vocals.

'Rolling Stones!' the hippie called out in the break between every song. 'Rolling Stones! …' It was hot and sweaty and loud and there was an alarming sense of events tipping out of control. The bruvvers from New Cross didn't like this guy's interventions. They were becoming irate. They told him to shut the fuck up but, whatever he was on – he was probably just drunk – it made no difference. I was in one of the galleries at the side; I didn't see exactly what happened, only the swirl in the heart of the crowd as the hippie was dealt to. It turned out they'd taken a fire extinguisher and beaten his head in. Someone called an ambulance but when it arrived the medicos weren't allowed inside. Nor were the cops and they didn't insist; it wasn't their turf. Instead, the broken hippie was carried outside and dumped on the pavement.

I don't know what happened to him or if anyone was charged. I remember the bruvvers with specks of blood on their cream silk shirts, their chests puffed out, their eyes shining with still unsated lust for violence, strutting around the Empire afterwards as if daring anyone else to have a go. No one insulted their Craze. Our other London gigs paled into insignificance beside this disquieting event. Afterwards, we gathered up our gear, accepted the money the bruvvers gave us, declined their offer of further supports of the Craze and trundled off into the night in Nick's little green Bedford van, anxiously, or not, watching the speedo click over.

Neil also remembers a gig at the London New Zealand Rugby Club where he and Chris Whitten 'jammed at length with Michael (Mr Ears 'can play anything') Houstoun', the now world-famous classical pianist from Timaru. I wasn't at that gig, nor at the cabaret shows Red Mole put on subsequently at the Albany Empire, because I had been asked to go back to New York. I was the advance man; my job, to lock in the dates for our next season at the Theater for the New City.

~

By that time we'd moved again, to the Angel Islington, where we were living in a tall old terrace house with Paul Carew and some others. How strange: I'd flatted with Paul seven years before in the Living Theatre house at 28 Sentinel Road in Herne Bay, when he and Sally were still together. He was the same, quiet, polite, perhaps a little melancholy, but the gulf in time seemed unbridgeable. I was pleased to be leaving London behind. It was class-ridden and claustrophobic; you could feel the heaviness of tradition, like a pall of funereal smoke, suffocating anything that promised real change. People said it took two years before you felt at home here; I didn't think I had that long.

Another thing I disliked about London was that the taxi drivers wouldn't pick you up. They'd pull over, ask where you were going and, if it didn't suit them, say, 'Sorry, I'm just going to have my lunch.' Even if it was five in the afternoon. So I walked to the station with my typewriter and my suitcase. Jan came with me. We said goodbye on the street before I descended the long escalator to the Angel down below. I was consumed with the notion that I was heading underground, like Orpheus perhaps. How mad was that? If she was anywhere, my Eurydice was up above. She was waving goodbye at the top of the stairs. I was the one going, melodramatically, to hell.

3

Going Back West

I had a window seat on the flight across the Atlantic, from which I could see to the north a wall of green ice at the Pole; or maybe it was the coast of Greenland. The fellow sitting next to me was a professor of Greek and he began talking about the difficulties of working out what the hexameters of Homer sounded like, how they scanned. It hadn't occurred to me that we could read the epics and yet not know how to speak or sing their lines. It seemed preposterous and gave, to my always susceptible mind, a sense of the thrilling strangeness of the worlds of the past. When we got to JFK I took a yellow cab into Manhattan, to Nance Shatzkin's apartment at 121 West 77th Street, where I was staying; she was away at her parents' place in Croton-on-Hudson.

Next morning I rode the subway downtown to 2nd and 10th to confirm, as I thought, the dates for our season at the Theater for the New City. But Crystal and George looked doubtful. They didn't seem sure. There was a problem, they said. The theatre might have to close during the dates we had previously been offered. Why? I asked. Oh, they said, it was a maintenance issue. They were laying new carpet in the foyer, the very one where we were standing. I looked down at the floor: yes, threadbare. But why not do it after we had finished our gigs? They shook their heads. Not possible. They were booked until the end of the year. It was now or never. They would have to cancel.

It was as if an abyss opened beneath me. How could I look the Moles in the eyes if they arrived and found they had nowhere to play? They were already rehearsing the new show in London. How could I disappoint them? Crystal was nothing if not shrewd. She could see the desperation on my face. 'I suppose there might be one solution,' she offered. 'You could lay the carpet yourselves. That way you could have the season and we could save on paying tradesmen to do it.' I realised I'd been set up. This had been worked out beforehand. But what could I do? I decided I'd rather face the wrath of the Moles than their dismay if I came up empty-handed. 'Yes,' I said. 'Yes, we'll do it.'

The Moles were furious, yet they did lay the carpet. And I still think I made the right decision. The alternative didn't bear thinking about. And it turned out there was an immediate, if unexpected, benefit for me as well. As soon as Nance returned to Manhattan I was relieved of any further managerial duties and reverted to my more comfortable, more leisurely, if not actually feckless role of part-time roadie, lighting guy and general dogsbody.

I also went down to 3rd Avenue to pick up copies of the books I'd written. I'd forgotten the overpowering odour of cat that greeted you when you walked into that super-heated interior. The other writers, mostly gay men, were tapping away as usual at their machines in the front room. Samples of the merchandise were shelved out the back, where the 1979 equivalent of a LGBTQI listings magazine was laid out at big wide tables. Florence gave me a copy of each of my six volumes. All were published under pseudonyms and the only title I remember is *Diary of a Well-Whipped Wife*, which was composed around a set of black and white bondage drawings. Something to do with punishing women for the temerity of their desires perhaps. An early shade of grey.

Florence understood that I wasn't coming back to work for her but she had a proposition: Why didn't I write a real novel? She would act as my agent and we would look around for a publishing deal. She thought something set in England might work. One of my pornos had taken place in a fancifully imagined British girls' school; I think that's where she got the idea. There was another fellow working there, David, the only other straight guy in the place, who was writing a literary novel; he'd often talked to me about it. Was it something I wanted to do as well?

I wasn't sure. I don't think I took the offer seriously. I didn't see myself as a writer of fiction, doubted that such invention was part of my skill set. I wasn't interested in making things up; I preferred the extravagant permutations of the real. I didn't know how to say any of this to Florence. I just thanked her, said I would think about it and get back to her; but I never did. That path not taken continued on without me, like the mysterious road beyond the gas station in Edward Hopper's 1940 painting, bending right in the darkening afternoon and running away through the trees.

~

The new show was called *Dead Fingers Walk*, a riff on the title of the 1963 William Burroughs novel in the same way that *Blood in the Cracks* referenced Bob Dylan's 1975 album, *Blood on the Tracks*. Burroughs' *Dead Fingers Talk*, a rarity now, was made out of three previous works: *Naked Lunch*, *The Soft Machine* and *The Ticket That Exploded*. He attempted to construct a new work by excerpting the explicitly

Dead Fingers Walk: Ian Prior, Deborah Hunt, Sally Rodwell, Alan Brunton,
John Davies, Theater for the New City, 1979.

sexual passages from the earlier books and then reassembling the remaining
material in a random manner, seeking the interventions of the Third Mind
perhaps. *Dead Fingers Walk* also had a relationship to earlier Red Mole material:
it was, radically reimagined, a detective story like *Slaughter on Cockroach Avenue*.
Frank Libra walked again.

We performed it in the small upstairs studio at the TNC; it was inventively
staged. The space was cut up so there was room in front for a skit, a song or
a dance to take place; there were three small, curtained puppet booths behind;
above on the right a large shadow-play screen; on the left a high platform. Six
separate performing areas, then, with the possibility at any point of dialogue
between any or all of them. The five actors – Alan, Sally, Deb, John and Ian – were
joined by a sixth, New York juggler John Grimaldi. Then there was the band.

The show was an hour long and included around 20 scene changes. There
were song and dance numbers: 'The Thorazine Shuffle', performed by patients in
a mental asylum; 'Cody the Missing Man', about an elusive drug dealer; and the
title song. The Shakey Islanders provided the music. The show's most innovative

aspect was the mix of live action and puppetry, both shadow and glove. I was up the back for this one. It was complex, yet exhilarating, to light.

Erika Munk in the *Village Voice* wrote:

Red Mole's work is surprising, quick, affectionate, beautiful to look at, extremely funny, never condescending and through-and-through political. The critical connections hover over the performance without being hammered in. Unforced, they sort themselves out, some during performance, some later. This unusual lighthandedness – given the subject and the complete lack of camp or nostalgia – comes from the production's speed and variety. There are bird-headed hand puppets, bird-masked people, shadow-puppets, live performers behind the shadow screen, a rock group and a juggler. Such small scale richness creates delight without illusion, leaving the mind free while the senses are pleased.

On the back of this review, the season at the TNC sold out, full houses every night. *Dead Fingers Walk* was one of those shows which seem like miracles at the time and continue to exist in the mind long after, bathed in a golden glow. It wasn't all new; there was at least one survival from London, what Munk described as 'a grisly and farcical hospital scene … It manages, while being very funny and a little scary, to create not only phobic shivers but hard recognition of institutional medicine's brutality and stupidity.'

The dead fingers walking were, of course, live puppets; the poster for the show was a diptych featuring a giant striped-trousered leg with a hob-nailed boot coming down hard; the Barry Linton Mole, looking nervous but intact, had escaped onto the other panel. The poster for the London version, where the show premiered at New Zealand House at the end of August, also featured the rather more harum-scarum White Rabbit logo, with top hat and cane, drawn by Deb Hunt. This was, so far as I know, with the exception of a few performances on our upcoming American and New Zealand tours, the end of White Rabbit Puppet Theatre. Red Mole had not abandoned puppetry; rather it had been incorporated into the mainstream of the performances, where it continued to play a vital part in the making of the shows.

The Shakey Islanders were about to disintegrate as well. There were a few more gigs around the hot spots of New York City: CGBGs, again, the Mudd Club, even, at last, Max's Kansas City (with Thor and the C.I.s). But Richard wanted to rejoin

Dead Fingers Walk: puppet booth, Theater for the New City, 1979.

his former band-mates from Red Alert, now busking mid-town as the Flying Sheep and soon to morph into the Drongos, and Chris Whitten had his eyes set on prizes more glittering than a musician supporting a group of travelling players could aspire to. There was one more brief tour with Red Mole, of the cities of the eastern seaboard, and then the Shakey Islanders were history too.

The Moles, remarkably, still had the Buick Le Sabre they'd bought in LA, but we were carless. From some Puerto Ricans in Alphabet City Neil and I purchased, for a few hundred dollars, a green 1969 Pontiac Le Mans V8 station wagon. It came without licence plates and so, in a satisfactorily clandestine manner, we bought a set off some other Nuyoricans. I remember the plates cost $12 and were handed over to us, wrapped in tissue paper, one night outside an apartment building near Tomkins Square Park in the East Village.

For that brief tour of Philadelphia, Baltimore and Washington I hired a U-haul trailer to carry the gear. We were living in the Bronx, in a walk-up – if a building had fewer than six storeys the owner didn't have to install elevators – and the depot was nearby. The day I picked the trailer up, early in October 1979, was also the day the Pope came to town: John Paul II, aka Karol Wojtyla, a Pole, only the second Pope after Paul VI to visit the US. Like his predecessor, he was going to address the United Nations, but he was also giving a mass at Yankee Stadium in the South Bronx.

Somehow my trip to U-haul became entangled with preparations for his motorcade. Thousands upon thousands of people lined the streets, in Pope T-shirts, waving Pope flags, buying Pope memorabilia: snow domes, medallions, coffee mugs. It reminded me of the parades which turned out to welcome the sarcophagus of Tutankhamen. Live Pope, dead pharaoh: celebrities both. No wonder we thought we were living in the era of the twilight of the gods.

~

In New York, when we said we were going to Philadelphia, people went, 'Oh yeah, Philly', in a manner that was only slightly condescending. The theatre gig was at the Wilma Project, founded in 1973 'to create theatrical productions of original material and to develop local artists'. Our predecessors there included the Bread & Puppet Theatre, Mabou Mines, Charles Ludlam's Ridiculous Theatrical Company, the Wooster Group, Ping Chong & the Fiji Company and Spalding Gray. In 1979 a Czech couple, Blanka and Jiri Zizka, were artists in residence and they went on, in the 1980s, to assume artistic control of the institution. Wilma was the name Virginia Woolf gave to William Shakespeare's putative, unsung sister.

I don't remember the shows in Philadelphia or the gig the band played at the Hot Club in a room where, Neil thought, the presence of Iggy Pop from the night before was still palpable. I do recall seeing the English group the Members there but that must have been on another night. Afterwards, looking for something to eat, we drove down South Street and saw, shining amid 10 dark and derelict blocks, a blue neon sign advertising soul food and, with typical naivety, pulled up outside and went in.

Everyone in the restaurant stopped talking when we walked in the door. Even though they served us gracefully enough, and the food – roast chicken, sweet potato, black-eye peas and gravy – was delicious, the chill never really lifted and it was a relief, when we were done, to walk out into the darkened street again. It felt as if we had, in some indefinable but ultimately unforgiveable sense, transgressed. Later I learned that South Street was accounted the oldest black street north of the Mason–Dixon Line. It was then facing demolition ahead of a new freeway but this was never built.

Martin Edmond, Jan Preston, New York, 1979.

Either that night or another we also spent a few hours in a bar where George Thorogood & the Destroyers used to play. They were from Wilmington, Delaware, just down the river, and had not yet recorded 'Bad to the Bone' or toured in support of the Rolling Stones; but I knew that, like Hello Sailor, they'd covered Bo Diddley's 'Who Do You Love?' A pretty young woman wearing tight white shiny jeans took a fancy to me and I remember the guy who booked us into the Hot Club urging me to go out the back with her for a while. Unfortunately I never got used to having sex in toilets, as so many people in those days did; it always seemed more emetic than erotic.

Jan was there too, watching this seduction unfold; I don't know what she thought. It wasn't the first time something like this had happened – there had been previous episodes in Auckland – and I half suspected her of indulging in liaisons of her own. I think, by mutual and unspoken agreement, we decided never to talk about these things. Curiously, or perhaps not, our love-making that night, on a mattress on the floor upstairs in someone's loft, was better than it had been for a while.

The other thing I did was go down to the Philadelphia Museum of Art to look at Marcel Duchamp's last work: *Étant donnés: 1. la chute d'eau / 2. le gaz d'éclairage: Given: 1. The Waterfall; 2. The Illuminating Gas.* He worked on it for 20 years and it was only unveiled, if that is the word, in 1969, a year after his death at the age of 81. It is made out of an old wooden door, nails, bricks, brass, sheet aluminium, velvet, leaves, twigs, a parchment dummy of a woman's body, hair, glass, oil paint, linoleum, an assortment of lights, a landscape composed of hand-painted and photographic elements and an electric motor housed in a cookie tin which rotates a perforated disc. It is held together by clothes pegs and paper clips and is extremely fragile: if touched, it would fall apart.

The work is installed away from the rest of the Duchamp collection. Down a cul-de-sac, set in a stucco wall, is a brick archway with a heavy, nail-studded wooden door. In it there are two peepholes at eye height. Through them you see, past a hole apparently blasted in a brick wall, a woman's naked body sprawled on her back across a bed of twigs in a landscape that includes a glittering tin-foil waterfall and, across a river, a line of trees. The woman has her legs splayed so that you look directly at her shaved vulva, which seems strangely deformed, like a wound or a mouth, with a clitoris prehensile as a tongue. Her lower legs are concealed behind the bricks, her face is covered by her hair and her outstretched left hand holds, or seems to hold, an illuminated gas lamp – like the Statue of Liberty perhaps. She didn't look enticing; she didn't even look dead; rather, it was as if she had never lived at all.

It's a disturbing image, partly because you can only look at it by yourself and so assume the position of a voyeur. Plenty of people have suggested that the work represents the aftermath of a rape and/or a murder. I can understand why they might think that, but to me it was about point of view: not only did it put you in an uncomfortable position; the work made you think about what you can and can't see and how you do or don't see it.

Others say that it is actually an act of love: Duchamp wanted to remember Maria Martins, the surrealist sculptor and wife of the Brazilian ambassador to the US, with whom he became obsessed in the 1940s and early 1950s. He used casts of her body parts to make the nude; all except that outflung arm, which came from his next lover and second wife, Alexina 'Teeny' Matisse, formerly Henri's daughter-in-law. I prefer Jasper Johns' description to any other: 'the strangest work of art in any museum'.

It took its place in my mind alongside half a dozen others I came across in stolen moments during our life on the road: the wall of Van Gogh paintings of orchards flowering in Arles seen at the eponymous museum in Amsterdam while my mind was still fizzing after smoking a joint; a basement room at the Tate in London lined with luminous, pulsating Mark Rothko works, like a temple dedicated to a some abstract, incoherent, subterranean god; three vast Monet lily ponds hung on three sides of a white, light-filled gallery upstairs at the Museum of Modern Art in New York, making you feel you had been transported to the garden at Giverny; the stark grandeur of Picasso's *Guernica* hanging by itself on a wall in the same building.

~

In Baltimore we played at the Maryland College of Art, one of the oldest institutions of its kind in the United States. Here the first public American showing of the works of Henri Matisse took place under the auspices of the Cone sisters, Claribel and Etta, in 1923. The institute had to close in 1968 because of riots following the assassination of Martin Luther King: Baltimore is accounted the northernmost southern city in the States. In the 1970s the college was a hotbed of the avant garde: John Cage, Allen Ginsberg, Walker Evans, Kenneth E. Tyler, Elaine de Kooning and Clement Greenburg all taught or worked there at some time or other.

Our appearances there – there must have been several gigs – is another gap in my memory. My sole surviving recollection of Baltimore is different. One evening we went down to the old port at Inner Harbor on the Patapsco River. The light was green and dying and the brick warehouse buildings between East Barre and Lee Street loomed against the sky as if gathering the darkness of centuries to themselves. Baltimore was, after New York, the largest immigrant port in the country. Here tobacco grown in Virginia was taken away in ships; here slaves from Africa and sugar from the Caribbean were brought and sold.

In a huge and gloomy second-hand shop I bought a jacket from a snaggle-toothed old woman. It was black and white striped and seemed to have been made out of the ticking that covered the kapok mattresses we slept on as children. I'm not sure why I liked it so much. Perhaps it was the woman herself who beguiled me: with her one remaining sharp and elongated tooth set in the upper gum of her wizened mouth, she was like a witch out of one of the fantastically dark and creepy inventions of Edgar Allen Poe. She cackled as I handed over the few dollars the jacket cost.

After Baltimore came Washington, where we performed at the New Zealand Embassy at 37 Observatory Circle and were billeted at the deputy ambassador's residence in the diplomatic quarter. He had a well-stocked wine cellar and while he was out, in his official capacity, attending a beer competition (the national brand, Steinlager, won a prize) we sampled what seemed to be unlimited stocks of velvety reds. Our official hosts were the embassy social club: Gentleman Jim and Jenny Stevenson were still stationed in Washington of the wide boulevards and leafy green trees; of vast and desolate black slums surrounding the privileged enclave from which white America seeks, or sought, to govern itself. We went to see *Monty Python's Life of Brian* and drove away afterwards singing, 'Always Look on the Bright Side of Life'.

~

There are just seven of us in the promotional photographs Joe Bleakley took out at Coney Island. Because the latest incarnation of the band had split again, we were reduced to just two musicians, Jan and Neil. Only four actors remained, John and the Gang of Three. I, in my Baltimore jacket and panama hat, carrying an umbrella, was the seventh member. In the image that we used, Alan in a white jacket, Sally in a tiger-striped coat, like parents of a dissolute brood, flank the rest of us. John in his cloth cap looks like the hero of a Jack London novel. Deborah and Jan stand on either side of him, Deb in a black-lined coat, Jan in shiny leathers. Neil and I are at the back, one in black and one in white, with a tower behind us like something out of Hieronymus Bosch's *Garden of Earthly Delights*, and half a derelict ride, a roller coaster perhaps. None of us is smiling. We are in Early Roman Kings mode, the gangstas about to go out on the road again.

Ian Prior, always the most fugitive of the Moles, decided not to join our cross-country peregrination. Perhaps he just wanted to stay in New York. In a booth in a mid-town coffee shop, Alan, Sally and Deb put to me that I might like to remain behind too. I suppose I would have been useful when they made their promised return after their New Zealand tour, and associated excursions, were over. I don't think they made the same offer, however, to Jan, who was more important to the enterprise than I was. She would go back home with them and I would stay behind? It seemed unlikely.

Alan Brunton, Neil Hannan, Deborah Hunt, John Davies, Jan Preston, Martin Edmond, Sally Rodwell, Coney Island, 1979.

Ian Prior, New York, 1979.

I should probably have thought a bit harder about this proposal than I did. I could have put it beside Florence's offer to agent a book for me and hunkered down to write. Who knows what might have happened? It wasn't that I didn't like living in New York. I felt quite comfortable there: its combination of village cultures allied with a magnificent impersonality suited me. Nor was I homesick. There were two reasons why I didn't stay.

The first was that it would have meant splitting up with Jan and I wasn't ready to do that yet – and anyway, it would have to be our decision, wouldn't it, not one instigated by the Moles? The other reason was more intrinsic: I thought the subject matter of the writing I was going to do was in the antipodes, and that I would have to go back there to reconnect with it. This turned out to be true.

~

The show we toured across America was called *Numbered Days in Paradise*. It premiered in St Peter's church hall at 336 West 20th Street on the night of 21 October 1979, a Sunday. It was part of an event called The Shared Season under the auspices of a triumvirate: the Labor Theater, Modern Times Theater and the New York Street Theater Caravan. We had to work around the set-up for another, forgotten production. The roof of the church hall was high and the ladder I used to climb up to adjust the lamps, rickety. On the other hand I was excited. The rig was made up of par cans, the same kind of lights used in mass formation by bands like the Ramones. 'Par' stands for parabolic aluminised reflector. Because they throw out a lot of wattage, they are employed as locomotive headlights and aircraft landing lights. I wasn't allowed to reposition any of the cans but I could repoint them, and I could change the gels.

I used the deepest, most saturated colours I had, sometimes putting two or three gels over a lamp. Reds, greens, blues and purples, with straw yellow and white light to add intensity. Given that the lamps couldn't be moved, the Moles choreographed the action according to the rig. If I positioned a deep red pool centre stage, say, Deb might hit that when she came out as Coyote. And so on. Because the roof was so high, the throw of the beams was long and the washes that poured down upon the stage attained a beauty and a power greater than anything else I had done so far. This was my third opening in New York and easily the best.

Numbered Days in Paradise was situated somewhere between a requiem mass and a gospel revival meeting. It took place in an intermediate zone, after the catastrophe but before its full effects are felt. The opening words of the scenario:

Seldom has there been more nervous expectation in a world of pain and desolation. The earth is drying up. We stand at the beginning of some mass confessional. The sun is about to rise, perhaps. Skinwalkers pass through a new landscape. Artefacts of the machine age litter the space. Cactus. Dogs howling. No birds. We are in the pits. Leaves fall from above. After the skinwalkers, the sky brightens. A group of country folk pass with large bird effigies. The sound of insects. Enter the fool – dances in silence except for the locusts. The fool sings a song.

The Fool was played by Deb in a coyote mask; she had a broom with which she swept up leaves scattered around the two wrecked car bodies that comprised the principal set for the show. These wrecks we hauled off the streets of Manhattan, manoeuvring them through the stage door and onto the boards where they were disposed towards each other and the audience in an open V. There were actors concealed within these car bodies and on cue they crawled out onto the stage. 'Two derelicts. Blankets and feathers, they are Indians or aborigines, maybe refugees from genocide on the Matto Grosso. They drink from bottles in brown paper bags and, when the bottles are empty, begin to clink them together to make a beat, which grows and builds and in the end transforms into a gospel song: "There's a Great Day Coming".'

Like all Red Mole shows, *Numbered Days* was short on plot and long on mood and atmosphere. Word-rich, too. The drama oscillated

Deborah Hunt, New York, 1979.

221

between despair and improbable hope. The song Jan and Neil and I wrote about the murdered or murdering drug dealer, 'Forbidden City', had an airing. There was another gospel chant, 'People Are You Ready?' A young man left his tribal homeland and went to the city, where he succumbed to the usual temptations. Upon his return, his people crucified him. We nailed together a rough wooden cross and John, about three-quarters of the way through the show, was hung upon it, bound with ropes. For the rest of the performance the shadow of his crucifixion fell eerily across the derelict car bodies.

Someday Afternoon screened. I projected a slide show depicting endangered species from the animal kingdom. I bought the slides from a mail order outlet; their Latin names were intoned as the images came and went. An anthem that was a paean to the corrupt nationalism that rules us still was sung: 'Over snowy mountains/Across the deep blue sea/O my country, my country/Your flag flies free.' A mysterious figure with a suitcase full of money appeared, bribing candidates in the upcoming, 1980, presidential election. The show ended with Sally and Alan, an old couple in rags at the foot of the cross, bickering as they try to coax a fire out of rubbish. They are the parental pair, the fool is their child and the crucified man the repository of all of their sins. 'Oh vacant earth,' wrote Alan, 'devoid of the tears of God, fructify thine inhabitants one last time, one last chance is all we are asking for. Open up the gates again.'

That October night at St Peter's Hall, like the first night of *Last Days*, like the debut of *Dead Fingers Walk*, was a resplendent opening. Even though our stance towards the religiosity of the material was ironic and sometimes even caustic, the show was capable of inspiring awe in an audience and on this occasion it did. It was a church hall, it was a Sunday and *Numbered Days* seemed to call down the sacred and manifest it both on stage and in the auditorium.

It included Alan's 'Chant of Paradise': 'Leaving the province of Tonola/and travelling northeast/through the country between two seas/you pass many castles on the banks of the river.' Sally read the words while John passed on stilts on his way to fissile heaven. We were taking *Numbered Days* into the landscape evoked in this chant. We would speak of paradise in the paradise of which we were speaking: 'Along the Oscura hills at 5 a.m./a faint glow spreads/Someone whispers in that desert/we don't know who/thirty minutes later/Mountain War Time/the order to fire.'

~

Before we left New York Neil's customised Fender bass guitar was stolen from a café on 45th Street in Manhattan. An audacious theft: Neil had put the guitar in its black travelling case just a hand's length away on the floor beside the booth where we were sitting; someone walking out must have picked it up. We saw nothing; it was as if it had been spirited away. But we also knew the score and, as soon as we discovered the theft, raced around the corner to 46th Street to see if the guitar had turned up in any of the pawn shops there yet. It had, but because of a city ordinance that said pawned goods had to be retained for a set period of time in case they had been stolen, Neil, bizarrely, was not allowed to buy his guitar back for a fortnight. Stoic, he borrowed another bass and went on the road with that.

We folded down the back seat of the Pontiac and packed all the musical equipment and all of our personal baggage into the rear of the station wagon. Jan and Neil and I sat side by side on the bench seat up front, with Jan in the middle and Neil and I taking turns driving. The car was, in Neil's words, 'packed to the gunnels – which caused two wheel bearing blow outs – one just before Richmond, Virginia on a Sunday night – managed to get that fixed at an off duty kind of garage where the "southern" mechanic did not say one word to us – but fixed the car – we drove on – only to have the opposite bearing blow out as we approached Knoxville, Tennessee.' I only remember the first of these two breakdowns: waiting beside the road on a rising curve in a green landscape near Roanoke on a Sunday afternoon, thinking about Walter Raleigh.

In Knoxville we played the Laurel Theater in Fort Sanders near the University of Tennessee. It was another converted church, a handsome wooden edifice built in 1898. When the Presbyterians drifted away, the Epworth Ecumenical Congregation took it over and for many years held services there. It was they who oversaw the transfer of the building, in 1969, to the Jubilee Community Arts, whose brief was 'to preserve and present the traditional arts of the Southern Appalachians'.

I'm not sure how Red Mole fitted this aspiration but, with our gospel-inflected show, we were certainly riding the zeitgeist. Earlier in the year Bob Dylan released *Slow Train Coming*, the first album in his Christian trilogy; Alan would get stern with anyone inclined to disparage what many believed was an incongruous, possibly cynical, career move. Republican Ronald Reagan, a millenarian Christian, was about to declare his candidature for the presidency. Jimmy Carter, the incumbent, was then a pious and upright Southern Baptist, although most people thought the rather more impious Ted Kennedy would be standing for the Democrats.

We played the Laurel on Monday, 5 November. The day before, in Iran, Muslim Students of the Imam Khomeini Line invaded the American embassy in Tehran and took hostage 52 diplomats and staff stationed there and kept them for 444 days. The crisis, described by *Time* magazine as 'an entanglement of vengeance and mutual incomprehension', effectively put an end to Carter's presidency. For us it meant that parts of *The Last Days of Mankind* suddenly became relevant again and we restored to the show 'The Madmen at the Gate Imitate the Loyal Burghers of Isfahan Lamenting the Passing of the Shah of Iran'. The repeated refrain, 'Who is this Ayatollah Khomeini? Who is this mad Mullah?', resonated. Even the kindly folk at Jubilee Arts were wondering that.

Jim and Jenny Stevenson too. After we'd left DC on the last tour Jim had been posted to Iran and they had been in Tehran only three weeks when the hostages were taken. New Zealand officials helped six Americans to escape – egregiously misrepresented in the 2012 film *Argo*. When the decision was made to return to New Zealand, Jim, as his obituary notes, 'was in charge of smashing the communication equipment with a huge mallet. Jenny was hosting a party for diplomatic wives when Jim rang and told her not to say a word but once everyone had left to quickly pack a small bag as they would be leaving that evening. After a circuitous route to the airport and a nerve-wracking wait in the departure lounge they were able to board a flight for London.'

~

We had to be in San Antonio by Saturday night for our next show and decided to go there via New Orleans. Meanwhile the Moles headed west through Memphis, Tennessee, into Arkansas, where they visited Levon Helm, the drummer with the Band, in Springdale near Fayetteville and sat on the porch jawing with him for an afternoon before continuing on south through Tulsa and Oklahoma City and Dallas for our rendezvous at the Alamo.

We were listening to talkback radio as we headed down Highway 40 towards Chattanooga and then on to Highway 59 for Birmingham, Alabama. Brash and ignorant voices proclaimed over the airways that we should 'nuke the Iranians back to the Stone Age'. That's an actual sentence I heard someone say. Did he know what he meant? The primary concern, then as now, seemed to be to keep the oil flowing into American refineries. On the other hand it didn't sound as if Jimmy Carter was prepared to heed advice of that kind. He was a southern gentleman after all, and the south could be surprising.

In Birmingham we parked on the street in a nondescript neighbourhood and stepped into a barber's shop. At the soul food restaurant in Philadelphia everyone had stopped talking and stared at these white folk who'd barged in without a by-your-leave. Here it turned out differently. When we said who we were and what we wanted there was a pause, then smiles all round, a proper welcome and a delicious meal of fried chicken at the adjacent restaurant. One thing Americans, black, white or Hispanic, shared, was an innate respect for entertainers; if you had a guitar, say, that was like a passport – to anywhere.

Cops were less easy to impress. South of Tuscaloosa we were pulled over and directed off the freeway onto a dirt road running parallel. Two men, with their hands on their guns, sidled up either side of the Pontiac. Neil was driving. One of them tapped on the window, asking to see his driver's licence and the car registration. His ID was in his bag in back of the wagon and he was given permission to fetch it.

The tension seemed to ease a bit and we were all allowed out of the car to stretch our legs while they told us why they stopped us. They had run a check on our New York plates. 'These here plates belong to a 1967 Ford Galaxy,' one of them said. 'But youall's driving a 1969 Pontiac. Can you explain how that came to be?' We could not. We pleaded ignorance. We said the plates came with the car. Registration papers? The Nuyoricans didn't give us any; just a cash receipt. Which we couldn't seem to find.

There was a bad moment when they asked us to look further into our luggage for that missing piece of paper. Jan and I had bought a zip-up suitcase with a woven, tapestry top in which we kept our precious items. These included a bag of dope that was just under one of Jan's two cocktail dresses which, folded carefully, so as not to get crushed, were sitting at the top of the case. They wanted me to unzip it. I did. There were five of us gathered around the open back of the station wagon when Jan, as was her wont, started talking – about her frocks, their velvets and satins, their glittering occasions. She was persuasive and at some point the cops lost interest in the search and started listening to her. 'Hey, Noo Zeeland! Is that up by Norway somewhere?'

They asked us where we were headed, advised us to fix the problem with the plates at the next place we stopped – City Hall, Jackson – then said, 'You leave our state behind, now.' At the state line in Mississippi, near a place called Cuba on Highway 59, there was a border station manned by armed police. They also wanted to know where we were going and advised us not to linger in their jurisdiction either. We might have been passing through the United States of Paranoia. We never did legitimise the plates: it would have cost too much and delayed us too long. The old ones were still on the car when I sold it to a black man in West Hollywood for $200. It had sprung a pin-hole leak in the petrol tank which, just before the sale, I plugged with chewing gum. I still feel bad about that.

~

New Orleans was gracious and melancholy with long, tree-lined avenues down which the streetcars sedately clanged. We were staying on Bienville with some people we had met along the way. Neil reckons the blokes in the household were trying to corral him and me so they could have their way with Jan; I don't remember that. My recall is that Neil fell ill and lay tossing, sweating and feverish, on a mattress for 24 hours, but his account says nothing about that.

He says we went down to the French Quarter and I remember that. On Bourbon Street it felt, like it did in Baltimore, as if the 200- or 300-year-old past of the city was still alive. Gentlemen in stove-pipe hats, high-collared shirts, embroidered waistcoats, tight denim pants and tooled leather cowboy boots drank bourbon in the bars or roistered drunkenly in the street with their high-toned women; you felt at any moment someone was going to pull out a gun and fire, not necessarily at another person, into the air perhaps. We went on down to Tipitina's on Napoleon Avenue near the junction with Tchoupitoulas Street on the banks of the Mississippi, hoping to see Dr John or the Neville Brothers play; and heard instead an excellent R & B band doing a cover of Talking Heads' version of Al Green's 'Take Me to the River'.

We carried on, through Baton Rouge and Lafayette and Beaumont, Texas, with a side trip to Port Arthur to pay homage to Janis Joplin. Somewhere along Highway 10 we stopped, in a dusty court outside some anonymous buildings, perhaps for a cup of coffee, and when we pulled away again I left my Baltimore jacket on the rooftop of the car and it blew away. I guess I was fortunate: my wallet was in my pants pocket. The jacket joined a long line of things gone astray or mislaid upon that trip. I made of list of them once but then I lost the list. I was only half there most of the time, in a fugue state, concentrating only upon completing the task at hand: driving, lighting, getting from one place to the next. There wasn't the time or the attention necessary to form memory traces. As a result, those few that remain tend towards the melodramatic.

It was night already, about 9.30, when we reached Houston. The town seemed huge and gloomy, sinister and somehow deserted too. In the murky dark we stopped to get something to eat at the first place we saw open, a yellow-lit café under the pillars of a freeway. There we met a Mexican, with one arm in a dirty sling and a whisky bottle in his other hand, who swore he was Freddy Fender and, to prove it, sang for us his 1975 hit 'Before the Next Teardrop Falls', a cappella and in Spanish. He was well liquored up but he could still sing, and was so affected by his own performance there were tears in his eyes too. We were in some kind of hobo jungle and it was hard to concentrate upon our burritos and keep an eye on the car full of gear parked outside as well. Shadowy figures drifted in the semi-dark like dead souls lurching towards a zombie apocalypse.

We carried on driving through the night and arrived in San Antonio in the early hours of the morning. Outside the Alamo we parked the car in the street and tried to get some sleep while dawn light fingered those old, bullet-scarred, adobe walls. The Moles arrived and then our hosts, an odd couple: Raoul, a stocky, macho Mexican and his thin, pale, Anglo buddy, whose name I've forgotten. Raoul was very solicitous of him and, indeed, of us. The Anglo had a brand-new black pick-up truck and everywhere we went, we went in convoy, us following the truck; they were afraid we would lose our way and determined to prevent this happening. That's probably why San Antonio was the one place I did lose the car, and had to wander the grid of anonymous streets for ages before I found where I'd parked it again.

~

We were playing in the rooms of the Mexican-American Unity Council at 2300 West Commerce Street, on behalf of Citizens Concerned about Nuclear Power and Mothers & Others Mobilized for Survival, at an event called the South Texas Festival of Energy and Light. We went to the Unity Council first and then to our billets. There were two shows scheduled, on the Saturday and the Sunday nights, but my memories of San Antonio concern Raoul and his nameless buddy. Their coddling made me irritable and that might have led to a blow-up at a party after the second night of the brief season. I was joking with John and Neil and I used the phrase 'a pack of pricks', an ironic self-description that was not meant to be taken seriously. We laughed.

Raoul must have heard something: either my original remark or a certain tone in the answering laughter. 'What did you say?' he demanded. A sudden silence in the room. His aggression was palpable. I met his eye. But how to explain? The phrase was self-deprecating but also functioned as a form of self-aggrandisement: we were Kiwi blokes who wilfully transgressed and yet adhered to a code. We were a pack of pricks. Did Raoul wish to be part of our fraternity? Or did he feel excluded from it? I wasn't prepared to venture further into these troubled waters. I just held his gaze. When he understood that was the extent of my reply he said, with manifest contempt, 'Are you all right?', and turned away.

The exchange perplexes me still. I think Raoul's machismo was offended but, given his close, possibly homoerotic relationship with his buddy, that machismo was already of some complexity. I also think he was sick of disparaging remarks made about his ethnicity and his people by entitled white folks, and may have felt that I had spoken another. And he had probably picked up on my irritability, which may have seemed like an insult to his hospitality.

Neil came to a similar conclusion: 'our Mexican hosts wasted no time in educating us, in the nicest possible way, about who really owned the place. Texas has a very similar history to New Zealand in the respect that the so-called gringo colonisers were initially invited in by the extant natives, but took it upon themselves to decide it was their manifest destiny to take over completely.' Yes. Another circle closed here: in San Antonio Neil made a trip out to the airport to collect his bass guitar, which Austin Trevett had recovered for him from the pawn shop and sent down to Texas courtesy of the airline he worked for. I think it may have had its own seat.

I'm going to leave it to Neil to describe the next stage of the journey, because the only two things I remember about Austin, Texas, are, first, that we stayed with people who kept a wide wooden bowl full of marijuana in the middle of their dining room table – visitors were expected to contribute to it what they could, and invited to take from it what they would; and, second, that we met there a wide-faced, blue-eyed, tangle-haired blonde called Casey, who travelled with us for the next couple of months. Well, there is a third: the grand boulevard called

Congress Avenue leading up from the Colorado River to the Texas Capitol where the State Legislature stands like a temple above the city on a hill. Sixth Street, the entertainment district, comes off that avenue.

'Seventy miles up the road,' wrote Neil, 'was one of the best gigs of the entire tour, at Esther's Pool (now called Flamingo Cantina) on 6th Street in Austin. This was a venue made for the type of theatre that Red Mole excelled at and for this night we revived the political cabaret from Carmen's Balcony days.' Austin entrepreneurs Michael Shelton and Shannon Sedwick had revived an old pool hall and opened a show named *Esther's Follies* on 1 April 1977. 'It was contemporary vaudeville, racy, daring, drug-fuelled and funny, which is probably why The Moles went down so well there too.' In 1979 6th Street was 'run down, low rent and hookers ... Esther's Pool was one of the single most significant factors in the development of Austin's entertainment district.'

It's good to know that Red Mole made a contribution to this revival and apposite to recall something Deborah said, many years later: 'Wherever we've gone we've found people or people have found us. They have honoured us with their presence.' All Red Mole's achievements, she suggested, were 'heart work'. In Ancient Egyptian ritual burial practice, the human heart was weighed for lightness of being against the feather of truth. Despite the vagaries of our existence and our occasional derelictions, even cruelties, this could stand for all that Red Mole did.

~

We drove west from Austin to the junction with Highway 10 and then on to El Paso, taking the Upper Emigrant Road, which runs to the north of the Edwards Plateau and intersects with the Lower Emigrant Road, out of San Antonio, near Comanche Springs west of Horseshoe Crossing on the Pecos River. These were military roads built in the mid-nineteenth century when gold seekers heading for the California fields could only pass safely through this bandit-infested, Indian-haunted land under escort, and perhaps not even then. Half a dozen forts were established along the way and their names, from Fort Inge to Fort Belknap to Fort Bliss, endure. It's about a 10-hour drive and we made it in style – until we hit the outskirts of El Paso.

There, in a poor Hispanic neighbourhood, one of the rear tyres on the Pontiac blew out. We had to unpack the wagon to access the spare and when we repacked it discovered that some light-fingered person or persons in the small crowd, mostly children, who gathered to watch us, had made off with Neil's mini-amp and our suitcase. The embroidered one with the precious things in it: Jan's cocktail dresses, my leather jacket, some vinyl records, the San Francisco curtains – though fortunately not the bag of dope.

I used to wonder where those elegant dresses ended up, who wore them. I imagined some young Spanish girl resplendent in pink satin and black velvet, and those translucent curtains closing the windows in some barrio or cantina. In the midst of our woes the Moles sailed past in their Buick and then, a few minutes later, their consciences pricked, came back. They pulled over, shook their heads at our predicament, smiled ruefully and carried on again.

The main thing we needed was money which, as usual, was in short supply. Perhaps they advanced us some. There might have been some agitation subsequently upon that score because, during our next season, in Albuquerque, accounts were drawn up and passed around: something that almost never happened. I still have the sheet of paper. We made, and spent, $1042 between New York and Austin; the income was itemised but its expenditure was not. After a couple of weeks in Albuquerque another $859 had been amassed, but again there is no indication of how that money was disbursed. I'm unable to assess the credibility of these figures. I guess we were, as always, at irregular intervals, handed some cash, and made do with that.

In El Paso we were so broke that, though we had enough money for the gas we needed to drive to Albuquerque, we lacked the wherewithal to buy anything to eat. We went busking on the promenade down by the water where elegant restaurants trailing vines lined the Franklin Canal, but none of the well-heeled Texans passing by deigned to give us a nickel or a dime. We decided to try our luck south of the border. We parked the car on Delta Drive and Neil stayed behind to look after the gear while Jan took her instrument and we crossed the bridge over the Rio Grande – a thread of silver in a wide white concrete culvert – and set up outside the stone wall of a church south of the strip in Ciudad Juárez, Mexico.

There were bars, dental parlours, brothels. It wasn't threatening but could have become so, especially after the sun went down. No one knew what to make of us. Jan was playing a keyboard she called a Tombo, after the name of the manufacturer. It was a melodeon with a long plastic tube through which you blew air; she was adept upon it and it had a certain novelty value. There was nothing for me to do but stand around and collect the money, should any eventuate. I felt like one of the pimps spruiking outside the brothels, except that I didn't, as they probably did, have a knife in my boot.

A man came from the souvenir shop, where he sold day-glo Christs, Elvises and skulls, with a pile of big round coins. Three children stopped and gawked; the one in the middle was wearing a horror mask she might have got from the souvenir shop man. They didn't have any money but others did. It was always tendered with a brief incline of the head, perhaps out of respect or perhaps in apology for both their own poverty and for ours. I think people felt that any gringos crazy enough to do what we were doing must have been in real need and hence, despite their own hardship, they gave.

After about an hour we decided we had enough and packed up to go back to America. You crossed a different bridge heading north; and there, halfway over, we were detained by officers of the border patrol wanting to see our passports. These, we explained, were in the car, over there in El Paso. You could see the Pontiac from the bridge. We hadn't thought to bring them with us. There hadn't been any problems going into Mexico.

One of the men, overweight, uniformed, wearing a belt hung with all kinds of hardware, looked contemptuously at me and spoke a sentence I've not been able to forget: 'We don't care who *leaves* the United States,' he said. 'But we sure as hell care who comes in here.' In the end, incredulous, like so many others, at our naivety, he detained Jan as a 'hostage' and allowed me to go back to the car for our passports, which he scarcely glanced at before waving us through.

The pesos the poor people of Juárez had given us turned out to be worth almost nothing in El Paso, but there was enough, about $10, to buy a roast chicken, which we ate down to the bones before getting back in the car and heading north on Highway 25 through Las Cruces and Truth or Consequences and Socorro and Los Lunas to Albuquerque, New Mexico.

El Paso was for me the low point on that trip. As we climbed up the valley of the Rio Grande, following the course of the great river towards its source in the San Juan Mountains in Colorado, I felt my spirits rising with the land, as if some rite of passage had been accomplished. As if I was breaking through, perhaps, into that paradise which is said to exist on the rooftop of the world.

~

BUS STOPS ON THE MOON

Under the auspices of the Community Cultural Affairs Program of the City of Albuquerque we were playing a two-week season at the KiMo Theater at 6th and Central: a pueblo deco dream palace built in 1927 and recently restored to some of its former glory. It was the brainchild of Oreste Bachechi and his wife Maria, Italians from Modesto who arrived in Albuquerque in 1885 and set up shop in a tent by the railway lines. They became liquor vendors and grocers and then moved into the entertainment business; by 1919, with a man named Joe Barnett, they were running the Pastime Theater.

The Bachechis hired famous Kansas City architects the Boller Brothers who had, by 1925, already built some 65 art deco cinemas across the Midwest of the United States. At Oreste Bachechi's suggestion Carl Boller and local artist Carl von Hassler, Bremen-born, of a Dutch father and a French mother, toured pueblos in New Mexico in search of inspiration; and came back with a vast and eclectic collection of motifs – from Zuni, Hopi, Navajo, Tewa, Mescalero, Apache and others – to be incorporated into the new cinema.

Purity was not their aim; variety and opulence were. The theatre is made of stucco designed to look like adobe and adorned in a way that seems simultaneously deco and pueblo. The interior, painted with dance and hunting scenes, includes plaster ceiling beams like logs; air vents disguised as Navajo rugs; chandeliers shaped like war drums and funeral canoes; wrought iron birds in the staircase banisters; and rows of buffalo skull lights with glowing amber eyes. The door knobs are kachina dolls. The name, KiMo, is Tewa, the language spoken by pueblo Indians living along the valley of the Rio Grande. It means mountain lion or, alternatively, king of the mountains.

For the KiMo Carl von Hassler painted a set of murals based upon the legend of the Seven Cities of Gold sought by conquistador Francisco Vázquez de Coronado during his 1540–42 expedition north from Mexico. For this he assembled an army of 300 soldiers and over 1000 Tlaxcalan Indians, as well as droving herds of livestock for food. Coronado never found the fabled cities, even though he went as far as Arizona, saw the Grand Canyon, traversed much of New Mexico and travelled north-east into what is now Kansas, where he encountered Wichita Indians. He did, however, destroy a Zuni pueblo at Hawikuh (= Cibola) and a number of other Indian towns, because they would not accept his demand that their inhabitants embrace Christianity forthwith – or else out of pique that they were not the fabulous storehouses of gold and jewels he wanted them to be.

232

Eight of the nine murals that Von Hassler painted, in oil, survive. (The ninth was destroyed to make a window for a radio station once situated in the building.) They depict, not mythical cities, but pueblos, or their ruins, still extant in the south-west; they use a palette of soft blue, rose pink, pale gold, leaf green and white; their resemblance to the Cities of Gold lies in their aesthetic rather than their subject matter.

Von Hassler, who for many years had his studio in the KiMo, was an innovator who sometimes, in the interests of longevity, baked his oil paintings in an oven. He worked on scaffolding six metres high to complete the murals in time for the opening of the theatre, a ceremony notable for appearances by Amerindian groups from nearby pueblos and reservations. A contemporary press notice predicted that 'numerous prominent tribesman of the Southwest will perform for the audience mystic rites never before seen on the stage'.

That association with local peoples continued. The staff at the KiMo included a young Mescalero Apache man, and on Thanksgiving Day his mother and other members of his family came into the theatre foyer with steel vats full of delicious hot food; Neil recalled 'home made quesadillas, the best I've ever tasted'. There was also green chilli and tortillas and, for dessert, sopaipilla, a fried bread with a core of liquid honey. From these gracious and generous people I learned what Thanksgiving really means: not a commemoration by Christian pilgrims praising the Lord for their survival, but a celebration of the time indigenous people saved their colonisers from starvation with gifts of food which included, presumably, turkey.

One of the legends associated with the KiMo is that of the ghost of Bobby Darnell, a six-year-old boy who was killed in 1951 when a hot water wall heater exploded. He is said to haunt the theatre still. There was a shrine to him, a blue-painted nook filled with bizarre and various offerings, and we were advised to leave out a string of doughnuts each night as propitiation against his mischief or his malice, which invariably manifested during performances. The doughnuts were hung on the water pipe that ran along the back wall of the theatre behind the stage and were always gone next morning. Neil remarked that Bobby must have liked Red Mole as no tricks were played on us; but I wonder.

I lit *Numbered Days* in Albuquerque from a board in an impromptu booth some rows back in the stalls on the left-hand side of the auditorium. One evening I noticed that the cross upon which John had been crucified, as usual, towards

Numbered Days in Paradise: John Davies, St Peter's Hall, New York, 1979.

the end of the show, was becoming unstable. The KiMo had a raked stage and, although the triangular base of the cross was heavily sandbagged, one of the sandbags had shifted, meaning the construction was beginning to tilt forward and was in danger of falling. John, tied hand and foot, was aware of his predicament and trying, surreptitiously, to free himself from the ropes that bound his ankles to the shaft.

Deborah, playing the Magdalene, knew what was happening too. She was crouched like a sprinter in the blocks ready to leap forward if – or rather when – the cross fell, to try to stop John smashing face first onto the boards. Both of them remained in character. The audience, small, passionate, as Red Mole audiences tended to be, were on the edges of their seats as the cross swayed, teetered and finally fell. Deb shot across the stage but she was too late. Luckily John had managed to free his feet and, although he hurt his knees when he crashed down, thereby saved himself from more serious injury. As one reviewer remarked, most of the audience thought the accident was part of the show.

~

The KiMo sometimes seemed dark and cluttered and labyrinthine, a place in which historical misunderstandings had become immured. Memories of old atrocities whispered along its corridors. Von Hassler's Seven Cities of Gold murals were apposite too. The central text of *Numbered Days*, 'Chant of Paradise', originated during *The Arabian Nights* at Carmen's Balcony two years before, 'details a journey from Tonala in Mexico northward into the American Southwest, ending somewhere in New Mexico as a nuclear explosion takes place'.

Why was it in the show at all? Not for local colour, as was the case with passing references in a shadow puppet play to Billy the Kid's execution in July 1881 by Pat Garrett at Fort Sumner to the east. Our concern was the development of the atom bomb at Los Alamos, north of Albuquerque, and the first ever explosion of a thermonuclear device at 5.29am on 16 July 1945 at Alamogordo to the south. The test was carried out in the Jornada del Muerto desert at what is now the White Sands Missile Range. Jornada del Muerto, Journey of the Dead Man, is sometimes translated as the Journey of Death.

The other routine that travelled with us from Wellington was 'Cripple Cockroach', the story of a galactic derelict who must tender a dollar bill to Sister Mercy before walking into a black hole in Times Square. Or, previously, Courtenay

Place. I wonder now about the relationship between paradise conceived as a thermonuclear explosion and a death foretold which, once paid for, comes as a blessed relief. Both are expressions of the vagaries of life, both are meditations upon last things and the strategies we use to endure a world made for destruction. We believed in the themes of these poems as much as we believed in ourselves.

Moreover, they gave a context for more homely routines: Deb's mutant Super Kid from *The Last Days of Mankind*; Sally's pilled-out drunken housewife, walking to oblivion on the collapsed sides of her high-heel shoes; John's stilt-walker stepping out towards paradise across the mesquite-haunted plains beneath the Sangre de Cristo mountains; my own lament, courtesy of the slides I projected each evening, for the species passed or passing from the earth. Many reviewers commented upon our optimism; it was genuine, but it was not earned at the cost of ignoring the calamities that surround us.

~

In Albuquerque we staged cabaret shows at the nearby Central Torta Café and lunchtime performances at the University of New Mexico in the historic district of Silver Hill. Also, by a process that seemed inscrutable, as had happened in Texas, we found gigs further up the line: in Santa Fe, the State capital 80 kilometres to the north, and in the mountain resort town of Taos, about the same distance north and a little to the east. I was sorry to leave Albuquerque, with its gracious, wide boulevards and sense of unhurried calm. I liked a small café opposite the KiMo, where a bowl of red or green chilli could be had, with tortillas, for just a dollar. You might wash it down with a bottle of Dos Equis, the Mexican beer everybody drank. And then order a sopaipilla for dessert.

I remember going into a thrift shop there, a supermarket full of second-hand goods, taking off the battered olive green suede ankle boots Ian Prior had found for me on the streets of New York – the same ones that had come back from Amsterdam with a bag of dope inside – placing them carefully among the other shoes for sale and pulling on instead a pair of handsome, calf-high, tan tooled-leather cowboy boots with Cuban heels, and walking out wearing them. They would carry me all the way back to New Zealand. We were often short of cash so we ate cheese or fruit in the aisles of supermarkets before disguising our depredations by buying chewing gum or cigarettes on the way out.

It was also in New Mexico that, for the first and only time, I saw our country's name mentioned in the headlines of an American newspaper. On November 29 the *Albuquerque Journal* reported that, the day before, 28 November, an Air New Zealand DC10 had flown into the side of Mt Erebus in Antarctica, killing all 237 passengers and 20 crew aboard. When we heard the news we were certain we must all know someone, or someone who knew someone, on that doomed flight. So it proved. And thus, for the first time in a long while, our thoughts turned towards home.

~

Neil caught a bus north to do pre-publicity for the show, *Dead Fingers Walk*, we were putting on at the Performing Space at 418A Montezuma Street next to the railway tracks on the Santa Fe line. He established a strong connection there, still extant, with our host George Koumantaros, a garrulous and enthusiastic Greek American. The advance man job fell to Neil because the Moles wanted to stay behind for a few days: Bob Dylan was in town.

Jan and I, meanwhile, took a detour. We went to Santa Fe via the Jemez Mountains, a spur of the San Juan Range which, like the Sangre de Cristo running parallel on the other side of the river, fingers south along the Rio Grande rift. The Jemez Mountains are volcanic; there are hot springs. We left the car in a parking lot and climbed for about 15 minutes up a steep rocky trail, through pine and spruce, to where the pools sit in natural declivities on the mountain side. There were two other people there, a young couple like us, bathing naked, so we took off our own clothes and joined them in the warm water of the lower pool, where you could sit among drifts of snow and gaze out north over the red rock San Diego Canyon and the rugged Pajarito Plateau. There are black bears and mountains lions in the Jemez, as well as elk, wapiti and beaver, but we saw only lizards and birds.

Our new friends were Daisy and Paul and we ended up spending the rest of the day with them. We adjourned to a bar, a log cabin knocked out of the woods near the town of Jemez Springs, and drank Millers beer through the afternoon. Daisy was pregnant and booked in for an abortion the next day; neither of them wanted to do it but both of them were scared. Paul had been a conscript in Vietnam and remembered patrolling through jungle that had been sprayed with Agent Orange. A jelly-like membrane clung to the leaves, he said, and 'for fun' he and his fellows used to ball it up between their fingers and flick it at each other.

They knew nothing about the hormone spray's toxic qualities, what the dioxin it contains can do to a human body. It was impossible not to think of the words of Sally's song: 'Just hanging around/Polluting the earth/While pretty women/Give monstrous birth.'

There was nothing we could do but listen. I had the feeling Daisy would have gone through with the pregnancy if Paul had been more supportive, but he was convinced that he had been genetically damaged. Maybe he was, but why didn't they do some tests, find out if the baby was healthy? Or were such things unavailable in the back woods of New Mexico in those far-off days? Perhaps Paul, like so many first-time fathers, was leery at the thought of the commitment a child represents. When we drove away they stood at the door of the bar, in the gathering darkness, waving to us, like babes lost in the haunted forest of the times.

As we made our way round the side of the mountain, heading east towards Pojoaque before turning south for Santa Fe, we saw below a scatter of lights like stars in the blackness at the bottom of a well: Los Alamos, the cradle of the bomb, where the top secret Project Y was established in 1942 in the buildings of what had been the Los Alamos Ranch School, a place to which the privileged young of America, including William Burroughs and Gore Vidal, went 'to gain health, strength and self-confidence'.

J. Robert Oppenheimer, the architect of The Bomb, knew Los Alamos too; he was sent there as a young adult in the early 1920s to recuperate from a bout of colitis. He would later, as the mushroom cloud bloomed above, quote the *Bhagavad Gita*: 'I am become death, the destroyer of worlds.' As if in fealty to that strange pronouncement, mingling the arrogance of power with something more fearful, there was a sudden scream of engines above: jet fighters flying to or from one of the military installations in New Mexico. This happened all the time: as if there were a war on or, more precisely, as if we were in a country under domestic military occupation.

~

There was another drama after we reached Santa Fe, one closer to home. We didn't usually all stay at the same place, but George's ranch house was big enough to accommodate all seven of us and Casey too; it had a mezzanine floor running around the walls of the large rectangular living area, with several staircases up and separate places for us to bunk down. One night when the lights had gone out and I was drifting towards sleep, I heard a cry in the dark. It was Sally and the occasion, I assumed, Alan's decision to leave her bed to go to sleep with Deborah.

Neil went over to comfort Sally. A chin-to-chin confrontation between him and Alan a few weeks later in Los Angeles, ostensibly about some other matter, had its origin in this act of kindness. Alan mellowed later, but then he usually responded to criticism, implied or actual, with aggression.

As for the dynamic that existed within the Gang of Three, it was as enigmatic as our finances. They always presented a united front; I never saw tension between Deb and Sal, for instance, nor any overt competition. And their ménage à trois would endure for some years to come. This is the only occasion I remember the veil slipping; characteristically, it was never referred to afterwards. Not that it was any of my business. I had other things on my mind. Where, for instance, was I going to find a film projector?

After *Dead Fingers Walk* we were going to do a version of *Numbered Days in Paradise* at the Performing Space, and for that I had to locate a 16mm projector in order to screen *Someday Afternoon*. I found different projectors in different places but the most common kind, manufacturer unknown, resembled a miniature cannon. Made of cast iron, with a rough grey-green surface known as hammer glaze, it was a powerful machine that became very hot if left on for too long.

Fortunately *Someday Afternoon* took only a few minutes to run; unfortunately I was incapable of remembering the correct way to thread the film and so, each time, had to start again from scratch. I could blame this upon the fact that every projector was a little bit different, but the real problem was my own ineptitude. Each evening before the show I would face the same conundrum; each uninterrupted screening was a relief.

After Santa Fe we moved north to Taos, where we played a series of cabaret shows at a local café, the Wayfarers' Inn in Kit Carson boulevard. The first time we drove there we stopped at the Pojoaque Pueblo where Neil, for $3, was given permission to record a Comanche buffalo dance, which was instantly incorporated into the subsequent Red Mole show. We shuttled back and forth between the inn and the Performers Space on Montezuma Street in Santa Fe a few times, playing each venue on alternate weekends. This was good for our finances and convenient too: our next gig, in Santa Monica, California, was not until 7 January 1980.

Thus we spent Christmas in Santa Fe, where people left out rows of farolitos, little lanterns, along the flat-topped adobe walls of their houses which, because

239

it was winter, were snow-capped as well. These lanterns were of the simplest construction – a brown paper bag quarter-filled with sand in which a lighted candle was placed – and great beauty, as they outlined with their golden glow the darker reddish brown of the adobe beneath the whiteness of the snow. They were to light a path for the baby Jesus so he could find his way to the manger in which he would be born again.

In Santa Fe, for the first and only time, we heard 'Hysteria' played on the radio. Even though the band that made it, Red Alert, no longer existed, wherever we stopped we took copies into the local radio station, and here they gave it a whirl. It might even have become a brief, minor, winter hit. The song came through on the car radio while we were driving and I thought it sounded good: high energy, nice fat sound, fast, punky, rock'n'roll:

> *Do you think we're happy*
> *Do you think we're free*
> *Do you think we live in a democracy?*
> *Everyone is being nice to everyone else*
> *I don't think we'll survive*
> *But I wish you good health*
> *Hysteria*
> *We're all living in hysteria*
> *America*
> *We're all living in America.*

In Taos we stayed in a solar house out on the mesa. It was half underground, made of mud brick, and built into the structure were walls in which rows of glass bottles were set. These walls faced south and west and gathered from the low sun energy that was stored in water tanks. In summer, when the sun was higher, the walls radiated heat and so kept the air inside the house cool. It was wonderful to sleep, without any interior heating, in a warm house while snowdrifts piled up against the outside walls. And the light that fell through the glass of the white or green or brown bottle ends had a dreamy, subaqueous quality, as if we were in an aquarium, or riding a spaceship.

It was like that out on the mesa: otherworldly. One day I walked west towards the Rio Grande. It ran unseen at the bottom of a deep, tree-filled ravine that seemed narrow enough to leap across, as characters do in cartoons. Taos is high, about 2000 metres above sea level, with a cold, bell-like clarity to the air. Out there I came across the ruins of an old sweat lodge, and inside I found the dried-up body of a long-tailed bird with iridescent blue-black feathers, highlighted with green and purple. I souvenired the wings and the tail; over the years, they slowly disintegrated into glittering dust. I never identified what bird it was; probably *Quiscalus mexicanus*, the great-tailed, or Mexican, grackle.

We also visited Taos Pueblo, the most northerly of eight villages built along that part of the valley of the Rio Grande. The pueblo has been there for 1000 years, the oldest continuously inhabited place on the continent. Gradual additions have made a thick-walled adobe structure like a ziggurat: five or six storeys high, two dozen or more dwellings long, a few houses deep. The entrances used to be in the roofs, reached by long external ladders which could be drawn up in the event of an attack.

The ladders remain but there are now conventional doors, painted a bright blue or green, contrasting with the brown-gold mud brick of the adobe. Bundles of red and green chillies hung from the protruding ends of wooden beams and you could smell bread baking in the free-standing round clay ovens out in the courtyards. The people of Taos Pueblo are private, not to say secretive, and we didn't trouble them for long.

~

We left Taos on New Year's Day and headed towards the Four Corners, where Arizona, Utah, Colorado and New Mexico meet. After Farmington, Shiprock; then across the border to Teec Nos Pos in Arizona. We were passing through Navajo territory. The only traffic we saw consisted of big old-fashioned low-riding wagons or sedans containing people of stately, impassive mien sitting three to a seat front and back, wearing wide hats and frilled black jackets and turquoise jewellery. After Teec Nos Pos, Moenkopi, aka Tuba City, which is on Hopi Indian land. Then we crossed the Painted Desert. There was a sign pointing away to the Grand Canyon but we didn't go that way, heading south instead to Flagstaff and west to Kingman, rolling down those wide beautiful American highways that make you want to drive forever, or until the gas runs out, whichever comes first.

As usual, we weren't travelling in convoy, but if Alan's poem 'Where There's Hope' is to be believed, the Moles did in fact run out of petrol on that journey and had to busk in the forecourt of a service station in order to raise the funds they needed to get to the coast. Just like what happened to us in El Paso. Maybe my suspicions about where the money went were not just erroneous but ungenerous; maybe they were as broke as we were. Alan wrote:

> *I'm going to do*
> *a little song and dance*
> *out here*
> *like Ronald Reagan in a pinafore praising Pabst Beer*
> *in 1954*
> *maybe some people will stop*
> *say:*
> *'look at that crazy arsehole holding out hope*
> *let's go shake his hand for good luck.'*

At Kingman we turned north along the eastern side of the Black Mountains. It was dark by now, we'd been on the road all day, and soon we saw ahead of us a strange white glow on the horizon. It grew in brightness and intensity as we crossed the pass into the Black Canyon and drove over the bridge across the Colorado River, with the mighty Hoover Dam on our right: a high curving concrete wall, unimaginably tall under the arc lights, with a prodigious amount of water, Lake Mead, which we could not see, stored behind it. The glow ahead of us was Las Vegas, like a great lightbulb, radiating enormous amounts of electricity into the vacant, starless, desert sky over the immensity of the Nevada Basin.

'Money (That's What I Want)' by the Flying Lizards was playing on the car radio as we turned into the strip. The tambourine sound in their version of the 1959 Barrett Strong classic sounds exactly like that made by silver dollars falling when someone playing a poker machine in a casino has a win. Jan was ill, feverish, pale and sweating, so we tucked her up under a blanket on the front seat of the Pontiac while Neil and I went into Caesar's Palace to check out the action.

It's true there are no clocks inside casinos, just cold-eyed beauties at the blackjack tables and men with guns around the roulette wheels. I put a coin in a one-armed-bandit and pulled the lever, but no pyramids lined up in row for me. I wasn't surprised: I've always found gambling implausible. Next to me a woman cradled a sleeping baby in the crook of one arm while, over and over again, she pulled the lever with her other hand. She was smoking too, the ashtray next to her filling up with butts.

It was dawn when we came out into the strip again; the sun rose in the rear-view mirror as we drove west through Paradise and Sloan to the state line and on across the Mojave Desert to Barstow. Neil again: 'Through the Cajon Pass, early on a light and airy morning, looking out across California towards the Pacific Ocean, had me channelling all the migrants who had made this journey before, the beauty and hope for this place was awe inspiring. We were booked in for a two week season at the Odyssey Theatre in Santa Monica, the weekend performances to begin at the very sophisticated hour of midnight.'

It was 1980 and we were back in LA, just 18 months after we first arrived in the US; I felt much older, while the city itself seemed hardly to have changed. Apart, that is, from the billboards on Sunset Boulevard. We stayed in West Hollywood in the house of a kindly, gay, melancholic Vietnam vet whom we met through the people at the Odyssey. Like Paul at Jemez Springs, Brad seemed to have mislaid some essential part of himself during the war. At the theatre on Sepulveda Boulevard, about 20 blocks back from Venice Beach, we set up around a production of Bertolt Brecht's *Mother Courage*, which was inconvenient but not impossible. We were nothing if not adaptable.

LA critics were neither as smart nor as generous as those in New York had been: notices ranged from the hostile to the bemused. Gretchen Henkel in *Drama-Logue* wrote that Red Mole 'served up a strange brew of music, sound effects and sketches. They've invented characters who are mutant freaks of our nuclear age, both grim and comic. The opening image is startling: a white-shrouded prophet intones the coming of the atomic apocalypse. The megaton angel comes down with its portent of doom. There are traces of vaudeville, new wave, punk, and 60s groups in their work.'

The *Hollywood Reporter*'s Ron Pennington was less sympathetic to what he called 'a punk vaudeville happening with most of the material concerning politics or ecology'. He thought the opening sequences shapeless, amateurish and uninteresting, but liked 'a dark poetic sketch about two characters called Cripple Cockroach and Sister Mary [sic] and their Christmas night on Times Square; a grotesque Mad Hatter tea party that would have given Lewis Carroll nightmares; and a hell and damnation sermon and revival meeting'. Alan's monologues were, he said, embarrassingly bad, but he may have taken offence, as so many Americans did, at the Ordinary Vernon's excoriating account of their country's politics and especially their foreign policy. In those days we felt we had succeeded if we managed to offend somebody, especially if it was a drama critic.

I was indeed older: I turned 28 in LA. There were no celebrations because I didn't tell anybody it was my birthday, but Lorraine, the gracious, sweet-natured woman who ran the box office at the Odyssey, somehow found out and gave me a card. I went down town and bought a black hat, a homburg, maybe because of the Procol Harum song of that name remembered from my teenage years. I was always buying hats in those days, as if seeking some elusive marker of identity, but I could never hang onto them for long. I would either lose them or they would be stolen, as this one was, from a party in Wellington, after we returned to New Zealand.

I also bought a dozen rolls of lighting gel in bright unsaturated colours from a newly released range: cerulean blue, straw yellow, rose pink; grass green, pale orange, lavender. They reminded me of the squares of taffeta from which Jan made the patchwork curtains in San Francisco. These were to light the band she and Neil were going to put together once we reached Auckland because, without ever really discussing the matter, either between ourselves or with the Moles, we'd decided to leave the troupe after the homecoming tour was over. Nevertheless this decision, in the way of such things, had somehow been communicated to the rest of the group. The Gang of Three already understood that this was what would happen.

LA in winter was as dark and gloomy as Houston. One night we went out to Madame Wong's in Chinatown. Toni and the Movers were excruciatingly loud, the drinks expensive and the punkoid waitresses slatternly and rude, it seemed, on principle; we didn't stay. I should have paid more attention: Toni was Toni Childs and members of her band went on to join the Bangles and Red Hot Chili Peppers. Outside it was as if the neutron bomb had gone off: massive architecture, not a soul in sight. The city stretched out vast and deserted under a louring sky; it was raining as if God could weep forever at the sight of his creation. We drove away down the boulevards and saw ahead of us, fizzing in the sombre air, red and green neon advertising Mexican food; we ate chilli and tortillas and drank tequila until we felt halfway human again.

On our last night at the Odyssey, 19 January 1980, my ineptitude at threading *Someday Afternoon* into the projector caught up with me. When it came time to screen the movie I switched on the machine and started the film running, but after just a few frames it jammed in the gate and burned up. The lighting booth was high on one side of the theatre, the screen across on the other; it was a long throw and the image, of emulsion smoking and curling and blackening, was inadvertently powerful. The audience thought that, like the toppling cross in Albuquerque, the immolation of Adam and Eve in the Garden of Eden was part of the show and applauded vigorously. So ended my American journey.

V

Exeunt

THE SEVEN OF US came into the customs hall at Auckland International Airport with a bulky, outlandish collection of luggage, including puppets and props, costumes and masks, as well as various items of electronic equipment upon which, perhaps, duty ought to be paid. We didn't declare anything, but the customs men, eyeing this heterogeneous pile of exotica, decided their professional reputation was at stake and embarked on a search. As luck would have it they started in on John's luggage first, which contained a laughing toy, bought in some magic shop in California. The men, by mistake, set this device off, and its hollow, mirthless, somehow derisive laughter, as if at some cosmic joke, began to echo around the hall.

'Ha ha ha ha,' it went, 'ha ha ha ha …' 'Can you turn that thing off?' they asked John, but he could not, whether by accident or design, seem to locate the toy, which went on laughing and gradually, incrementally, the besieged customs men lost heart. I remember the moment they gave up and began replacing what they had removed from John's bag; remember the way, stony-faced, they waved him through and the rest of us after. And so everything we had brought back with us, perhaps illegally, including amplifiers and microphones as well as other imponderables, was allowed into the country. Which, predictably enough, seemed quaint, even antique. 'My word,' said Deb's father in the terminal. 'My word, it's good to see you, girl.'

We hit the ground running. Our first gig was at Sweetwaters, the rock festival outside of Ngāruawāhia, where we headlined the third night, Monday 28 January, coming on at 9pm for an hour before Billy TK and the Powerhouse closed the weekend's proceedings. Exalted company: Split Enz played the Saturday night nine o'clock slot, Elvis Costello and the Attractions the one on Sunday. We found ourselves among friends: Hello Sailor, just returned from Australia, were on the bill; Midge Marsden, Limbs and Neville Purvis too. Our performance was divided into sequences: black, green and white. It began with giant effigies and ended in fire. Along the way we did the 'Endangered Species' from *Numbered Days*, 'Apocalypse Blues' from *Last Days*, the 'Chant of Paradise' and the gospel song, 'People Are You Ready?'. Our avant-punk evangelical show was prodigious, alarming and equal in intensity to any of the rock'n'roll shows.

That was, alas, the high point of our return tour. We were travelling under the auspices of the New Zealand University Students' Arts Council with Graeme Nesbitt as our impresario, road manager and chief supplier of substances. No longer did we have to seek our own accommodation, or drive ourselves from gig to gig; no longer did we have to lug and set up our own gear; we had roadies. And hotels. Gone was the time of sleeping side by side in the one motel bed, as Neil and Jan and I had done somewhere in Arizona. We were given every consideration, every comfort, all the necessities; though I noticed that the NZUSAC stopped short of supplying a drink rider.

Our next gigs were in Wellington and so down we flew to the capital. The rendezvous point was a house at 335 Willis Street that functioned as an arts centre. I have a memory of the seven of us arriving there on a sunny afternoon, strutting in, fanning out, taking possession of the territory. It was another Early Roman Kings moment. We had perfected a certain style of intimidation, necessary if you were to be taken seriously on the road in the States. We had learnt how to walk in as if we owned the joint. Curiously, my cousin, who was there that day, also remembers that encounter, albeit from the other side. He and others who were there felt as intimidated, as unsophisticated, as uncool, as we intended them to – though it was mostly just bravado.

Later that day we were driven out to Breaker Bay, where Jan's brother Ted lived and where she and I were going to stay. Alan was with us in the car, in one of those moods of mordant glee he was subject to: chortling, crowing, like one who has seen at last the truth behind the lies, the reality behind all illusions. Wellington did look peculiar: I couldn't get used to the way the houses were built so close to each other and yet separate too. It must have been the effect of having spent so long in cities where the streets were lined with uninterrupted facades. I looked at

Red Mole street parade: Sally Rodwell, Neil Hannan, Deborah Hunt, Jan Preston,
John Davies (on stilts), Hamilton, 1980.

the lines of white-painted, red-roofed wooden houses straggling along the sides
of the hills and felt a shiver of recognition and dismay: each one looked so lonely,
so alone on its green slope. It was a premonition of a larger alienation.

We played the State Opera House again, just two years since we'd performed
Ghost Rite there. The show was *Numbered Days in Paradise*, with two burnt-out
car wrecks on stage and the frame of an old couple arguing before, after and
during the unfolding of apocalypse. Bruce Mason described the opening image:
'Centre stage a young man in white pantaloons, wearing a huge white fanged
headdress, plants in either hand, slowly revolving, clockwise. On sound, bird
noises and jungle drums. He could have been a figure from a Solomon Islands
shark cult. After some minutes of this, a gigantic monolith with a cut-out face,
in aspect both savage and mournful, was guided cautiously on stage and stayed
there, glaring at the audience.' But he soon became impatient. Drama was not just

image, he complained, but action. Fifteen minutes, by his reckoning, was too long for the effigy to turn. And the performance that followed 'lacked coherence and forward pace'. He had, he said, nothing but admiration for Red Mole's 'largeness of vision and sublime courage'; it was our execution that was at fault. 'The gags are not good enough, the dancing under par, the vaudeville parodies slack, techniques primitive: I ask, in a word, for style.' By which he meant a shaping of the script. He found this towards the end of the show – perhaps he'd got used to our peculiarities – but not in the preliminaries.

It was well meant, but I couldn't help wondering if he had come up against our limitations or his own. Either way we were being asked to return to a tradition we'd already rejected. Passéist theatre had caught up with us again. The invigorating sense we had in New York, that an audience or a critic might have a role to play in putting together the meaning of the spectacle, was lacking. Mason again: 'Red Mole might well retort that they seek, through parodies of old dramatic rituals – vaudeville, cabaret, film, rock concert – a spectrum of images to disturb, perhaps blow, the mind.' Well, yes. But no. The remarks on style followed, without consideration of the possibility that coherence and forward pace might proceed via images rather than through the hoary old devices of character and plot.

Maybe the sound was bad that night. Mason said he could not hear Alan's monologues, that the words of the songs were garbled. His most damning comment was that we were unable to fill the space – despite the fact that we had enlisted a drummer, a guitarist and two back-up singers. As for the lighting, I was overwhelmed by the size of the rig at my command, and by the complexity of the lighting board I had to operate. It was brand-new, computerised and looked like something you might find in the cockpit of a jet airliner. The actors and musicians may not have felt out of their depth; I certainly did. It was an intimation that I, too, had reached a limit, both of what I could, and what I wanted, to do.

~

That tour, which lasted six weeks, seemed interminable. We played *Numbered Days in Paradise* in the main centres and did an ancillary tour of cabaret shows to universities, tied in with orientation as the new terms began on the various campuses. At some point the title morphed into *Bus Stops on the Moon*, an apt reflection of the way we were feeling. That exhaustion, after more than a year on the road, showed up on stage too. There was a raggedness to some performances, or the shrillness that comes from trying to insist upon what is not actually present in the auditorium. Maybe Bruce was right.

We needed not just a rest, but an opportunity to come up with new material. Local critics were fierce when they detected survivals. When 'The Opium' was revived for a show in Auckland, the response was vicious: How dare this group come back here, all puffed up from their experiences in New York and London, and expect us to put up with acts we've seen before? Yet no one would have minded if the Rolling Stones, say, played a song that everybody knew; indeed they would have complained if they had not. Perhaps there were revelatory moments for people who hadn't encountered us before, and even for some who had. But my feeling was that we no longer connected with New Zealand reality. Going, they say, is not the same thing as coming back. Having stepped beyond the limits of the unknown world, we had returned unfit to live comfortably within the known.

The last gig of that tour was on 8 March 1980, a Saturday night, in the Auckland University chemistry building on Symonds Street. After it was over Alan came with us to the door to say goodbye. He gave Jan a hug, then shook my hand. 'Hail and well met,' he said. And then, turning away, unable to resist the lure of a rhyme, 'Never got a laugh yet.' I laughed. We found a place to live in St Marys Bay, with Kate Hill, the painter, and her son Reuben. The following night, Sunday, we gathered around the TV set for the premiere screening of *Red Mole on the Road*. Could anything more poignant be imagined? There we were, in our former incarnations, full of energy and optimism, setting out on the journey of a lifetime which had now, definitively, ended.

~

So the split was amicable. Later that year Jan collaborated with Sally and Deborah on a women's collective performance called *Electric Eyeland*. She composed the score for a film they made, *Second Sight*, with Melanie Read directing and Caterina De Nave producing. Neil stayed on for one more show, doing the music, with Rick Bryant and others, for *Lord Galaxy's Travelling Players* at the Maidment Theatre. It was about the Dutch-born exotic dancer, courtesan and alleged spy, Mata Hari, played by Deborah; in the archive there is an excoriating photographic still of her naked execution.

Neil, too, was ready to move on. Harry Lyon, ex-Hello Sailor, had been at that last performance of *Bus Stops on the Moon* in Auckland and he and Neil

Lord Galaxy's Travelling Players: Deborah Hunt and ensemble,
Maidment Theatre, 1980.

got talking. With Jan, and, initially, Steve Osborne on drums, they formed Coup d'Etat. As their lighting guy, I got to use my new gels and, later in the year, to light that other Hello Sailor spin-off band, Dave McArtney and the Pink Flamingos. They were great days, or rather nights; but that's another story.

For me leaving Red Mole had become a psychological necessity. As long as I worked alongside Alan, I wouldn't be able to achieve the autonomy I needed to write the things that were in me to write. I'm not saying he obstructed me; quite the opposite. He was competitive but he always gave me encouragement, from the days of *Spleen* until I worked as a pornographer in New York; from the Undertaker to the 'Endangered Species' lament that was part of *Numbered Days*. It was just that the largeness of his talent, and the prodigious energy he owned, didn't leave a lot of room for other contributions. I'm sure he understood this too. It was probably a relief for him not to have me around, watching his every move, picking up every little crumb that fell from his table.

Alan did ask me to work with him one more time during the year we spent in Auckland. He and fellow poets Dave Mitchell and Ian Wedde, with a band called the Four Gone Conclusions – Bruno Lawrence, Bill Gruar and Wilton Rodger – were embarking on *State of the Nation*, a poetry and jazz excursion Ian described as 'a ramshackle touring show [which] felt like, and probably was, the last rites of male egotism that had seemed fresh back in 1969'. Alan asked me to come along and do the lights for them but I said no – for the same reason I left Red Mole. My frailties, I thought, my vulnerabilities, would be exacerbated if I spent too much time around larger talents than mine. Or perhaps my arrogance was so great I lacked the humility necessary to subsume myself to a larger enterprise. Or maybe I'd just done enough of that already. Deborah lit those shows.

~

When *State of the Nation* played Auckland in August we went along to the Maidment to see it and afterwards, in high good humour, repaired to the Windsor Castle in Parnell where the Crocodiles were doing a farewell gig before going to Australia. Bruno had previously been their drummer and came on for a guest spot with other former members, including bass player Mark Hornibrook. Towards the end of the show, as was their wont, the police arrived. About 20 of them came into the bar and took up positions around the walls, facing inwards, waiting for the bell that would go off at 11pm, marking the end of the evening's entertainment. They would then begin to harass punters into leaving and arrest, often violently, those who were slow to do so.

It was understood that musicians were exempt from this policy of deliberate intimidation and so when some of the cops tried to hustle Mark Hornibrook, people objected. Suddenly Peter Dasent, keyboard player with the Crocodiles, who had been defending Mark's right to be there – 'He is in the band, he played on the album' – was grabbed by the neck, dragged backwards in a chokehold out of the room and thrown into a waiting paddy wagon. It was too much. A crowd of about a hundred gathered outside the pub demanding Peter's release.

The cops responded by making more arrests. Bruno was next. Then I felt a bony arm wrap round my neck and my Cuban heels bouncing on the macadam up Parnell Road as I, too, was dragged in a chokehold to the wagon. Seconds later Jan was thrown into a kind of annex, for female prisoners, between our enclosure and the cab. Her handbag was hurled in after her, its contents spilling across the

253

grey metal floor. She told me later there was a roach among the detritus, which she had the presence of mind to swallow before the police found it.

We spent several hours in the back of the wagon as the cops drove around town picking up strays: young Polynesian kids having a fun fight on K Road, drag queens, drunken apprentices, an aristocratic Fijian couple who'd had the temerity to be seen leaving a nightclub. Then several more hours in the lock-up at Central, where the habitual violence of police towards their charges was amply demonstrated – I saw one dragging a punk along by his green hair – along with their recourse to unremitting foulness of speech. Ironic, since Peter Dasent had been arrested for obscene language. They said he said Mark played on the 'fucking' album.

One young cop with a clipboard was enjoying pretending that he was about to let us out and then not doing so. When I said, 'Does your mother know you are doing this?', he blushed scarlet and left the room. We were bailed soon afterwards, around dawn, and made our way home under pellucid skies, with a sick feeling in the guts and, in my case, a bruised neck that took a couple of weeks to heal. Clearly the cops were practising for their exertions during the following year's Springbok Tour. We defended ourselves when the matters came before court and we were all acquitted. The police lied, as they always did; we had credible witnesses; the magistrate soon figured out what really happened.

Later, when my chapbook *Streets of Music* came out, and I launched it at Dave Mitchell's Poetry Live! at the Globe Hotel I delivered a rant (not in the book) about the experience: 'Burnt sienna sunrise on the cold skyline', it began. 'Venus blazing in azure.' It was the night we heard that John Lennon had been shot dead by a deranged fan in New York City. As I made my way up the hill to the pub before the gig I saw Alan sitting alone in a bus outside the Auckland Public Library waiting to go back to Mount Eden; we exchanged mute, companionable greetings. It was my first book launch.

~

My malaise was curious. I felt I was under surveillance. As if, when I walked up St Marys Bay Road to Three Lamps in Ponsonby, eyes were watching me. Knowing eyes, hostile eyes. On the face of it, this was absurd. I was nobody, doing nothing much, why would anyone care? But feelings can be imperious and do not always require validation from the so-called real world. And aspects of my circumstances might have helped to explain my paranoia. Our living situation, for instance.

The house in Hackett Street was a lovely old wooden villa built on the side of a hill looking north across the Waitematā. It was unrenovated but in good nick. I had a study; there was a spare room for guests. A sitting room with a fireplace. The bedroom where Jan and I slept had a banana palm growing over the veranda outside the window and you saw glimpses of the blue sea through its ragged green leaves. There was a lawn at the back which the landlord, Don Gifford, mowed every few weeks; otherwise we never saw him. That lawn was quite private and no one used it much, so I dug up a flowerbed running parallel to the wall of the house and planted a crop of marijuana there. It was a sun trap; the plants flourished throughout the wet, warm spring and the hot rainy summer that followed. They made a glorious resin.

There was, however, a problem. In the house next door lived a robust and forthright 80-something-year-old woman who broadcast a community hour weekly on 1ZB and spent the rest of her time spying on the neighbourhood. She was a Christian, an Anglican. Her kitchen looked out over our house and part of the lawn. You would see the white lace curtain at its window twitch when a visitor came to our front door, which was down that side, though we mostly used the back door. One day a film producer who lived a few houses up the street told Kate that the twitcher had informed some police who lived behind us that I was growing marijuana plants along the wall at the back of the house.

I soon worked out that they were firemen, not cops, and uninterested anyway in my crop. Then I went to visit the twitcher. She served tea and biscuits and introduced me to her stroke-afflicted husband. Slack-jawed, drooling, wearing pyjamas, a tartan dressing gown and a checked cloth hat à la Andy Capp, he dragged himself wordlessly through the darkened house. She was inclined to wring her hands at her predicament; I murmured that of course I cared. Then, choosing my moment, I made a point of looking out the window of her kitchen and commenting upon the lush growth on my tomato plants which, by craning your neck, you could just see, and asked if she'd noticed them yet? She flushed and denied all knowledge of them, but I could tell from the look in her eye that I would have no more trouble from her. So it proved.

The situation in the house on the other side was intractable. A widow in her forties, with two teenage sons, lived there. The boys were radio hams who spent hours every day, and most of the night too, it seemed, bent over their short-wave sets, which were installed in a small basement room contiguous with the top corner of the back lawn. You would hear them talking to like-minded shut-ins in Japan or California, in Papakura or on Mars. Nothing wrong with that, except that our stereo picked up their transmissions. When we played our David Bowie or Blondie or Clash or Bob Marley or Marianne Faithful records bursts of static, mysterious underwater sounds or spectral voices interrupted the music. It drove us crazy, but when I went over to talk to the widow, a thin woman with desperation in her eyes, she shrugged her shoulders and said she didn't know what to do either.

The amount of dope I smoked in those days might have contributed to my paranoia: I once overheard someone say, 'You mean that guy who always looks like he's out of it?' But the base-line was elsewhere: a self-scrutiny originating in my desire to write and my evident failure to do so. I had left Red Mole to follow my vocation, but where were the results? I recall Kevin Williamson, the artist, whom I knew from Huntly College, asking me what I was doing. I didn't know how to answer and, in the face of my silence, he said, not unkindly, 'Just mucking around?' It was a bitter blow, and fed a mounting sense of anxiety; I had to do something.

And so, before Christmas that year, I conceived a plan of going to visit my old home town of Ohakune and writing an account of the excursion. I asked my then brother-in-law, Barry Thomas, if he would like to come along and take some photographs. These would be used to illustrate the work when it was published. Barry agreed, I took the train down, he drove up from Wellington and we spent a few days touring the Waimarino before going our separate ways. I asked him to focus upon images of dereliction and he obliged, producing a fine set of black and white pictures, highly evocative and, at the same time, achingly sad.

Even though its themes were loss and decay, the writing of what I called 'A Quiet Corner of Paradise' was a joy. I used the voice I'd found in 'The Abyss of Cities' and adopted the routine I'd followed when writing pornography in New York. I sat down each day in a state of pleasurable anticipation that was almost always answered by an assembly of words and sentences I could read back later without wincing or blushing. It went on like that for a month and then it stopped. One day an American guy I knew called Tim – he used to buy the excess of the dope I was growing – rang up with the offer of a job. He was looking for crew members for the shoot of a feature film being made in Auckland by a bunch of his fellow countrymen.

I'd appeared by then as an actor in a few films, like *Someday Afternoon*. I'd written an unproduced script, an adaptation, with Richard Turner, of the Maurice Duggan story 'Along Rideout Road That Summer' and proposed, or had proposed to me, several others, including the one that became Leon Narbey's *Illustrious Energy*. I thought screenwriting might be a way of earning a living while my 'real' writing proceeded elsewhere and in my own time. So I said yes to Tim and went to work on a movie with the working title 'Shadowlands'. It was released as *Dead Kids* (*Strange Behavior* in the US). I never saw it, yet the events of my time on that crew marked me indelibly and intensified the alienation and paranoia I was already feeling.

That story is too long to tell here. Suffice to say that the distress I suffered was caused as much by my own ignorant and/or arrogant actions as it was by the brutal and unpleasant people I had to work with – not so much the New Zealanders as those who occupied the higher echelons of the hierarchy: Americans, Australians and especially South Africans. I was soon relieved of my position as driver of the make-up van and third assistant to the director and shifted to the art department, alongside Russell Collins, an old Mole. When the producer, John Barnett, refused to pay our per diems, we sabotaged set-ups – hiding bones in a cemetery – until he came across with the money. One of the strangest things about the shoot was that we spent our time altering Auckland locations so that they looked like places in the Midwest of the United States: the teen slasher movie we were making was set in the small town of Galesburg, Illinois.

So I never finished 'A Quiet Corner of Paradise'; it would be another 10 years before I returned to the writing of prose. The part I did complete remained unpublished until a later version became the title piece of my 2007 book, *Waimarino County*. After the shoot was over I felt more desperate than ever to get away. At the same time Jan was having trouble with her band. When the record company's decision about what the next single would be went against her, she decided to leave Coup d'Etat.

People tried to talk her out of it but she was adamant. Where would she go? What would she do? Many musicians we knew were, like the Crocodiles, relocating to Australia. Why didn't we follow suit? I barely thought about it. I knew there was a film school in Sydney, that they taught courses in screenwriting.

I could enrol there and learn the craft. The money I made from selling the rest of my dope to Tim was just enough to buy an air ticket. I said, 'Yes, why not? Let's go.' As casual as that sounds. It never occurred to me that the move might turn out to be permanent. I didn't appreciate that some choices are, or become, irrevocable.

~

The Moles were going away too: not to Australia, back to New York, 'for the duration,' Alan said. They had a bitter pill to swallow. The invitation to the Third South Pacific Festival of Arts in Port Moresby in mid-1980 had come to nothing. As a Red Mole press release put it, 'No further written communication has been sent informing the group of Cabinet's decision, or change of plans of the selection committee.' It went on to suggest that Red Mole were only ever on the bill as a place holder until a suitable indigenous theatre group could be found – or invented. Roma and Brian Potiki's radical agit-prop troupe, Maranga Mai, were contenders, but they were probably deemed politically unacceptable too. Internal Affairs chose an ad hoc group of Māori actors instead. When the official New Zealand contingent did fly out to Port Moresby there were 40 empty seats on the plane. Red Mole asked, reasonably enough, why could they not have been offered those seats? They were, after all, adept at last-minute solutions. But it would seem the problems with their attendance were never really logistical.

That press release was picked up by a number of newspapers and called forth a tart rejoinder from Hamish Keith. He said that his verbal invitation was always conditional and that Red Mole should have understood that. As for Volkerling's letter, that, too, was conditional. Keith did not speculate any further on the matter, and neither did Red Mole – or not publicly.

The minister of arts in those days – the first in our history – was Allan Highet, MP for Remuera, an accountant and a former amateur opera singer, a liberal in the Muldoon government. He was by no means a yes man. In the lead-up to the 1981 Springbok tour he suggested that, should it go ahead, in his capacity as minister of sport he might withdraw lottery funding from the New Zealand Rugby Union. That doesn't mean he supported Red Mole's participation in the festival. It seems likely that, if Cabinet did rule Red Mole out, Muldoon was instrumental in the decision. He was probably aware of our relentless satire about him, going back five years at least. He might have known he was the Pig.

The other notable aspect of the press release is a rare, non-rhetorical account of what we were about:

> Red Mole's work is far-reaching, covering not just a large variety of techniques of theatre, but also techniques of puppetry, shadow puppetry, mask making, voice production, dance and movement, music, song, acrobatics and publication of newspapers, books and poetry. Members of Red Mole are also skilled in set design, lighting, making of props, stage effects and costume design (for which the group won an award in New York). Red Mole feels that as a small touring group they have a lot of skills to share with other Pacific performers.

All of this was true, but wouldn't have cut any ice with Muldoon and his cronies. With the loss of the gig at Port Moresby, the possibility of Red Mole's participation with Black Tent at the festival in Tokyo also disappeared. New York was probably always the final option; it became the only one.

The press release might also have mentioned how hard-working they were. *Lord Galaxy's Travelling Players*, the Mata Hari show at the Maidment in March, was followed by *I'll Never Dance Down Bugis Street Again*, a burlesque version of the Mr Asia story. It toured for 13 weeks, from April to June, in both islands, in venues as various as Auckland's Mainstreet, the *Aranui* during a Cook Strait ferry crossing, the Golden Eagle Hotel in Greymouth. The Sam Ford Veranda Band went on that tour and also contributed to a *Radio with Pictures* special, *Life is a Zoo*, directed by Tony Holden, which featured four songs from the Bugis Street burlesque show.

The latter part of 1980 was devoted to workshops, lectures and performances: *State of the Nation*; the women's show, *Electric Eyeland*; the film *Second Sight*; a series of talks Alan gave in Hamilton under the title *What Are You, An Alarm Clock? The Redmole Version*, which played in Auckland and Wellington before and after Christmas, respectively, was their last outing and then, early in 1981, the Moles did go back to New York, island hopping across the Pacific from Samoa to Niue to Papeete in Tahiti and thence to Los Angeles.

~

The final New Zealand shows, appropriately enough, were at the Last Resort in Wellington towards the end of January. Their next appearance was in New York in July, at the Pyramid Theater on 42nd Street, a space Nance Shatzkin found and which the Moles inhabited, and refurbished, in rather the same way we inhabited, without refurbishing, Carmen's Balcony. In a peculiar reiteration of what happened with *Goin' to Djibouti*, that first show back in New York was also called *The Redmole Version*; but it was a different version and split into two parts: *The Early Show* and *The Late Show*.

Ian Prior, who'd stayed in Manhattan, came in to light it. Artist Rick Killeen made shadow puppets. Otherwise the performers were the same group that crossed America: Alan, Sally, Deb and John, with the addition of Tracy Trevett. The next year, 1982, Red Mole put on their third production at the Theater for the New City: *The Excursion*, set in ancient Egypt was, from the photographs, as visually splendid as *Ghost Rite* had been. It was meant to highlight Deb's mask-making abilities and included material from sources as diverse as Flaubert's *Letters*, his *Travel Notes* and the December 1981 *Declaration of Martial Law in Poland*. A key text from that show begins 'Baboon, we have travelled far ...'

When it was clear that we were going west and they were going east, and it might be a while before the twain should meet again, we went around to the Moles' flat at 45 Marlborough Street in Mount Eden to say goodbye. It was another of those shadowy, curtained, seemingly underground locations they favoured. After dinner Alan fired up a carousel projector and started going through slides. Some beautiful shots came up: beams of blue and red and green light falling vertiginously across car body wrecks before which four emblematic figures stood: the mother and the father, the crucified child, the fool in motley sweeping up leaves while crying out helplessly against the doom of the times.

'Who lit that show?' Deborah asked. Sally, in her rich and lovely voice, said my name, but I already knew. They were shots of the first performance of *Numbered Days in Paradise*, in St Peter's Parish Hall on 20th Street, Manhattan, the one for which I'd only been able to change gels and repoint lamps. Seeing those magnificent images I felt redeemed. However fraught things might have been, however extreme my fugue states became, however many failures I endured or was responsible for, it all seemed worthwhile. The quotidian translated, howsoever briefly, into the eternal; light made solid again; the ineffable, which could neither be unseen nor undone, accomplished.

Coda

I DID WORK WITH RED MOLE ONE MORE TIME: when I arranged for *The Book of Life* to come to the Belvoir Street Theatre in Sydney in 1990. My credit for the show says I did the lights but actually, for the first and only time in my life, I was the sound man. This was not onerous. The score, by Jean McAllister and Tony McMaster, was pre-recorded; all I had to do was cue tapes and make sure they started and ended in the right places.

Red Mole were a rump. Deborah had gone, via Mexico, to Puerto Rico, where she still lives and works as an internationally loved and respected mask-maker and performer. John went in 1984 from New York to Japan to study Noh theatre, then back to Aotearoa and a life of teaching and theatre-making. Ian Prior, too, at some point, returned to New Zealand to live and work. It was just Sally and Alan, with Stewart Shepherd, their designer, doing walk-on parts. They played Duncan and Luanne, a couple of nerdy door-knocking evangelists with a message that became increasingly bizarre, deranged and menacing as things devolved. It was a good show but hardly anybody came.

There was a shadow puppet play to 'It Was Night in the Lonesome October', Alan's Baltimore poem about Edgar Allan Poe; a line of tiny ships crossing the stage, rehearsing the transportation of nuclear waste to Johnson Island in the Pacific; Sally's monologue as a bent dentist's besotted receptionist; and Stewart's miniature stage, where mysterious alternative actions unfolded. Dominic Wong in the *Sydney Review* wrote: 'The show is both creepy and funny and this mood never lets up as the work whizzes through with its wild metaphors and non-stop dream-like action. Perhaps the best thing about it is that it never takes itself too seriously.'

For Red Mole aficionados like me the best came last. A series of black and white slides of Island Bay, Wellington, where Sally and Alan had bought a house, was projected, to music, and just when it seemed Duncan and Luanne were sentimentally reconciled to each other and to life on earth, footage of Joe Bleakley's bird on a wire, from *Slaughter on Cockroach Avenue,* passed wonkily across the screen, blowing all solemnities away.

After the last show of that week-long season was over I waited with Sally and Alan outside the theatre for their taxi to arrive. Elizabeth Street, 11pm on a clear spring night, looked stark and strange. Noir. They were going back to my flat in Darlinghurst because I'd moved out to stay with my girlfriend in Newtown for the duration of the season. Everything used in the production, all the costumes and masks and props, including the shadow puppet screen, was packed into one trunk: an economy of means they duplicated for the travelling shows they took to Europe and to the Americas during the rest of the decade and into the next millennium too.

What I recall is Alan's stance, like a figure of outward: whatever the disappointments of the season might have been there was nothing behind him, he was intent upon the next task, the next journey. And yet the look on his face belied that attitude. Beneath his flinty determination was an awareness of grief and pain, the knowledge of the passing of time that would not come again. Sally was beside him, as always, courageous, committed and optimistic. Their pact was intact and inviolable: don't look back. The cab came, we loaded up *The Book of Life*, cracked a few jokes and off they rode into the night.

That was the last Red Mole show I saw, though Alan and I continued to work together on literary projects. He facilitated the publication of my first book, *The Autobiography of my Father*, putting me in touch with Michele Leggott, who gave the manuscript to Elizabeth Caffin at Auckland University Press. His imprint, Bumper Books, published two long essays of mine, one on the 1970s, the other on the Pacific. The last time I saw him was in Wellington in the winter of 2000 when I was attending to matters consequent upon the death of my mother. I bought a bottle of good red wine and went out to Brighton Street in Island Bay to have dinner. It was soup and toast – they always were abstemious eaters. When we finished one bottle and were about to start on the next Alan asked Sally, 'Shall we rinse the glasses?'

The Book of Life: puppet ship, Belvoir Street Theatre, 1991.

Despite his characteristically boyish celebration of the work they had just been doing on the house – 'It was a good day, wasn't it?' – he seemed older than when I had seen him last, which wasn't very long before. The wealth of his experience, of lived life and of the poetic and theatrical traditions he was heir to, had given a gravity to his person which, for all that he wore it lightly, was far-seeing, compassionate and, if not acquiescent to fate, comprehended its vagaries as much as its gifts. The aggression he'd so often shown – which, he once admitted, was based upon fear – had gone. It still seems cruel that he should have died so young, with so much left undone; I particularly regret the absence of the reminiscences he intended to write. However, most of them may already be encoded in the poetry: if you know how to excavate those 77 levels of meaning.

At the same house, six years later, I had my last meeting with Sally. It was the autumn of 2006 and I had gone around for dinner again; their daughter Ruby, then in her early twenties, made dessert. Lilicherie McGregor was there. Three times during the evening Sally and I went outside to smoke cigarettes. On each occasion she brought up the question of her wish to die, which she had discussed with me and with others over the course of the four years since Alan's death from a heart attack in Amsterdam on 28 June 2002; years during which, nevertheless, she wrote and directed four shows. My sister's suicide many years before had a bearing on why she wanted my blessing for her own. Alan died on the same day that Rachel did.

I had always before, as we feel we must, advised her to hang in there, seek professional help, wait for things to get better, let time heal her wounds. The third time out the back, however, puffing away on our fags, in the face of her importunities, I heard my reassurances begin to sound hollow, placatory, in bad faith. I gave up pretending I knew what she should do and said, 'Well, if that's what you want.' It sounds strange – it was – but when Sally heard that, tears of gratitude started in her eyes. She really couldn't live without Alan, or perhaps it is better to say she did not know how to mend a broken heart. Who does? She gave me a hug and we went back inside.

In a personal sense Sally and Alan were crucial for me, they overlooked my growing up, in loco parentis perhaps: sometimes stern, always encouraging, often funny, invariably tolerant. I felt, whatever else was going on, they had my best interests at heart. This was a role they fulfilled with respect to many other people too. Also, maybe erroneously, I feel I never gave enough back to them while they were here, thinking there would be time enough for that later. And this is never the case; all we ever have is now.

As for their theatre, I am only able to write about those first seven years; which were followed by another 25, during which works were made more in accord with the European and American (including Latin American) avant garde than with the popular forms explored while I was with the troupe. Their New York shows in the 1980s, including a loose trilogy – *Childhood of a Saint*, *Dreamings End* and *Lost Chants for the Living* – were followed by, among much else, *Circu Sfumato* and *Playtime* in New Mexico and *Playtime* and *Hour of Justice* in Amsterdam. *Hour of Justice* was the show they took with them back to New Zealand in 1988.

Productions from the 1990s and early 2000s included a dozen more original shows; a Greek tragedy (Sophocles' *Antigone*, as both theatre and film); Shakespeare (*Romeo and Juliet*, with a Samoan cast); Beckett (*Krapp's Last Tape* and *Krapp's Last Video*); Russian and Futurist plays; several other films and videos, including *Zucchini Roma*, a partial, eccentric Red Mole history. They founded a company, Roadworks, to facilitate the work of younger practitioners. Sally joined the Magdalena Project, an international association of women working in contemporary theatre. Alan taught agit-prop to members of the Seafarers' Union for use in their struggle against the bosses.

Theatre is ephemeral and only the bones of documentation survive; in Red Mole's case the archive is extensive and has not yet been properly assessed. Their work will, I hope, live on in publication and in performance: a rich legacy that can only grow with the years. Then there are the souvenirs. I don't have much: a few scripts, a letter or two, brochures, some photographs. A complete, if crumbling, set of *Spleen*. A glove puppet someone gave me in Sydney: robust, insouciant, a hamburger wearing a Stars and Stripes hat; I think it must have been the star of *After Midnight at the Kentucky Burger Bar*. And a helmet mask I made at Costley Street in Auckland in 1978. It's a black head of Anubis, the Egyptian jackal god of the dead, which sits on a high shelf in my bedroom – as a reminder of mortality, I suppose.

Most precious, indeed invaluable, are memories of theatrical moments which, though they cannot be reproduced, remain determinants of the life that goes on after them. For me they include a scene from *Ghost Rite* which, because I was a part of it, I never saw: six hieratic figures, wearing Anubis masks like the one I have, lift from a bier the body of a pharaoh, crook and flail crossed upon its breast, and bear it hence to await reincarnation in the Duat. It reminds me of an ancient quatrain, transcribed from the walls of a tomb:

> *We set out now in the boat of millions of years*
> *Your love in my flesh like a reed in the arms of the wind*
> *On the far horizon the ancient sun rises again*
> *Our souls will be birds on the distant roads of the sky.*

Notes on sources

The main sources for this memoir are human memory and the Brunton Rodwell papers (B/R papers) in Special Collections/Kohikohinga Motuhake at the University of Auckland – the Red Mole archive, which includes the records of the White Rabbit Puppet Theatre. I quote from them courtesy of the copyright holder, Ruby Brunton, and with the advice and consent of my co-literary agent at the archive, Michele Leggott.

The memories are my own, amplified by those of Neil Hannan and Richard Kennedy; Deborah Hunt, John Davies, Jean McAllister, Tony McMaster, Stan Mitchell, Nance Shatzkin, Joe Bleakley; Brian Potiki, Redmer Yska, Richard Turner, Craig Miller, the late Malcolm McSporran; Ian Wedde, Joe Wylie, Jenny Stevenson, Jean Clarkson, the late Arthur Baysting and the late Barry Linton.

The Brunton Rodwell papers consist of 28 boxes arranged in 22 series. I mostly used Series 8 and 9, Red Mole publicity and production materials respectively; the White Rabbit files in Series 10; Series 11 and 13, which contain the photographs and the coloured slides; and Series 19, where the *Spleen* material is kept.

Although there is an inventory of the archive, references to it are, perforce, imprecise. For the rest I have tried, not always successfully, to match the quotations in the text to their place of original publication or, alternatively, to their unpublished source.

Notes are keyed to page numbers

p. 20   Amamus: 'Amamus Culture Shock': *Salient*, Vol. 37, No. 24, 18 September 1974.

p. 21   Grotowski: Giuliano Campo, *Zygmunt Molik's Voice and Body Work: The Legacy of Jerzy Grotowski*, Routledge, Taylor & Francis Group, 2010.

p. 22   'shouting erotics': chorus of 'Billy Goat Gruff Song'; Russell Haley, *The Walled Garden*, Mandrake Root, 1972.

p. 26   Redmer Yska: pers. comm., 7 February 2018.

p. 28–29 *Sexus*: see 'Acting Out', curated by Stephen Cleland, Adam Art Gallery, 6 May – 9 July 1976: http://stephencleland.net/ACTING-OUTJACK-BODY-JOHN-MILLER-EDWARD-BULLMORE-VALIE-EXPORT-SARAH

p. 29   Cornelius Cardew: draft constitution for the Scratch Orchestra, *Musical Times*, June, 1969.

p. 37   Michele Leggott: 'Leaving Luang Prabang: A Tale of Two Travellers', *kmko* 4, September 2007: www.nzepc.auckland.ac.nz/kmko/04/ka_mate04_leggott.asp

p. 38   Peter Fantl: descriptions from Red Mole publicity material, B/R papers, Series 8, n.d. (1975–78).

p. 39   Jenny Stevenson: pers. comm., n.d. (2018).

p. 42   'You'll never last': I don't know who said this; it was quoted often down the years.

p. 44   The gamelan: https://gamelan.org.nz/history/

p. 44   Cathy Wylie: 'Sonic Spectrum', *Listener*, 12 April 1975.

p. 45   Murray Edmond: 'From Cabaret to Apocalypse: Red Mole's Cabaret Capital
Strut and Ghost Rite', *kmko* 4, September 2007: www.nzepc.auckland.ac.nz/kmko/04/
ka_mate04_murrayedmond.asp. See also his PhD thesis, 'Old Comrades of the Future:
A History of Experimental Theatre in New Zealand 1962–1982', English Department,
University of Auckland, 1996.

p. 45   Alan Brunton: 'The Commissioner for Enlightenment: Alan Brunton talks to Chris
Bourke', *brief* 28, 'Alan Brunton', ed. Jack Ross, Spring, 2003: www.nzepc.auckland.ac.nz/
authors/brunton/brief/bourke.asp

p. 46   Ian Wedde: pers. comm., 17 March 2018.

p. 46   Deborah Hunt: 'Old Comrades of the Future'.

p. 50   'Sunrays and Pain': *Salient*, Vol. 38, No. 12, 20 June 1975.

p. 53   Charles Baudelaire: 'Spleen', trans. Robert Lowell, *Imitations*, Faber and Faber, 1962.

p. 54   Alan Brunton: 'Questions and Answers: Alan Brunton, John Geraets', *brief* 19, March
2001: www.nzepc.auckland.ac.nz/authors/brunton/questions.asp

p. 54   Sunny Amey: quoted in 'White Rabbit Puppet Theatre, a Chronology', B/R papers, Series
8, n.d. (1976).

p. 57   Mountain Jim Jantipur: *Spleen* 1, n.d. (1975).

p. 57   'New Jerusalem Sonnets': *Big Smoke: New Zealand Poems 1960–1975*, Auckland
University Press, 2000.

p. 57   Brent Southgate: www.nzepc.auckland.ac.nz/features/bigsmoke/bs_o-y.asp

p. 64   Charming Cole Tundra: *Spleen* 2, n.d. (1976); see also Alan Brunton, *Slow Passes,
1978–1988*, Auckland University Press, 1991.

p. 67   Flick Bromide: *Spleen* 4, n.d. (1976).

p. 67   Richard Turner: pers. comm., 23 March 2018.

p. 69   Brian Eno: Eric Tamm, *Brian Eno: His Music and the Vertical Color of Sound*, Da Capo
Press, 1995.

p. 69   Phil Manzanera: Jim DeRogatis, *Turn on Your Mind: Four Decades of Great Psychedelic
Rock*, Hal Leonard Corporation, 2003.

p. 70   'Cripple Cockroach': Alan Brunton, *Beyond the Ohlala Mountains, Poems 1968–2002*,
Titus Books, 2013.

p. 71   'We climbed …': 'Taking Tiger Mountain', track five, side 2, Brian Eno: *Taking Tiger
Mountain (By Strategy)*, Island Records, 1974.

p. 71   Barry Gustafson: *His Way: A biography of Robert Muldoon*, Auckland University Press,
2000.

p. 72–73 RP: review of *Ace Follies*, *Greymouth Evening Star*, 24 September 1976.

p. 74   Mike Nicolaidi: review of *Ace Follies*, *Evening Post*, n.d. (August 1976).

p. 75   Lee Hatherly: source unknown, but she was in the audience that night; n.d. (1976?).

p. 75   Fortune Theatre: 'The Incredible Ace Follies'; *Spleen* 6, n.d. (1976).

p. 76   Colin McCahon: letter to Peter McLeavey, n.d. (1976), kindly forwarded to me by Peter
Simpson.

p. 78   *Towards Bethlehem*: scenario in B/R papers, Series 9, n.d. (December 1976).

p. 84   Alan Brunton: *Salient*, Vol. 40, No. 4, 21 March 1977.

p. 84   Carmen: source unknown; for more on Carmen, see interview with Jack Body, Sydney,
1991: www.pridenz.com/carmen_interviewed_by_jack_body.html

p. 84   *Cabaret Capital Strut*: the A4 outlines are in the B/R papers, Series 9, n.d. (1977).

p. 90   Lawrence MacDonald: 'And I Wonder … Who Wrote the Book of Life? Red Mole and Carnivalesque Theatre', *Illusions* 18, 1991–92.

p. 90   Ian Fraser: 'Moles in the Foundations', *Listener,* 12 November 1977.

p. 92   Murray Edmond: 'From Cabaret to Apocalypse'.

p. 93   Joe Wylie: pers. comm., n.d. (2019).

p. 96   Neil Hannan: 'Red Mole Diary 1977–80', Phantom Billsticker's *Café Reader*, Summer, 2017; I quote from a longer, unedited version Neil sent me in February 2018.

p. 100   Sally Rodwell: interview, publication unknown, B/R papers, Series 8, n.d. (1993).

p. 104–05 Redmer Yska: pers. comm., 7 February 2018.

p. 105   Ian Wedde: 'A brief history of derangement and enterprise: Alan Brunton 1946–2002', *Listener*, 3 August 2002: www.nzepc.auckland.ac.nz/authors/brunton/recollections/wedde.asp

p. 111   *Slaughter on Cockroach Avenue*: scenario in B/R papers, Series 9, 1977.

p. 111   'Rangitoto': Baysting/Hannan, Crossing the Tracks, Mascot, 1978.

p. 112   'Oh Fat Daddy': Martin Edmond/Jan Preston, Crossing the Tracks, Mascot, 1978. See also *The Midge Marsden Collection*, SDL (Scoop de Loop), 2017.

p. 115   Adrian Kiernander: *Act: Theatre in New Zealand*, Vol. 2, No. 10, December 1977.

p. 116   John Davies biography: Red Mole publicity, New York, n.d. (1980–81); B/R papers, Series 8.

p. 118   Deborah Hunt: pers. comm., 27 September 2019.

p. 123   *Ghost Rite*: typescript in my possession.

p. 124   *Ghost Rite*.

p. 126   *Ghost Rite*.

p. 127   Antonin Artaud: *The Theater and its Double*, trans. Mary C. Richards, Grove Press, 1994.

p. 128   Hans Bones: 'The Message of Hans Bones', *Beyond the Ohlala Mountains*.

p. 130   'Liberty Bus': Alan Brunton, 1978.

p. 133   Simon Wilson: 'Dig Tunnels Deep: Two Views of Red Mole', *Salient*, 13 March 1978.

p. 133   John Ghent: *Auckland Star*, n.d. (March 1978).

p. 134   Murray Edmond: 'From Cabaret to Apocalypse'.

p. 136   *Crazy in the Streets*: playscript published in 'Hamilton Hometown', *Landfall* 180, December 1991.

p. 145   Howard McNaughton: *Press*, n.d. (May 1978).

p. 161   'Hysteria': Edmond/Preston, 1979.

p. 162   Richard Kennedy: here and following pages, pers. comm., 28 February 2018.

p. 180   Sally Rodwell: Introduction, *Goin' to Djibouti*, Alan Brunton, Bumper Books, 1996.

p. 180   Sally Rodwell: Introduction.

p. 182–83 Noel Carroll: review of *Goin' to Djibouti*, *Soho Weekly News*, 18 January 1979.

p. 183–84 Sally Rodwell: Introduction.

p. 184   Erica Munk: review of *Dead Fingers Walk*, *Village Voice*, Vol. XXIV, No. 33, 24 September 1979; Terry Curtis Fox's review of *Goin' to Djibouti* appeared in the 15 January 1979 issue.

p. 184   Theater for the New City: https://en.wikipedia.org/wiki/Theater_for_the_New_City

p. 186   Karl Kraus: see Marjorie Perloff, 'Avant-Garde in a Different Key: Karl Kraus's *The Last Days of Mankind*', in *Critical Inquiry*: https://criticalinquiry.uchicago.edu/Avant_Garde_in_a_Different_Key/

p. 186   *The Last Days of Mankind*: There are several versions of the scenario in the B/R papers, Series 9, n.d. (1979).

p. 192   Sally Rodwell: interview with Jane Bowron, B/R papers, Series 8, n.d. (1994).

p. 196   Manifesto: Alan Brunton, B/R papers, Series 9, n.d. (1974). The first version lists 25 propositions, from which, at a later date, these five were selected; the bracketing of (the) in the first proposition emphasises that Red Mole was also a lovers' pact.

p. 200–01 Neil Hannan: 'Red Mole Diary'.

p. 204   Time Out: Ros Franey, *Time Out*, 17–23 October 1979.

p. 208   Neil Hannan: 'Red Mole Diary'.

p. 212   Erica Munk: review of *Dead Fingers Walk*.

p. 214   The Wilma Project: https://wilmatheater.org/about/mission-history/

p. 216   Jasper Johns: this remark is widely quoted but usually left unsourced: www.nytimes.com/2019/02/18/t-magazine/jasper-johns.html

p. 220   *Numbered Days in Paradise*: typescript in my possession.

p. 222   'Chant of Paradise': *Slow Passes*.

p. 223   Neil Hannan: 'Red Mole Diary'.

p. 223   Jubilee Community Arts: www.nps.gov/parkhistory/online_books/sero/appalachian/sec15.htm

p. 224   Jim Stevenson: Obituary, New Zealand Law Society: www.lawsociety.org.nz/news-and-communications/people-in-the-law/obituaries/obituaries-list/james-richard-allan-stevenson,-1947-2018

p. 226   Neil Hannan: 'Red Mole Diary'.

p. 229   Deborah Hunt: video interview (unused) for *Zucchini Roma: A Life in the Theatre*, dir. Sally Rodwell, Red Mole, 1995; Red Mole archives held in Ngā Taonga Sound & Vision, Wellington: www.nzepc.auckland.ac.nz/authors/brunton/brief/edmond.asp

p. 232   KiMo Theatre: pre-publicity for the opening in the *New Mexico State Tribune*, Albuquerque, n.d. (1927).

p. 235   Michele Leggott and Martin Edmond: 'Notes for Beyond the Ohlala Mountains': www.nzepc.auckland.ac.nz/authors/brunton/ohlala-notes.pdf

p. 235   Los Alamos: John D. Wirth and Linda Harvey Aldritch, *Los Alamos: The Ranch School Years, 1917–1943*, University of New Mexico Press, 2003.

p. 240   'Hysteria'.

p. 242   Alan Brunton: 'Where There's Hope', *Beyond the Ohlala Mountains*.

p. 243   Neil Hannan: 'Red Mole Diary'.

p. 243   Gretchen Henkel: review of *Numbered Days in Paradise*, Hollywood Drama-Logue 10–16 January 1980.

p. 243   Ron Pennington: review of *Numbered Days in Paradise*, Hollywood Reporter, Vol. CCLX, No. 2, 14 January 1980.

p. 249–50 Bruce Mason: review of *Numbered Days in Paradise*, Evening Post, 11 February 1980.

p. 251   *Red Mole on the Road*: documentary: www.nzonscreen.com/title/red-mole-on-the-road-1979

p. 253   Ian Wedde: pers. comm.

p. 260   The Excursion: see *brief*, 28: www.nzepc.auckland.ac.nz/authors/brunton/brief/excursion.asp

p. 261   Dominic Wong: review of *The Book of Life*, *Sydney Review*, October 1990.

p. 266   Quatrain: see booklet accompanying Silvana Alasia and Lo Scarabeo, *The Egyptian Tarot Deck*, Llewellyn Publications, 2000.

Photograph acknowledgements

It has not been possible to identify all of the photographers whose works are reproduced here, nor to source every image to the person who took it. Most of the prints and slides are in the Brunton/Rodwell papers in Special Collections at the University of Auckland library and many of these are uncredited; almost certainly commissioned and paid for at the time; or given by the photographer in a spirit of solidarity. In lieu of a complete log, then, what follows is a list of those who are known to have worked with Red Mole and the period during which they did so:

Richard Turner photographed *Cabaret Paris Spleen* and Black Power. Arthur Baysting and Di Cadwallader, among others, recorded *Vargo's Circus*. Michael de Hamel, in Dunedin, documented *Ace Follies*. Bryan Staff took photographs for *Spleen* and of *Cabaret Capital Strut*. Gaylene Preston also made a visual record of that period. Larry Jordan was another who took live shots at Carmen's. There were no usable photographs of *Whimsy and the Seven Spectacles*, *Siddhartha*, *Cabaret Pekin 1949*, *Towards Bethlehem*, *The Adventures of Sir Real Janus* or *Slaughter on Cockroach Avenue*.

Some *Ghost Rite* images, by an unknown photographer, appeared in *Art New Zealand* #8, illustrating a piece by Terry Snow. Stuart Page recorded Christchurch performances on Red Mole's *Goin' to Djibouti* tour, including pictures of *Our World* and *Crazy in the Streets*. The pictures taken at Ziggy's are unsourced but Peter Frater may be responsible. Robert Alexander, in New York, photographed *Goin' to Djibouti* and *The Last Days of Mankind*. Joe Bleakley took the publicity shots and the individual portraits from New York in 1979; and the images of *Dead Fingers Walk* and *Numbered Days in Paradise*. Colleen Forde photographed the 1991 Sydney performances of *The Book of Life*.

Joe Wylie's and Barry Linton's posters are used by permission; in Barry's case, from his daughter, Lily Linton. Joe Wylie recalls the ethos: 'As far as rights or ownership matters, my understanding was that the Moles owned what they'd commissioned and paid for. It's all part of your/their legacy.' The covers of *Spleen* #2 and #3 are by Jean Clarkson; the latter was made into a poster with the legend: *Seen a Spleen? Coming right at you!*

271

Grateful acknowledgement is made to Special Collections at the University of Auckland library for permission to use material from the Brunton/Rodwell papers and especially to team leader Nigel Bond, archivist Katherine Pawley, and cultural collections assistant Ian Brailsford, who scanned the slides. Mayu Kanamori re-photographed the black and white pictures and enhanced the images; for which, many thanks.